Cambridge Opera Handbooks

Benjamin Britten
Death in Venice

T0328434

Benjamin Britten, 6 February 1976, at The Red House, Aldeburgh

Benjamin Britten
Death in Venice

compiled and edited by
DONALD MITCHELL

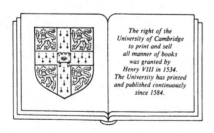

The right of the
University of Cambridge
to print and sell
all manner of books
was granted by
Henry VIII in 1534.
The University has printed
and published continuously
since 1584.

CAMBRIDGE UNIVERSITY PRESS

Cambridge
London   New York   New Rochelle
Melbourne   Sydney

Published by the Press Syndicate of the University of Cambridge
The Pitt Building, Trumpington Street, Cambridge CB2 1RP
32 East 57th Street, New York, NY 10022, USA
10 Stamford Road, Oakleigh, Melbourne 3166, Australia

© Cambridge University Press 1987

First published 1987

British Library cataloguing in publication data

Benjamin Britten, Death in Venice. – (Cambridge opera handbooks)
1. Britten, Benjamin. Death in Venice
I. Mitchell, Donald
782.1'092'4   ML410.B853

Library of Congress cataloguing in publication data

Benjamin Britten: Death in Venice.
(Cambridge opera handbooks)
Bibliography.
Discography.
Includes index.
1. Britten, Benjamin, 1913–76. Death in Venice.
2. Operas – Analysis, appreciation. I. Mitchell,
Donald, 1925–   . II. Series.
ML410.B853B42   1987   782.1'092'4   86-23231

ISBN 0 521 26534 7 hard covers
ISBN 0 521 31943 9 paperback

Transferred to digital printing 2004

ME

CAMBRIDGE OPERA HANDBOOKS
General preface

This is a series of studies of individual operas written for the opera-goer or record-collector as well as the student or scholar. Each volume has three main concerns: historical, analytical and interpretative. There is a detailed description of the genesis of each work, the collaboration between librettist and composer, and the first performance and subsequent stage history. A full synopsis considers the opera as a structure of musical and dramatic effects, and there is also a musical analysis of a section of the score. The analysis, like the history, shades naturally into interpretation: by a careful combination of new essays and excerpts from classic statements the editors of the handbooks show how critical writing about the opera, like the production and performance, can direct or distort appreciation of its structural elements. A final section of documents gives a select bibliography, a discography, and guides to other sources. Each book is published in both hard covers and as a paperback.

Books published

Richard Wagner: *Parsifal* by Lucy Beckett
W.A. Mozart: *Don Giovanni* by Julian Rushton
C.W. von Gluck: *Orfeo* by Patricia Howard
Igor Stravinsky: *The Rake's Progress* by Paul Griffiths
Leoš Janáček: *Kát'a Kabanová* by John Tyrrell
Giuseppe Verdi: *Falstaff* by James A. Hepokoski
Benjamin Britten: *Peter Grimes* by Philip Brett
Giacomo Puccini: *Tosca* by Mosco Carner
Benjamin Britten: *The Turn of the Screw* by Patricia Howard
Richard Strauss: *Der Rosenkavalier* by Alan Jefferson
Claudio Monteverdi: *Orfeo* by John Whenham
Giacomo Puccini: *La bohème* by Arthur Groos and Roger Parker
Giuseppe Verdi: *Otello* by James A. Hepokoski

To the memory of Peter Pears

Contents

x   *Contents*

Illustrations

All the production photographs are of the first production, the Maltings, Snape, June 1973.

xi

Preface

In a very real sense the inception of this book dates back to the early autumn of 1970 at Horham. Britten had asked me to visit him there at Chapel House and as we trudged round the margins of a very muddy Suffolk field before lunch he told me that he had quite definitely decided to go ahead with *Death in Venice* and asked me to begin the formal negotiations with the Mann family for the acquisition of the necessary rights. I picked up a Suffolk flint as Britten spoke and have retained it to this day as a keepsake.

The composer got his opera written and the contributors, in turn, got this book written. I thank my collaborators most warmly for their chapters and for their patient consideration of the many queries and suggestions I put to them. To one of the contributors, Philip Reed, the present Research Scholar at the Britten–Pears Library, I owe a quite particular debt, not just for his admirable chapter, but for the generous and painstaking editorial assistance he has rendered me throughout the production of the book. If I had not been able to rely on his skills and energy, this book would not have been seen through the press as speedily as it has been. Of course the responsibility for unnoticed errors (there will be some but not, I hope, too many) is mine alone.

Without virtually unrestricted access to the extraordinary documentary riches of the Britten–Pears Library and Archive at Aldeburgh, this book could certainly not be what it is. I am deeply grateful to the institution and its Trustees and especially to its Archivist, Rosamund Strode (who is also a contributor), and to the Librarian, Paul Wilson, whose contribution is none the less valuable for being as it were unseen. I should also like to thank our indefatigable copy editor, Vicki Deathridge, and Penny Souster, the music books editor of the Press, who supervised the publication of the book with a stimulating combination of enthusiasm and rigour. Jill Burrows kindly undertook the provision of the index.

Finally, we may be sure that the opera itself would not have been written at all had it not been for Peter Pears, the man and the artist. The opera was dedicated to him by the composer in all possible meanings of the word. It was my intention to surprise him on publication with the dedication of this Handbook. Alas, his death intervened and makes the dedication a posthumous one. But his incomparable achievement as the first Aschenbach will live on for as long as the opera itself survives; and as this book would seem to suggest, Britten's last work for the opera house is likely to have a very long future. It will not be forgotten while the world continues to value feats of high civilization.

London, November 1986   D.M.

Acknowledgements

We are indebted to Faber Music Ltd, the copyright owners, for permission to reproduce the music examples which appear throughout this book.

We gratefully acknowledge permission to reprint the following illustrations: p. xviii and Plate 13 (© Anthony Crickmay); p. ii, Plates 2, 12, 14 and 25 (© Nigel Luckhurst); Plates 11 and 16 (© Mrs Brenda Garner); Plate 26 (Warner Bros. Inc. © 1971 ALPHA CINEMATOGRAFICA S.R.L.). For permission to reproduce and transcribe Britten's manuscripts: the Trustees of the Britten–Pears Foundation (Plates 1, 3, 5, 6, 8, 17, 19, 20, 21, 22 and 23; music examples in chapter 4 (Exx. 1, 7, 9, 11); chapter 8 (Ex. 13); chapter 9 (Exx. 4, 7, 9, 11); the Trustees of the Britten–Pears Foundation and Donald Mitchell (Plate 4; Ex. 1 in chapter 1); the Trustees of the Britten–Pears Foundation and Myfanwy Piper (Plate 7); the Trustees of the Britten–Pears Foundation and HRH The Princess of Hesse and the Rhine (Plate 18). Plate 24 appears by kind permission of The British Library Board and the Trustees of the Britten–Pears Foundation. The excerpts from Britten's letters are reproduced by permission of the Trustees of the Britten–Pears Foundation and are copyright ©1987 Trustees of the Britten–Pears Foundation and not to be reproduced without written permission.

Peter Pears, the first Gustav von Aschenbach,
Act II scene 9: 'The pursuit'

1 An introduction in the shape of a memoir
DONALD MITCHELL

If this Handbook has a singular feature, it is this. Among its contributors are many who were working alongside the composer to help him bring his new (and, as it turned out, his last) opera to completion. Perhaps there will be other symposia on and about *Death in Venice*, but unless the contributors gathered together here are duplicated, I do not think that any one of them will be able to claim to give in quite the same way an account of the evolution of the opera, with all its attendant problems, of the revisions and modifications that both preceded and followed its première, of the hundred technical considerations affecting the course of its creation, which in this Handbook has its source in the recollections of those who, often on a day-to-day basis, were involved in the complex network of tasks associated with the launching of a major musico-theatrical undertaking. Everything of course had to be, and was, subordinated to the making of the music, to the composer's need to get his work written; and there were few activities by Britten's colleagues who had responsibilities in spheres other than the strictly compositional which now would have any significance if it were not for the music, which lends them, so to say, retrospective importance. Everything was geared, and so was every*body*, to making it possible for the composer to get on with his composing, plagued by as few practical doubts and uncertainties as was humanly possible. This was not to be the case with *Death in Venice*, nor had it been the case with *The Rape of Lucretia* and *The Turn of the Screw*; indeed, Britten perhaps had more than his fair share of ill fortune when choosing texts for his operas in which copyright or an associated right was invested.

This sort of unforeseen difficulty is described by Rosamund Strode in her authoritative chronology of the opera's composition, in all its multifarious dimensions, a contribution which is absolutely central for the symposium as a whole and a brilliant illustration of the immediacy which is at the heart of it. Miss Strode will have put paid

1

for ever to the idea that the creation of an opera requires no more than a text, a composer with ideas, and a large stock of blank manuscript paper. As she so convincingly shows, the impact of many other factors and events, and especially the intervention of the unforeseen, influence not only chronology but also the actual shape and character of the work itself.

In precisely the same way, the contributions of Myfanwy Piper, the librettist, and Colin Graham, the producer, allow us fascinating insights into successive stages of the work's assembly. These dialogues with his librettist and with the producer – I like to think of them as *duets* even – were fundamental to the process of Britten's composition, something that is not surprising in the case of the words (though even here it is of special interest in *Death in Venice* how many major textual decisions had to be made in the light of the shape the work took, as its composition progressed) but perhaps somewhat less to be expected in the case of the actual staging of the opera. But there was never any question of Britten as it were presenting his producer or designer (John Piper) with a finished musico-dramatic work that it was then their responsibility to get on the stage. On the contrary, the practicalities of the staging – not only stage movements, but timing and duration – how long did the Traveller require to accomplish his metamorphoses into Elderly Fop, Gondolier, Hotel Manager, and so on? – were from the very start intimately involved in, were part of, the compositional process. There was nothing new about that, of course. When composing *Peter Grimes*, Britten had asked his designer, Kenneth Green, to let him have a sketch – a suggestion – of how the stage might look: it was an essential aid to getting the work under way.[1] How things were going to look, how singers were to move, and where – much of all this was plotted *along with the music*.

And naturally enough, Britten's own ideas about his new opera changed as the work began to materialize. Both Colin Matthews (in his scrutiny of the 'Venice' sketchbooks, pp. 55–66) and Mervyn Cooke (in his study of the Balinese dimension, pp. 115–28) fascinatingly explore the fine detail of the sketches, revealing the options Britten pursued and (no less significant) those he discarded. One comes very close here to the inner workings of creativity. 'Inspiration' is an exceptionally difficult word to define though we use it all the time and think we can unerringly recognize it when we hear it. There were a couple of occasions that I can recall when Britten talked to me about the particular materialization of two of the leading musical ideas in the opera (though the word 'inspiration' never passed his lips). The first concerned the famous 'view' theme, which crops up continuously throughout the ensuing contributions. (In its final form it first appears as Ex. 2 in Peter Evans' synopsis (p. 79) but see also Colin Matthews, Exx. 2 and 4, p. 57 and 59.) This particular theme, Britten said, came to him as it were quite out of the blue and virtually in its entirety, and he hastily jotted it down ('on the back of an envelope') when he was travelling through France with the Pipers in January 1971, a trip which had as its *raison d'être* discussion of the forthcoming opera. Britten confessed to me his surprise that, when it came to getting down to the actual composition of the opera, he found his sketch useful. Normally, he went on to say – and perhaps this is the most interesting part of the recollection – when early ideas (inspirations?) came to him too soon, in too finished a state, too complete, for those very reasons he was unable to import them into the composition. Thus the 'view' theme was a notable exception to the rule.

The second passage Britten talked to me about involved another theme, and this time an absolutely critical one – Tadzio's theme, which is scrutinized from very many angles by many of the contributors but first appears as Ex. 3a in P. Evans (p. 79). Here, Britten told me, he had brought his composition sketch to the point of Tadzio's first entry *without*, it seems, any clear idea of what the boy's musical profile – his distinguishing theme – was to be. He put down his pen (or pencil, rather) and did not resume work on the opera until the next day. As soon as he recommenced composing, the theme came to him, perhaps not altogether surprisingly because he was a great believer in the therapy of sleep and rest and the ability of his unconscious to help out with solving compositional problems. What was surprising, and at the same time a tribute to the methodology of the composer's unconscious, was the character and special properties of the theme itself, which, to quote Britten's own words, 'used up the notes that had been left unused the night before'. Precisely what he meant by this can be examined in Colin Matthews' chapter on the 'Venice' sketchbook (see his Ex. 4, p. 59). He replicates the sketch itself and the table of pitches which shows Britten systematically ticking off the notes that had been conscripted: once Tadzio's theme had materialized, all twelve pitches of the chromatic scale were consumed. Mervyn Cooke's chapter further shows (pp. 124–25) the subtle symbolism involved in the extrapolation of the boy's haunting melody. This passage had always struck me as a *locus classicus* of the extraordinary degree of calculation that in fact is involved in what we deem 'inspiration'.

I mentioned Britten's changing ideas as work on the opera progressed, something of which I was powerfully reminded when Rosamund Strode (see p. 29) turned up in an old file some notes I had made in Edinburgh, in 1971, of a conversation with Britten about *Death in Venice*.[2] I had quite forgotten these and although Miss Strode also quotes from them, they strike me on reading them through as worth transcribing in full, since they give a faithful account of how Britten envisaged the opera two years before its first performance:

> Royal Circus Hotel
> Royal Circus
> Edinburgh EH3 6SL
> BB/DM
> 4.V.71
> Taxi in E!

D in V
3 levels of action

1) Narration (Aschenbach
   reading from his Diary,
   v. spare musical accomp't:
   his intellectual questing
   & doubts);

2) The Beach (together with
   visible Beach perc. orch: Boy
   & his family, etc.)

3) Venice, the Hotel, etc.

4) Pit orch. (Orchestra
   not yet decided)

5) To be produced *in
   the round* at *Snape*

6) only Two principals
   PP as Aschenb. &
   JS-Q as symbolic figure
   of death, singing all
   6 roles – Hotel Manager,
   Gondolier, etc., etc.

7) Chorus of men &
women, to sing all other
crowd scenes, minor roles
or whatever.

8) Two Acts – about
2 hrs. overall.

Certain features of this document are worth a moment's consideration. Myfanwy Piper, in her account of working with Britten on her masterly libretto for *Death in Venice*, has suggested (see p. 49) that at one stage he had contemplated Aschenbach *speaking* (not singing) as he read from (or wrote in) his diary; and this seems to be borne out by my notes which refer to Aschenbach 'reading from his Diary, v. spare musical accomp't'. That description must have been Britten's own, and it indicates that in May 1971 he had not yet decided that it was the solo piano that was to serve the recitatives; or perhaps it was settling for recitative that finally determined that the 'v. spare musical accomp't' should take the form of a piano? One wonders what the 'spare' musical accompaniment might have been, had he pursued the spoken diary idea. But in any event, what he ultimately chose to do was as close to speech as fixed pitches can get, while the piano perfectly articulates the particular soundworld that Aschenbach in his monologues inhabits (see Plates 1 and 2).

For the rest, while there were fascinating ideas that were modified by sheerly practical considerations – Miss Strode remarks on the abandoning of the idea to produce the opera 'in the round' at Snape – there were also many that stayed the course: much of what he talked about in the taxi in Edinburgh in May 1971 actually happened along the lines of my hasty notes (though the opera turned out to be significantly longer than two hours in duration – 2 hours 25 minutes in all).

An idea that both stayed with the composer and yet was modified (again, no doubt, on practical grounds) was the concept of the independent percussion orchestra to characterize Tadzio, his family and the games on the beach. This is clearly outlined in my Edinburgh notes, which also, however, refer to Britten's notion of a 'visible' percussion band, i.e. an *on-stage* percussion ensemble. Britten would soon have realized that this was not a practical proposition, especially in view of the integration of the percussion band into the continuity of the music. Eventually the percussion band was assigned to the pit, along with the main orchestra, though maintaining its independence. But the Edinburgh notes rather interestingly show how

6

1 The end of Aschenbach's recitative preceding Act II scene 8 in the composition sketch (The Britten-Pears Library and Archive)

2   Peter Pears in Aschenbach's first monologue, Act I scene 1: Munich

in May 1971 the three distinct planes of musical activity and characterization were already separated out in Britten's imagination and even to some degree territorially differentiated. (The actual constitution of the pit orchestra, it seems, had still to be determined.) There was no specific mention, I notice, of an 'oriental' dimension, though it strikes me now of course that the very idea of the 'visible' percussion band, particularly when it was envisaged as accompanying the games on the beach, must have directly stemmed from Britten's experience of Balinese dance and music during his round-the-world trip in 1955/6, where the instrumental ensemble (the gamelan) is a *seen* part of any performance (the classical Noh drama of Japan too, with its visible musicians, may have been another influence). In any event, the oriental dimension was to show up as a major feature of *Death in Venice* in the music of Tadzio, his family and his comrades, music for which Britten turned to the resources he had developed so powerfully since his *Pagodas* ballet of 1957 and which perfectly embodied the elements of the text, exotic and alien, which are part of Mann's novella. (See also Carnegy, pp. 175–6.)

The origins of Britten's encounter with oriental and, more specifically, Balinese music date back to a period which preceded his actual visit to that island by some fifteen years, to his wartime residence on Long Island, New York, and his friendship with the remarkable Canadian-born composer and ethnomusicologist, Colin McPhee (1900–64).[3] It is not my intention here to go over again the history of this crucial, and until relatively recently, unsuspected and unexamined first brush with Balinese music which was eventually to have such profound consequences for the development of his compositional techniques.[4] Sufficient here to refer to Mervyn Cooke's pioneering contribution (see pp. 115–28) which for the first time scrutinizes in detail the gamelan dimension of *Death in Venice*, and its function, and places it precisely in relation both to Balinese music and to precedents in Britten's own work.[5] The *Pagodas* was, of course, a major precedent, and one of Mr Cooke's illustrations (see Plate 20, p. 118) shows the composer addressing an *aide-mémoire* to himself on p. 5 of the Venice sketchbook in the shape of a listing of the constituents of the percussion orchestra he had assembled for the gamelan music in his ballet of 1957. But the seeds of the Pagoda-land music had been planted much earlier and flowered not only in the ballet but in 1973, in this last opera of all.

My Edinburgh jottings represent a conceptual stage in the evolution of the opera. All my other recollections are bound up with the work after its composition had been completed. Rosamund Strode spends some time on the revisions made to *Death in Venice* after the first run of performances at the Aldeburgh Festival of 1973, in the preparation of which Britten was unable to participate and none of which he was able to attend. It was not until 12 September of that year that he actually saw and heard the work, a private performance mounted for him at Snape.

There can be no doubt that the special and painful circumstances attending the composition of the opera – Britten's ill-health while labouring to bring the score to an end, his continuing ill-health after his heart operation in May 1973 – affected his judgement of his music. It was not, I hasten to stress, a question of his illness pre- or post-operation affecting the quality or distinctiveness of his ideas, but, rather, his illness undermining his confidence in his own judgement of what (and if any) revisions needed to be put in hand. There was nothing strange to Britten about the process of revision. What was new, perhaps in the case of *Death in Venice* was Britten's own uncertainties and even a kind of indecisiveness about some of the revisions which engaged his attention *after* he had the chance to experience his opera in the theatre.

Part of this uncertainty was undoubtedly due to his physical condition, to the disruptive impact of the operation. I can remember coming on him in the libary at the Red House with a full score of the opera before him. He was working on an orchestral revision with evident concentration but also with a conspicuous anxiety. I cannot now recall the exact location of the revision but it was a comparatively minor decision that was worrying the composer, perhaps no more than the respacing of a single chord or the reallocation of a single pitch. He explained to me, with a sigh, that since his operation he had sometimes found it difficult to be absolutely sure that what his hitherto impregnable inner ear had dictated was precisely what he was seeking as a resolution of the problem. It may have been a moment only of acute depression; and indeed the opera and the ensuing late works speak for an ear and instrumental imagination that had lost nothing of their former power. (Christopher Palmer's chapter (see pp. 129–53) abundantly expounds the singular sound-world the opera creates and then marvellously inhabits. Nonetheless, an incident of the kind I have just related must have shaken Britten's self-confidence and contributed to his occasional self-doubts.)

Because of the peculiar circumstances of the first staging of the opera – the composer absent and incommunicado – it was natural enough, though I had not myself had the experience before, for Britten to enquire of his friends and associates (and the conductor, Steuart Bedford) if there were things in *Death in Venice* that had troubled them, things that had not worked. (This was after he had seen the production for the first time in September 1973.) No doubt this consultative process had always been part of the normal post-première evaluation, the means by which decisions about revisions (if any) were arrived at. What was new to the situation in 1973 and 1974 was, I think, the composer's own unsettled state of mind. Whereas in the past he would have at once exercised his own judgement or accepted the advice of others because he immediately saw the point of it, in the case of *Death in Venice* he seemed uncharacteristically indecisive.

His 'tell me what bothered you', 'tell me what was wrong' interrogation did not quarry anything momentous out of me. On the contrary, I had been convinced by Britten's sustained mastery of an epic dramatic form ever since I had first heard the opera (more of that first unveiling below). But there were two or three musico-dramatic details which did seem to me to require his attention. One aspect of Act I that had troubled me, for example, was Aschenbach's gondola journeys. (See also Strode, pp. 41–2.) There were times when it had occurred to me that these were vestigial in the extreme: they needed articulating more clearly and at greater length if they were to register more effectively with audiences, if indeed the ritornello-like function of Aschenbach's ceaseless to-ing and fro-ing was to be established. Nor had the abstract, non-realistic staging done much to help make these journeys by water visually substantial. An example of this crucial passage in its final form may be found in the published vocal score between figs. 115 and 117. But at the first performance, this specific gondola trip had comprised only one unmeasured bar of Gondoliers' cries, preceded and rounded off by a flourish that was an indication of Aschenbach getting into and then out of the gondola. This, I felt, was taking economy and compression too far, and I pressed Britten to reconsider the concept of the journeying music.

He did: and in the case of the ferrying back to the hotel from fig. 115, he did so in a characteristically ingenious way. In the first place, he returned to what he had originally composed (15 bars from the landing stage to the Lido, as against the six (approximately) that were heard at the first performance: a cut had been imposed here before the première). But in addition he wrote a new vocal part for Pears – 'But where? Where shall I go?', etc. – to which the existing

3 From Britten's copy of the dyelined vocal score (in Colin
   Matthews' hand). This shows the gondola music (figs.
   115–118) that was ultimately restored, and the composer's
   later addition of a vocal part for Aschenbach (The Britten-
   Pears Library and Archive)

(original) journeying music now formed an accompaniment. What had previously been purely instrumental in execution (but for the Gondoliers' cries) was thus made vocal: and Aschenbach's participation further intensifies our sense of his overpowering claustrophobia and his compulsion to 'find a clearer sky, a fresher air' (see Plate 3).

The new and transforming vocal line, one notes, did not entail in overall length the addition of a single bar; and it is this fact, the solving of a problem which at the same time reasserted the proportions of the original ritornello (as had been established by the end of January 1973), which is perhaps the most interesting and significant of all. It suggests that the composer should have trusted himself rather than the counsel of others, especially where matters of musical duration and proportion were involved, for it was precisely in these spheres that his judgement was patently superior.

For me, this opinion is not modified but strengthened rather by his initial doubts about the length and pacing of the Prologue and Act I of the opera, doubts which assailed him while he was busy with the composition of the work. In a fascinating letter to his librettist, written from Germany on 6 February 1972, he concentrates on the problem of duration and formal proportions:

In order to look at what I had done from a distance – I played it all through, and made the alarming discovery that as far as the arrival of the hotel guests, the duration is at least 45 minutes – before Tadzio, the False Departure, any of the Ballets! I cannot see, at this rate, how the whole Act could be less than 1½ hrs [in the event it proved to run for 1 hour 20 minutes], and tho' shorter, Act II can't be too short – at least one hour [in its final form, 65 minutes]. I have been through it carefully from the musical point of view only – and I think in my excitement I have been too generous, & I have made lots of little cuts (some rather distressing ones – but right, I think), and also played it again (this time to Peter [Pears]). I may have saved 2 or 3 minutes, but not more, & I think we must look at it all again, very closely. . . . I feel the Guests' conversation may have to go, some of the Gondola journeys, & I feel now that some of the 'spoken' comments will have to be shorter, & some even to go altogether. In playing the Prologue last night I was immensely struck by how the first comment ('spoken') reduces the dramatic tension. I think we must discuss each point to see if it is dramatically essential, to see if we haven't already made it another way. . . .[6]

An altogether absorbing letter – it also contained news for the librettist of Peter Pears's suggestion that a counter-tenor should undertake the Voice of Apollo – which reminds us, if we should need reminding, of how closely involved he was in the evolution of the operas – and Britten's reaction (a cautious 'excellent') to Mrs Piper's surely somewhat unworldly proposal that the boys in the beach games should dance naked (an idea that was fortunately not pursued: see also Piper, p. 50). But what concerns us here is Britten's clearly expressed anxiety about the formal proportions of the first act of his opera; and his list of 'points' for consideration interestingly includes Aschenbach's journeys by gondola, one of which I have just discussed, and the first recitative, on which I comment below (the Guests' conversations (fig. 66, *et seq.*) were retained).

The case of the gondola-ritornello is of special relevance to my argument that we should trust the composer and that composers should trust themselves. Britten's 1972 letter undeniably shows him nervous about duration well before the work was completed, let alone being rehearsed. It is not surprising in all the special circumstances surrounding the first performance of *Death in Venice* that the journeying music at fig. 115 was singled out for a cut. But as I have shown, once Britten was himself convinced that this was a misjudgement, he returned the passage to its original (January 1973) proportions; and I hope had the satisfaction of realizing that his composer's earlier instinct had been right all along. As we shall see a little later, the first recitative, about which he had had an early attack of anxiety as well, was also to come up for debate; but that story needs separate telling and consideration. First, and by way of contrast, I want to document a later revision with which I had something to do – one that, far from revealing any indecisiveness on Britten's part, disclosed the precise opposite: not only an instant decision but also instant revision.

What was involved in the small but significantly revised timing of the announcement to the Hotel Guests that dinner was served ('Signori! Il ristorante, a vostro servizio!': Act I scene 4) is outlined in the chapter by Rosamund Strode (see p. 43). The further gloss that I would wish to add here is this: that no sooner had Britten seen the point of my submission than he called for a pencil and on the blank half of the appropriate page in the interim vocal score, which he rested on his knees, he sketched out with lightning rapidity exactly what needed to be done to transpose the entry of the Hotel Waiters.[7] (I reproduce on Plate 4 the page with Britten's revision inscribed on it, at the top of which I added the date and place where the amendment was made: 'Horham 2 October 1974, after lunch'.)

I tell the story because in the brief moment that it took Britten to sketch the revision, I had a glimpse of that extraordinary practicality

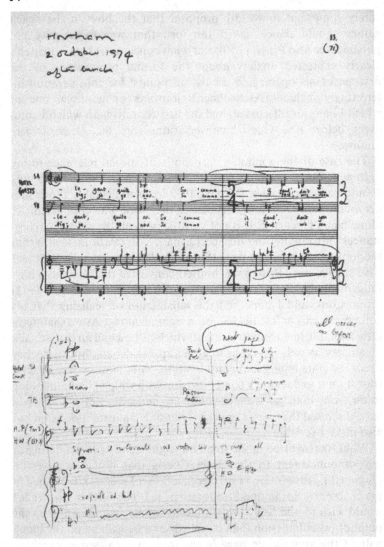

4 A page from the interim vocal score, Act I scene 4, showing Britten's revision of the announcement in the hotel that dinner was served (Collection: Donald Mitchell)

and decisiveness for which he was renowned in the theatre, a legendary ability and capacity to solve problems on the spot if the need was there. I was reminded at the time that this was a gift that must have served him well in the 1930s in the GPO Film Unit and Group Theatre, and in the broadcasting studio – a gift indeed that was sharpened by the techniques that those areas of activity necessarily entailed. It was the immediacy that was so striking; and when I read in 1976, a description by Christopher Isherwood[8] of the production, in 1936, of W.H. Auden's *Ascent of F6*, the tiny vignette of the Group theatre's resident composer –

I remember . . . Ben as pale, boyish, indefatigable, scribbling music on his lap, then hurrying to the piano to play it

– transported me back to Horham in 1974, when just for a minute or two I had an uncanny glimpse of the ever resourceful, speedy and skilful composer of 1936, nearly forty years on but as speedy and resourceful as ever, and with his music still on his lap.

This tiny incident shows all the old decisiveness, which would doubtless have been brought into play at this very point if Britten had heard the work in rehearsal. My next recollection (the last I have in the area of revisions) concerns the question of the first recitative, a passage with a pre- (see Britten's letter above) and post-first performance history. I shall begin with an obvious discrepancy.

Students of the vocal score and of the recording made under the composer's supervision will have noticed for themselves the oddity that the recording of the opera apparently adopts a cut that in the vocal score is offered only as an option.[9] What has to be emphasized in this context is chronology: that the recording *preceded* publication of the vocal score, and that the seeming paradox of the 'authentic' recorded performance not matching up with the 'authentic', i.e. complete, text of the opera, had its origins in Britten's uncertainty about how successful he had been with the pacing, the timing, of the opera's Munich prologue, which as we have seen, had surfaced as early as February 1972.[10]

I have no doubt that any suggestion made to him after the première that the opera was slow in getting underway and, more specifically, that Aschenbach's first meditative recitative, in which he ponders whether he should allow 'impulse' to be his guide (vocal score, pp. 16–17), was an unnecessary (or at least disposable) postponement of his ultimate decision, 'So be it! I will pursue this freedom', would have reactivated the composer's old anxiety that he had been too 'generous'.

My view was (and remains) quite other. *Without* the first recitative Aschenbach appears to make up his mind to undertake the journey 'to the warm and lovely south' much too easily. It is in the first recitative that we first encounter Aschenbach's introspective irresolution, appropriately manifesting itself when, in the opera, for the first time, the burden is placed on him of having to come to a decision. The loss of the recitative would entail a significant loss to the prompt establishing of Aschenbach's characteristic vacillation.

Britten in fact came to regret the omission of the first recitative from the recording, which itself was made, one might add, at a time when he was in low spirits and physically at low ebb. The restoration of the recitative in the vocal score (with an accompanying note simultaneously offering it as an optional cut) was perhaps a not very happy attempt (I think now) to reconcile the vocal score with the recording. It was an eruption of anxiety that in the event had an ironic outcome. For practical reasons, it proved not possible to introduce the cut into the original production because this then left insufficient time for the Traveller to rematerialize in the guise of the Elderly Fop. Thus it was only in the recording that the eventually unwanted and impractical cut was made. I am pretty confident that now the composer would wish us to forget his Aschenbach-like indecision ('I am become like one of my early heroes, passive in the face of fate', and so on) and rid the published version of his work of the evidence of an interim confusion.

My last memory of all is in fact of a performance of the opera, one that preceded all rehearsals for the première and was given by the composer himself at the piano one day in London, in his studio at Halliford Street, N. 1, shortly after he had completed the composition sketch in December 1972. I was the only member of the audience, but the composer appeared in multiple guise: he impersonated all the vocal roles, and summoned up from the keyboard with those preternaturally long fingers of his, the unique colours of his Venice orchestra. It was a brilliant demonstration of what Peter Pears remarked in a television interview in 1985: 'Ben somehow had a command over the keyboard with his fingers which came . . . flashed like lightning from his very being. But it was amazing what colours he could get. He thought a colour and he could do it.' Even the percussion did not defeat him. Rhythmic patterns he knocked out on the piano rest. As for the voice, everything was delivered in that inimitable *sotto voce* that was always a feature of these spell-binding occasions; and yet I cannot remember a single major expressive or dramatic point that Britten did not succeed in making. The climax of Act I – 'I love you' – and the orchestral epilogue that rounds off Act II: I was not more profoundly stirred by those inspirations when I came to hear them in the theatre. It was a first exposure to *Death in Venice* that I shall not forget.

Britten was no lover of the telephone (for which we may be grateful: it made him a prolific letter writer), but there were two or three phone calls he made during the composition of *Death in Venice* which have lodged in my memory. One of them, made quite late at night, was to tell me that he had reached the climactic point of Act II, the death of Aschenbach. It may have been, indeed, that he had actually passed that point. I cannot now be absolutely certain. But what struck me at the time about this brief phone call, and what I remember still, was its *necessity*: this was an absolutely critical moment for the composer, for his opera, for the opera's protagonist. There was no way round Aschenbach's death. It had to happen. It had to be composed. The burden of that enactment, of that imagined and yet so real death, showed up in the telephone call, which was a way perhaps of sharing the burden a little. (Peter Pears, I recall, was away at the time.) It was for me a singular experience, without precedent and never repeated. It brought home very vividly just how profoundly Britten was involved in the fate of his doomed hero.

There was more than one phone call, naturally, in connection with the recomposition of the Strolling Players' scene (Act II scene 10) concerning the bizarre copyright snag that Rosamund Strode untangles on p. 38. Britten's reaction to this setback, after the initial shock, was entirely decisive and spirited. As soon as he saw that a substitution had to be made, he simply got on with it, at high speed. It was doubtless in connection with this untoward event that he sent me a page of manuscript paper with a couple of the Strolling Players' tunes written out, though not quite in their final shape. On the verso of the page I found a sketch, inscribed 'End of D in V', which embodies the very moment preceding Aschenbach's death, the event that was to prompt the phone call I have described above.

This is clearly an early sketch – there is another and later one in the Venice sketchbook (p. 29) – for the preparation of the climactic event of Act II. I transcribe the sketch below (Ex. 1), and below it, the version at which Britten finally arrived (Ex. 2). It is fascinating to observe in the sketch that already at this stage he had in mind the precise pitches of Aschenbach's cry of protest – 'Ah, no!' – and with them, the accompanying percussion (gamelan) chords; and most significantly of all, an indication of the tuba's lethal intervention, though this was to become more elaborate in the final compositional state. Likewise, the sketch ends with an indication of the first of the off-stage choral cries, 'Adziù' – in Britten's sketch 'Tadziù!' – written at the identical pitch we know from the finished score. What differs is the music that links Aschenbach's cry of pain to the first, partial articulation by a quartet of voices of his name (the 'Adziù' which is so close at this terminal point to 'Adieu'). Whereas the sketch seems to show Britten envisaging Tadzio picking himself *up* after his struggle with Jaschiu (hence the *ascending* figuration) to the accompaniment of his own characterizing instrument (vibraphone) and in a shape closely related to the original form of his characterizing theme – the later sketch still preserves this feature – the final version shows a much more complex picture. There, after Aschenbach's cry, the momentum of the boys' fight is liquidated in the percussion orchestra's punctuations, based on the principal motive of the music which has accompanied the struggle. At the same time, Britten retains the characterizing vibraphone music, though in a more elaborate formu-

Ex. 1

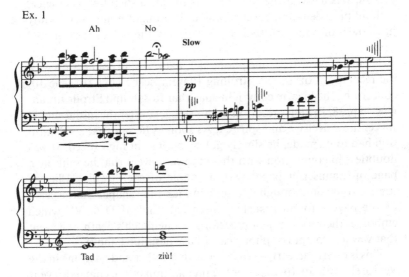

[This example is an exact transcription of the original sketch and does not attempt to correct its idiosyncrasies and inconsistencies.]

Ex. 2

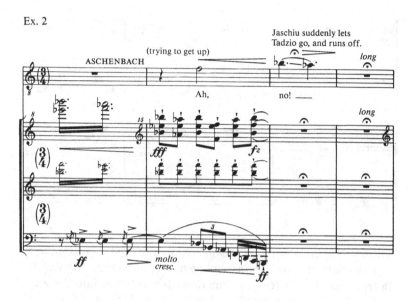

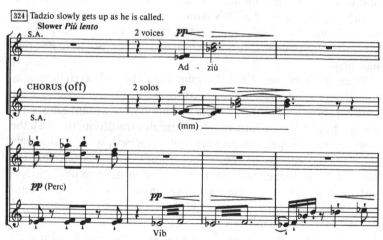

Ex. 2 (*cont.*)

lation – one moreover which is interrupted by and then combined with the punctuations. The ascending motion, however, is retained – Tadzio regaining his feet, walking towards and finally into the sea – and in fact leads us onwards and upwards, and by way of Aschenbach's expiration on Tadzio's name, rising on an inverted outline (ascending) of Tadzio's own pitches, arrives at the high point at which Tadzio's theme enters and from which it descends, in its original form.

What distinguishes the final version from the early sketch, we may think, is the exceptional compositional craft. A rather simple sequence of events – the cry, Tadzio's recovery, the distant echo of his name – has been transformed into a complex transition, in which the boys' aggressive energy is progressively dispersed, while at the same time Tadzio recovers his poise and distant voices recapitulate the boy's name as Aschenbach has first heard it in Act I scene 5. No less importantly, the whole passage functions as a marvellously contrived lead-back to the final recapitulation of Tadzio's theme, at its original pitch and in its basic shape (fig. 325).[11] To be sure, the sketch documents ideas that were to be crucial to the passage. But for their composition into a multi-layered transition we have to look to the final version.

Death in Venice was Britten's last opera, written in circumstances of great stress and later revised here and there in circumstances that were scarcely serene. It is tempting to read into the work, and perhaps especially because of the coincidences between Britten's personal history and the history of his protagonist, a particular aware-ness on the composer's part of mortality, of the possibility (somewhat nearer than hitherto) of his own death. But Britten survived *Death in Venice*, and though physically frail, went on composing, and died still full of ideas for future works. The opera, as it happened, turned out to be a kind of last testament, at least in terms of Britten's contribution to the musical theatre, because of his untimely death and because of the strange parallels that sometimes run between life and art. But it might have been otherwise.

In one respect, however, the opera was undeniably a 'testament' (though it need not have been a last one) and also autobiographical in character. *Death in Venice* embodies unequivocally the powerful sexual drive that was Britten's towards the young (and sometimes very young) male. It is true that this was by no means the first time that this deep-rooted side of his nature had profoundly influenced the topics of his musical dramas. But it was certainly the first time that it had been expressed so directly. Are we any the wiser for drawing this parallel between life and art, between a composer's history and the work he creates? I reject outright the idea that our knowledge of a composer's psyche will somehow 'explain' his music. In Britten's case, and particularly where sexual preferences are involved, psychologizing is too often used not to elucidate or illuminate the *work* (which is something quite different from the author of it) but, rather, to *explain it away* (we then no longer have to devote any thought to it). But in fact the parallel in this instance tells us something significant about the work, about the composer's approach to his art, and about the composer. Britten was a composer of parables long before he actually used the word to describe his Church operas; the concept of 'parable-art' was defined and discussed by Auden in 1935 ('that art which shall teach man to unlearn hatred and learn love'), the onset of a period when the poet and composer were most closely and productively to collaborate.[12] *Death in Venice* is scarcely less of a parable than, say, *The Burning Fiery Furnace* (or one might have introduced, with equal relevance, *Owen Wingrave*). In the last opera, parable-art operates on different levels, one of the most important of which – possibly the most important – embodies the struggle of the artist to create, the labour of creation; and more specifically the obligation to keep in balance the opposed forces of Apollo and Dionysus, order and chaos, form and feeling. Interestingly enough, this was again an issue that had been raised by

Auden, this time in his now famous letter to Britten, written in America in January 1942, just before the composer's return to wartime England. Auden wrote: 'Goodness and [Beauty] are the results of a perfect balance between Order and Chaos, Bohemianism and Bourgeois Convention. Bohemian chaos alone ends in a mad jumble of beautiful scraps; Bourgeois convention alone in large unfeeling corpses.'[13] The very theme, one might think, of *Death in Venice*. It is clear, indeed, that Auden's words went on resonating in Britten's mind, as they would have done with any thoughtful artist. What he wrote to Kit Welford, his brother-in-law, in March 1942, while he was still in America, seems in fact to echo Auden's January letter:

I am so pleased that you have thought things out so carefully. From a very different angle I have come to an identical point-of-view (re discipline and obedience) – but in art, as you know, the bias is to the other direction, that of anarchy and romantic 'freedom'. A carefully chosen discipline is the only possible course.[14]

This would suggest that his friend's analytical letter about the 'dangers' that beset him 'as a man and as an artist' made a striking impression on him, was long meditated on, and finally discharged in the shape of *Death in Venice*.

Auden of course did not invent the Apollo/Dionysus dichotomy. He spelled it out, however, in the context of his own and Britten's homosexuality. Thomas Mann also spelled out the age-old dichotomy and chose to enact it in terms of Aschenbach's hopeless infatuation with Tadzio. We know now how deeply rooted his novella was in his own experience and inner life. Britten, likewise. His last opera unfolds, parable-like, his long-standing preoccupation with the problems and perils of the artist, dangerously poised between the Apollonian heights and the Dionysian abyss: the opera on one plane is about the making of itself, in the same way that Proust's great novel is itself the great creative undertaking which the novel is about. But on another plane, and intensely so – perhaps more intensely than for Mann – the Aschenbach/Tadzio relationship/dichotomy functioned for Britten as a parable of his own life, though with a fundamental difference; and it is precisely this difference which distinguishes the work of art from the persona of the artist. There can be no doubt of the degree of engagement Britten brought to *Death in Venice*, of his identification with Aschenbach. How could it be otherwise? He must often have been stirred to feelings exactly like those of his hero. But it is precisely at this point, where life and art seem to merge, that we have to be most wary. We should acknowledge the paradox that *Death in Venice* exemplifies: the integrated work of art that culminates in the disintegration of its protagonist, without itself disintegrating. We encounter a similar paradox in *Tristan* which is dedicated to a transcendental nihilism and yet by its very existence contradicts that philosophy, while Wagner survived to complete the *Ring* and compose *Meistersinger* and *Parsifal*! In *Death in Venice* too, life and art radically diverge. Although we are wholly right to perceive Britten's opera as autobiographical in a very special sense, the parable it tells on this level nonetheless does not spell out the tale of Britten's life. Aschenbach, his hero, is fragmented and finally destroyed by his obsession, at once a curse and source of inspiration. Britten, on the contrary, and like Wagner (at least in this respect), was a survivor. Not only was he able to hold in balance the Apollonian/Dionysiac confrontation in *Death in Venice*, which enabled the opera to be written, but also to hold the same balance, at whatever cost, in his own life. Without this balance he could not have functioned as the artist he was.[15] The parable-opera ends for Aschenbach tragically and unproductively, a difference that makes my last point for me: that while the opera ends with the protagonist destroyed (Dionysus uppermost), there was no comparable defeat in the composer's personal history. There was certainly struggle and conflict, and it would be trite, sentimental even, to summon up Apollo to provide a neat conclusion. But in sum, his life – that 'carefully chosen discipline' already articulated in 1942 – was a victory.

Quite apart from the subject of the opera, the compositional processes involved in it have also sometimes seemed to lend strength to the 'last testament' notion, simply because we find in *Death in Venice* an astonishingly comprehensive exploitation of virtually all the resources of music which Britten had ever fed into his own creativity. There is the gamelan dimension, boosted by the Far East trip of 1955–6, but which we now realize to have had its roots in the 1940s, and indeed first showed up in Britten's first full-length theatrical work, *Paul Bunyan* (1941), before making a major début in *The Prince of the Pagodas* in 1957.[16] There is alongside the gamelan element, the heterophonic principle, which again can be traced back to *Bunyan* (and to works post-*Bunyan*, *Grimes* among them), which was to emerge most prominently, and much later, in *Curlew River* (1964), and thereafter profoundly affected Britten's compositional techniques.

There is, on the other hand, the conspicuous twelve-note com-

ponent; and juxtaposed with that, Britten's unshakeable commit-
ment to tonality and long-range tonal planning, about which
Eric Roseberry (pp. 86–98) writes so stimulatingly. This is a rich
enough mix, one might think, and one made richer still by the cross-
fertilization of one resource with another, e.g. the heterophonic
treatment, stripped of all exotic associations, of the diatonic orchestral prelude to Act II.

Death in Venice not only anthologizes all the musical resources
and techniques available to the composer but also conscripts useful
precedents from earlier operas – for example, the choral dances from
Gloriana must have been in Britten's mind when contemplating how
'The Games of Apollo' might be formulated. But there are aspects of
Death in Venice that seem to me to extend even farther back, to his
post-college years, when he was earning a living in the documentary
film movement. It was in the 1930s, through the combination of an
exceptionally acute ear and a brilliant talent to persuade from a
handful of instruments the sonority to replicate a sound from the
'real' world, that Britten developed the documentary gift that stood
him in such good stead throughout his life in the opera house. This is
a kind of mimicry raised to the nth degree and makes a final appearance in Act I scene 2, 'On the boat to Venice', where Britten marvellously contrives the sound of the ship's siren, and the engines' throbbing into life (see Palmer, Ex. 1, p. 132), the thud of the pistons, the
hiss from the prow as it cleaves the water – a pocket anthology of the
sounds, mechanical and natural, of a ship at sea, extrapolated from
a pair of trombones[17] and an ensemble of drums sometimes played
with unconventional means, e.g. domestic scrubbing brushes. It is an
acoustic illusion generated by the skill acquired by the youthful
composer-in-residence of the GPO Film Unit.

And so one could go on: about the orchestration, for example,
which is a positive compendium of Britten's orchestral techniques,
and a dozen other features of the opera. But none of this suggests to
me that he was consciously pouring into this 'last' opera all the
musico-dramatic experience of preceding decades, as if he were
documenting everything that had meant something to him. I read
Death in Venice somewhat differently, as one of those characteristic
works of Britten which was a summation of a crucial period of his
creativity, a retrospective, and yet at the same time, a *prospective*, a
looking forward to works as yet unwritten, a mapping out of territory that was to be explored. I see *Grimes* in that double perspective,
and likewise *Death in Venice*; and there are many other key works

which similarly consummate a period and initiate a fresh one. This Handbook tells us a good deal about the sources that fertilized *Death in Venice*. What longer future in Britten's *oeuvre* the opera might have fertilized – that now we shall never know.

2 A 'Death in Venice' chronicle[1]

ROSAMUND STRODE

Nineteen months after the heart operation he had undergone in May 1973, Benjamin Britten was interviewed for *The Times* by Alan Blyth. In the interview ('Britten returns to composing', 30 December 1974) he said, concerning *Death in Venice*, 'I wanted passionately to finish this piece before anything happened. For one thing, it is probably Peter's last major operatic part; for another, it was an opera I had been thinking about for a very long time, and it had already been postponed once.'

With his larger works a considerable period of gestation was not at all unusual for Britten, although exactly what constituted 'a very long time' in this case is not quite clear. It seems, however, that *Death in Venice* was well in mind by 1965 at the latest. His own copy of the text is the New Adelphi Library edition (1929) of H.T. Lowe-Porter's English translation of Thomas Mann's story, and although it has the owner's autograph on the flyleaf (written, perhaps, at some time during the 1950s or 1960s) it is undated. But the first positive step was taken early in September 1970, when Britten asked Myfanwy Piper if she would like to write the *Death in Venice* libretto for him.[2] Britten had just finished the full score of their previous collaboration *Owen Wingrave* (due to be produced for television that November) and in the breathing space thus afforded he was already planning his next major work.

He wrote to Thomas Mann's son, Professor Golo Mann (whom Britten had known in New York in 1940) to see whether his idea would be favourably received by the author's widow and family. On 14 September Golo Mann answered warmly, assuring Britten of the full support of his mother and himself over the *Death in Venice* project (see Carnegy, p. 168). He also mentioned Visconti's film, at that moment being made in Venice (see P. Reed, pp. 178–83), but did not anticipate any serious troubles arising on that account. In fact here he was wrong; contractual complexities with Warner Bros. were not finally to be resolved for almost two years.

26

Those first three years of the 1970s were exceptionally busy for Benjamin Britten, and to appreciate fully the task he set himself in writing *Death in Venice* one needs to know something of his other commitments at this period. At the start of 1970 he was still writing *Owen Wingrave*, finishing the composition sketches in February, just before he and Peter Pears went for a six-week tour of Australia and New Zealand, both with the English Opera Group and on their own. They returned as the reconstruction of the Maltings Concert Hall at Snape, gutted by fire at the start of the 1969 Aldeburgh Festival, was nearing completion, and Britten conducted the first concert in the rebuilt hall on 5 June. During the next three weeks he conducted three performances of Mozart's *Idomeneo* and four other concerts (including the first performance outside the USSR of Symphony No. 14 by Shostakovich, dedicated to Britten, and the world première of the Cello Concerto by Arthur Bliss with Mstislav Rostropovich as soloist) and played the piano for a memorable recital of Schubert's last songs performed by Peter Pears and John Shirley-Quirk. At Snape in July Britten conducted recordings for Decca of *The Rape of Lucretia*, Mozart's 'Prague' Symphony K. 504 and his own Violin Concerto with Mark Lubotsky.

In August he finished the full score of *Owen Wingrave*. That September at Snape there was a week of Britten operas, given by the English Opera Group, during which he conducted two performances of *Lucretia* (it was at about this time that he approached Myfanwy Piper over *Death in Venice*) and in the same month he played for a television recording of Schubert's *Winterreise* with Peter Pears, conducted a recording of Purcell's *The Fairy Queen* for Decca at Snape and a concert performance of the same work in the Queen Elizabeth Hall, London. The whole of November was devoted to the television production of *Owen Wingrave* at Snape (rehearsals and filming) and the opera was recorded for Decca at the Kingsway Hall, London, at the beginning of December. Back immediately to Snape, now cleared of the *Owen Wingrave* set, for yet another Decca recording (Britten's Piano Concerto with Sviatoslav Richter) followed by a fund-raising gala concert given in the presence of Her Majesty Queen Elizabeth the Queen Mother at the Royal Opera House, Covent Garden; Rostropovich was the principal guest artist. Two recitals with Peter Pears in Germany rounded off the year's concerts; an exceptional year in many ways, with extra commitments because of the Maltings fire in 1969. Improvements to the rebuilt concert hall had entailed special fund-raising events, and some Decca recordings (planned for the

1969/70 season, when the hall was not available) had had to be fitted in whenever possible.

The visit to Germany at Christmas provided the opportunity for a meeting with Golo Mann. By the end of 1970 it was apparent that legal complications did indeed exist with regard to the agreements already made between the Estate of Thomas Mann and Warner Bros. concerning film rights, but it was hoped that these could quickly be resolved. Professor Mann was consistently helpful and encouraging, and Britten felt that he could now start seriously to think about *Death in Venice*. To avoid accusations of plagiarism or of being at all influenced by Visconti's work, Britten was advised not to allow it to be known publicly that he proposed to write an opera based on Thomas Mann's story (though in fact he in any case preferred to keep his compositional plans as private as possible) and, when Visconti's film was eventually released, that he ought not to see it. On 6 January 1971 he wrote to Myfanwy Piper, cautiously optimistic and ready to hold preliminary discussions. A holiday in France by car with the Pipers and Peter Pears was arranged for the end of January (in the meantime Britten wrote his *Canticle IV: Journey of the Magi*, for performance in June) and they set off on the twenty-sixth of that month.

Once abroad, with John Piper driving and Peter Pears map reading their way through France, Britten and Myfanwy Piper sat in the back of the car talking over their ideas of *Death in Venice* and working out a preliminary scenario. On returning home she wrote enthusiastically to Donald Mitchell and began drafting the libretto, sending pages to Aldeburgh from time to time during the following weeks for Britten's comments, while discussions on the complex scenario continued. The producer's involvement in a new opera from the earliest possible moment was absolutely necessary to Britten, and two days after returning from France he met Colin Graham in London.[3] It was obviously important to start making outline plans for the opera at once, and on 2 March discussions were held with Graham and the English Opera Group management regarding the possibility of producing the new work at an autumn season of opera at Snape the following year, in September 1972.

Over the succeeding months, Britten's punishing schedule of work continued; the Third Suite for Cello was finished on 3 March, Bach's *St John Passion* recorded for Decca at Snape at the beginning of April and a performance of it given there on Good Friday. Later in April he and Peter Pears went to the USSR with a large party of musicians for a week of British music, with concerts in Leningrad and Moscow.

The return home was immediately followed by a week's concert tour in the north – Rosehill (with performances of Bach) and Edinburgh where, on 4 May (postponed for a year owing to Peter Pears's illness in April 1970) Britten's Op. 84 *Who are these children?* was given its first complete performance. In Edinburgh that day Donald Mitchell noted down some important decisions about *Death in Venice* which Britten told him during a taxi journey across the city. He learned of the various levels of action planned (Aschenbach's narrative; the beach; Venice) and that there were to be only two principals – Peter Pears and John Shirley-Quirk – with minor roles taken by members of the chorus. The constitution of the orchestra was not yet determined, but the opera was to be in two acts. And (most interesting, perhaps) he noted that it was 'to be produced *in the round* at *Snape*'. (See also Mitchell, pp. 4–6.)

Britten then came back to Aldeburgh in time to see the first showing of *Owen Wingrave* on 16 May (the Pipers came to stay for that) and to prepare for the Festival. He made a cautious statement to the Press on 1 June; *The Times* the following day carried Alan Blyth's report:

Benjamin Britten is writing a new opera to be given at The Maltings, Snape, in September 1972. For contractual reasons the subject cannot yet be announced, but the composer told me yesterday that he was 'clearing the decks' in order to spend all his composing time over the next year on this work. He is also planning a large-scale solo piano piece for Sviatoslav Richter.

(Alas, that work for Richter was never to materialize.)

At the 1971 Aldeburgh Festival Britten conducted two orchestral concerts, the Mozart *Requiem*, and two performances of *The Dream of Gerontius*, one of them given in Cambridge. Playing the piano, Britten accompanied vocal duets, gave a performance of *Winterreise* with Peter Pears, and played for a programme entitled 'Three Voices and Piano'; this concert included songs by Purcell, Wolf and Schütz, and the new *Canticle IV*, sung by James Bowman, Peter Pears and John Shirley-Quirk.

In July, work was again resumed on the *Death in Venice* scenario and a second draft prepared. On the fifteenth of the month the agreement between the Estate of Thomas Mann and Benjamin Britten was signed at the Mitchells' Sussex home. But although this now removed all legal obstacles concerning the use of Thomas Mann's story as the basis for Britten's opera, negotiations for full clearance in relation to the film rights ceded to Warner Bros. (these unfortunately included television and, even more important, radio rights for several years) were still to drag on for another twelve months.

A week at the end of July was taken up by a recording for Decca at Snape of *The Dream of Gerontius*, with the London Symphony Orchestra and Chorus. In August the new scenario became the basis for the most detailed discussions so far, including the probable size of the orchestra and – from Colin Graham – the number of chorus members needed, an analysis of which singer could double what characters, and the minimum number of costumes required. A meeting was held with Sir Frederick Ashton (who had produced the première of *Albert Herring* in 1947) to talk over the choreography of the ballets. During this period unexpected stress arose with the resignation of the Aldeburgh Festival General Manager, Stephen Reiss, whose views on the future of the Maltings diverged too sharply from Britten's for them to be reconciled; the crisis was painful and worrying. More conducting for Britten at the end of August: rehearsals and two performances of *The Turn of the Screw* at Snape and two more at Sadler's Wells Theatre three weeks later. Further activities in September included a Promenade concert performance of *The Fairy Queen* at the Royal Albert Hall, two big recitals, and a recording for Decca of Mozart's 'Little G minor' Symphony K. 183. But *Death in Venice* was starting to move; at the beginning of September Myfanwy Piper had finished the draft of the Act I libretto, and at the end of the month Britten, realizing that he needed more time (after all he had not so far written down a single note of the new work) decided that the first performance should be postponed. Instead of September 1972 as originally planned, it would now take place nine months later, in June 1973 at the twenty-sixth Aldeburgh Festival.

October 1971 was almost entirely spent abroad, again with the Pipers – but this time they aimed for Venice, to soak up its character and atmosphere once more and absorb it into the fabric of the opera. During the week spent in Venice, Britten bought the small sketchbook described by Colin Matthews (see pp. 55–66); a gondolier had been found who still knew the traditional cries, and they were noted on the spot by Britten, with the words taken down by Peter Pears. Back home once more, the planning continued; the June 1973 date seemed impossible for Colin Graham, who was not only booked to produce *Owen Wingrave* at Covent Garden that May (a production which of course involved others from the *Death in*

Venice team) but he had also been previously contracted by Glynde-bourne to produce *The Marriage of Figaro* there in July 1973. Hap-pily he finally agreed to the June première, and Glyndebourne released him from the Mozart engagement. (The notion of present-ing *Death in Venice* 'in the round' at Snape was relinquished as impracticable by the end of the year, when the new General Manager of the Aldeburgh Festival, William Servaes, showed that it would have resulted in a loss of almost a fifth of the available seating in the hall.)

Meanwhile a disturbing factor came to light. On a previous visit to Venice in 1968 Britten had picked up a serious viral infection, which had left him less robust than before and with a weakness to the heart. In November 1971 his general health was not good and he was told that this was largely due to his teeth. This was dealt with by major dental extractions, and more days were lost.

The time had now come for the plans about *Death in Venice* to be made officially public, and a press release was issued by the Aldeburgh Festival Office on 6 December. This also announced that the first performance of the opera at the 1973 Festival, to be given by the English Opera Group, was to be directed by Britten himself. The news was widely reported by the Press the next day, confirming what had, by this time, become a rather open secret.

'Who really understands the workings of the creative mind?' says Aschenbach, at the beginning of Act II. Because of the way in which Britten worked (hammering out the shape of the opera with his librettist, first as a scenario and then in greater detail as pages of the draft libretto reached him, planning the music in his head all the time) it is not really possible to give precise dates for the composition of *Death in Venice* except where very occasionally, when writing to Myfanwy Piper or to others, he happened to mention the place he had just reached. The first bars of the composition sketch were prob-ably written at Aldeburgh before Christmas 1971, but he could not really settle down to hard work until, on 10 January 1972, he went on a month's visit to his close friend the Princess of Hesse and the Rhine at Schloss Wolfsgarten, near Darmstadt. She had more than once provided him with the perfect conditions for work, and in those four weeks much was achieved. In the middle of his stay Myfanwy Piper came for another period of work on the libretto; by the end of January she was struggling with the second beach ballet, that is scene 7. On 6 February Britten wrote to her from Wolfsgarten to say that on playing the music through to Peter Pears (who had recently joined him in Germany) as far as the Hotel Guests' arrival in scene 4, he was seriously alarmed to find that it already amounted to forty-five minutes in length, and that was after he had made several small cuts. They would, he warned her, have to look at everything very carefully, leaving out what was not absolutely necessary, if the duration of Act I was not to become too long. (See also Mitchell, pp. 12–16.)

By mid-February Britten, back in Aldeburgh, was apparently at scene 5 ('O Serenissima, be kind') and a fair copy of the libretto – of those sections for which he had already written the music – could be typed to that point. At the end of February the Pipers came to stay for two days of hard work, and Myfanwy, writing on 3 March, informed Britten that she would get on with the Players' scene – that is, scene 10, well ahead of the point which he had actually reached in the composition sketches. But he had to know what she would be suggesting, and it was already clear to her that this scene had peculiar difficulties and would prove especially awkward.

Towards the end of March the demands of concert-giving took over once again; at Snape on Good Friday Britten conducted Bach's *St John Passion* and he played in a chamber concert on Easter Day. He visited the Pipers early in April, and had several engagements to fulfil later in the month. Meanwhile arrangements were in hand concerning the vocal score of the opera. And indeed with a busy composer like Britten, planning ahead to ensure that the music he had just written would actually be available when needed by the artists who were to perform it was an important task in itself. In the case of an opera the problems proliferated; the conductor, producer, designers, lighting and technical staffs all needed scores as soon as it could be managed, solo singers had to have their copies in order to learn the notes and to begin to interpret their roles, and their coaches required something to play from. The full orchestral score had to wait. Britten already knew that his work on the opera would have to be set aside for several weeks while the Aldeburgh Festival took place, and this provided the ideal opportunity for somebody to begin making the vocal score. (This part of the job was one which I had myself declined to undertake when first coming to work for Britten as his music assistant; it needed pianistic ability and a composer's mind, attributes which I have never possessed. But I always checked these scores, and put in the words for the singers; this combined approach seemed to work well.) An arrangement was made with the gifted young pianist Graham Johnson, then in his last year at the Royal

Academy of Music, for him to do the preparation of the vocal score, using photo-copies of the composition sketches and supervised by me. It seemed an ideal plan, since he was later to act as rehearsal pianist for Peter Pears in his formidable task of learning the part of Aschenbach, but in the event the whole thing proved too difficult for him – he was simply not experienced enough – and it was evident that he would not be able to keep up the pace. So in mid May he had to be relieved of the vocal score, and someone else found. In due course Graham Johnson did, happily, more than adequately fulfil the role of coach to Peter Pears.

On behalf of Britten's publishers, Faber Music, Donald Mitchell was fortunately able to recruit the young composer Colin Matthews to take over the vocal score. Eighteen months before this he had worked as an assistant to his elder brother David in preparing, against time, the fair-copy full score of *Owen Wingrave*, so he was already known in Aldeburgh. It was a happy introduction, and from that moment Colin Matthews played an increasingly important part as another music assistant to Britten.

On 28 April Britten had sent a card to Myfanwy Piper bemoaning the fact that he would have to stop work on the opera until July; 'All I want to do is get on with D in V' he said, then 'However I hope it will be the better for keeping.' In May he and Peter Pears went to Camogli, near Genoa, for a ten-day holiday before attacking the Festival; he wrote a long letter to Myfanwy Piper about the opera, now resigned to the two-month break before he could resume writing, 'But I can't stop thinking about it.' He said he had come 'to a grinding halt' in the big final scene of Act I, 'the idyllic one'. (Scene 7 was, in fact, called 'The Idyll' for a long time; for the first performance, and in the published libretto, its title was changed to 'The Feasts of the Sun', only later becoming 'The Games of Apollo'.) At Camogli Britten had had the idea of using the chorus to describe the actions performed in the beach games of 'The Idyll', and Myfanwy Piper readily accepted this new approach to what had become a real difficulty for both of them. At the end of May there was a fund-raising concert in the National Gallery (in aid of the fund to buy Titian's painting of 'Actaeon') at which *Canticle IV*, performed by the artists for whom it had been written, received its first London performance. As far back as February Peter Pears had suggested the use of a counter-tenor voice for Apollo in *Death in Venice*; now that she had heard James Bowman in *Journey of the Magi*, Myfanwy Piper, too, realized the exciting possibilities that this quality of sound could provide, both in 'The dream' (scene 13) and, she now proposed, in 'The Idyll'.

The 1972 Aldeburgh Festival was to be the last one in which Britten took an active part; despite his noticeably deteriorating health, it seemed as strenuous for him as ever. The most demanding event was a concert performance of Schumann's *Scenes from Goethe's Faust*, which had already taken up a good deal of time and effort both from Britten and his staff in editing, preparing and organizing the music and rehearsals for so complex a work, also scheduled to be recorded by Decca at the beginning of September. He accompanied Dietrich Fischer-Dieskau and Peter Pears in two big song recital programmes, played for part of a chamber concert, conducted two performances of *The Turn of the Screw* and an orchestral concert at which Rostropovich (then not allowed to leave Russia) was to have been the soloist. The Festival was followed by a fortnight's holiday with the Princess of Hesse in the Shetland and Orkney Islands (home of her Geddes ancestors) and it was not until the second week in July that the opera could be taken out of the safe again.

With the choral dance solution to 'The Idyll', that scene seemed at last to be manageable, and work on it, by both librettist and composer, proceeded steadily, punctuated by unavoidable summer incidents. In mid July Dmitri Shostakovich (in England to receive an honorary degree) paid his only visit to Aldeburgh. He and his wife stayed at a hotel in the town for a couple of days, coming to the Red House when possible. On one of those occasions Shostakovich spent two hours alone in the library looking at the composition sketches (up to the beach 'Idyll') of *Death in Venice*; a compliment from one composer to another, and evidence of the high regard and affection in which Britten held his Russian colleague.

Right at the end of the month, after repeated efforts on the part of Donald Mitchell and Britten's own legal advisors (Isador Caplan in London and Abraham Friedman in New York), notification came at last that Warner Bros. agreed to waive any rights that might exist with regard to radio broadcasts of Britten's opera, while retaining all television rights until the date of expiry of that part of their agreement with the Estate of Thomas Mann. (As the date concerned was in fact 31 July 1973, the prospect was fortunately not a daunting one.) Also at the end of July another composer came to Snape: William Walton, whose seventieth birthday was celebrated there by a weekend of music, with a gala ballet performance. At this, Britten played one of Mendelssohn's *Songs without Words* for 'The Lord of

Burleigh' - a short solo (choreographed by Sir Frederick Ashton) danced by Deanne Bergsma, who was to create the role of Tadzio's mother the following year. Two more performances at Snape of *The Turn of the Screw* followed at the beginning of August (the Pipers came for one of these) and final arrangements were made for the *Faust* recording; the first part of Colin Matthews' vocal score (up to Aschenbach's 'So be it' three bars before fig. 138) was carefully checked, and sent back early in September for reproduction. Research work at the British Museum (now the British Library) on published versions of the ancient Delphic Hymns, needed for Apollo, was undertaken by Roderick Biss, then a senior member of Faber Music's staff.

Late in August Myfanwy Piper wrote a long, closely considered letter to Britten about the still worrrying problem of the act divisions, making new suggestions as to a possible solution to a recent idea of Britten's that the work should be in three acts, not two (see also p. 36 and Plate 5). And at some (unrecorded) point during the summer Britten decided not to conduct the first series of performances of *Death in Venice* himself, but to invite Steuart Bedford to take it on. But next he had the recording of Schumann's *Faust* for Decca.

In spite of the Festival performance three months earlier, this was a difficult assignment; several distinguished soloists (not all of whom had sung in June), a large amateur chorus, Wandsworth School Choir and the English Chamber Orchestra all took part and (as usual) the precisely worked schedule had to take into account the availability of the artists rather than the shape of the music. By the end of the recording sessions Britten found himself utterly fatigued by the effort involved - indeed this *Faust* recording was the last time he ever conducted. The Pipers came for a fleeting visit in mid September (by now scene 9, 'The pursuit', was under discussion) and a period of solid work began after one more interruption, an event which, though small in itself, was to prove the historic beginning of the Britten–Pears School for Advanced Musical Studies. A weekend course for singers at Snape was prefaced by a song recital by Peter Pears and Benjamin Britten; the programme included songs by Wolf, and *Winter Words*, the Britten song cycle being studied at the course. That recital, too, turned out to be poignantly historic in its own way, for although this partnership was yet to perform again in Germany, it was their last full recital in England.

By October the English Opera Group had made firm arrangements for fifteen performances of *Death in Venice* at home and abroad, including Edinburgh and Venice, between June and October of 1973; Myfanwy Piper was sending more materials for the Players' song in scene 10, and Britten spent a week at Wolfsgarten, during which he attended a performance of *War Requiem* in Darmstadt in which Peter Pears was singing. In Suffolk again, and after consultation with his doctor, it was decided that Britten, whose state of health now gave rise to serious concern, should undertake no more conducting or big engagements but concentrate solely on completing the opera, the one thing that mattered most to him. Recording sessions of two large orchestral works by Frank Bridge (*The Sea* and *Enter Spring*) and a remake of Mozart's Symphony in G minor K. 183, arranged for the second week of November, were abandoned, but later in the month he played for the recordings of his own *Tit for Tat*, *Who are these children?* and *Canticle IV*, and some songs by Schubert and Percy Grainger. Last-minute arrangements were made for Steuart Bedford (already booked to be present at the sessions as a keyboard player) to conduct a scheduled record of instrumental and choral arrangements by Grainger, though Britten remained on hand during the sessions themselves. And by 7 December Britten could write to Donald Mitchell of *Death in Venice*: 'Thank goodness it *is* getting on quite fast now – that horrid period of delay being over.' He reached the end of the opera on 17 December, and although reconsidering the very last section took him up to Christmas Eve, the composition was officially complete.

But there yet remained the vexed question of act divisions; 'The Idyll' looked like a separable piece, though it was too short to stand alone as an individual act, or indeed if so extracted it would not make very much difference to the timing of the whole. Britten played through the entire opera on 31 December to a tiny audience including the Pipers and Colin Graham. Afterwards he made the final decision: the existing pause bar before fig. 189 should be the end of Act I, and Act II would begin with a repetition of the same bar (cf. Plate 5).

The next matter to be taken in hand was the full score, and the final part of the vocal score. (The second part, consisting of scenes 7, 8 and 9, was ready just before Christmas.) Britten had a useful meeting at the beginning of January 1973 with David Corkhill, who had succeeded James Blades (recently retired) as timpanist of the English Chamber Orchestra. Several points of detail concerning the notation of the glockenspiel, vibraphone and marimba were clarified, and Britten and Peter Pears went off to Germany for ten days to fulfil concert engagements in Bavaria. Meanwhile I had myself been

5 The page from the composition sketch which shows that initially there was no break between Acts I and II of the opera: the music was continuous (The Britten–Pears Library and Archive)

preparing the first pages of the full score (putting in all voice parts, stage directions, clefs, instrument names, bar-lines etc.) so that Britten could at once make a start on the detailed orchestration when he returned home. The final draft of the libretto could now be typed straight through as a preliminary step towards its publication by 16 June, especially important since (as with all of Britten's late operas) the vocal score would not be on sale for some time to come.

With the appearance of the dyelined vocal scores had come that nightmare known to all connected with the publication of music: every subsequent change to the existing text, whether new material in the way of revisions, or flaws so far unnoticed must, however small, from now on be noted and circulated to everyone who possessed one of the incorrect copies. In the case of *Death in Venice* this was further complicated by the three-stage vocal score, and as the full score gradually emerged, it, too, had to be kept up-to-date. Britten was still dissatisfied with the closing bars of the opera, and there were to be other changes. Colin Matthews finished the third section of the vocal score (from fig. 235 to the end) by the end of January, and it had to be issued immediately, before the revisions to the end were available. From February onwards Colin then helped out with the full score; I still went ahead of Britten, who usually worked at great speed at this stage of scoring, and Colin Matthews followed behind, filling in some of the more routine instrumentation, or anything else Britten asked him to do (cf. Plate 6). We were all conscious of the fact that at all costs Britten's strength must be spared; it was known that he was to undergo thorough medical examination once the score was done, and the need for it was all too apparent. The first instalment of the full score (176 pages of the final 723) went to London on 19 February – it was, of course, imperative that Alan Boustead, the skilled copyist engaged to make the instrumental parts, should be brought onto the scene as soon as possible – and then a quite bizarre situation arose. In the Players' scene Britten had used what he thought to have been a traditional popular Italian tune as the basis for the Leader of the Players' first song 'La mia nonna always used to tell me'. It transpired that it was not a traditional tune at all, but a 'popular number' still in copyright, for the use of which its publishers made quite unrealistic demands, in terms both of percentages (due on every performance of the opera) and other conditions generally. Britten's response to this news was to rewrite the entire song, making use of a non-copyright tune sent to him by the Italian publishers Suvini-Zerboni. Ten pages of vocal score between figs. 243 and 260 had to be replaced on this account.[4]

6 A page from the full score, Act I scene 5, showing the combined hands of Britten (wind, percussion, harp, piano and strings), Colin Matthews (percussion and piano, following the composer's example) and Rosamund Strode (all vocal parts and preparatory ruling-up). The manuscript is in pencil throughout. (The Britten–Pears Library and Archive)

From quite early on in the composition of the work, Aschenbach's recitatives had presented particular problems. It was important, by overhearing his thoughts, for the listener to understand his character and actions, but keeping out inessentials (as Britten had mentioned when writing to Myfanwy Piper on 6 February 1972: see also Mitchell, pp. 12–13) was absolutely necessary if the opera was not to become unwieldy. As he received his vocal scores and began to learn his role, Peter Pears too began to have positive ideas about Aschenbach, and on occasions made suggestions for verbal changes which he preferred to the original words. In some respects cutting and adjusting recitatives was not difficult (for most of the time the accompaniment was for piano only) but the three main protagonists – composer, librettist and singer – worked hard over several weeks to reach their definitive version. In particular the Phaedrus monologue in scene 16 caused much trouble, and it had to be rewritten to a new text at the very end of March. At the beginning of this scene there were revisions, too, to the instrumental passages between figs. 301 and 303, and right at the end of the opera some slight readjustments were made to Tadzio's tune on the glockenspiel.

There had been just two recital engagements for Britten during the spring: with Norma Burrowes and Steuart Bedford he and Peter Pears took part in a gala concert on 1 February at St James's Palace in aid of the Royal Academy of Music's 150th Anniversary Appeal, and in mid March they went to Wolfsgarten to celebrate the sixtieth birthday of the Princess of Hesse. On 30 March Britten saw a cardiologist in London, and as a result of the consultation he was taken into hospital for thorough investigation a fortnight later. The tests there showed that an immediate operation for the replacement of a heart valve was essential; this was a bitter blow to Britten, who had hoped that he might be able to attend some of the rehearsals and performances of *Death in Venice* and postpone any treatment until later in the year. He went into hospital on 2 May and five days later underwent a long operation. It stabilized his heart condition for the next three years, but a slight stroke sustained during the operation unfortunately resulted in the impaired movement of his right side.

Although Britten was in hospital throughout May, work on the opera proceeded according to plan, and for Peter Pears, John Shirley-Quirk, Colin Graham and Steuart Bedford its production rehearsals were prefaced by the first staged performance of *Owen Wingrave* at Covent Garden, in sets designed by John Piper. Production rehearsals on the new opera began, and the detailed lists of corrections continued; two collated lists I distributed in May gave 346 separate corrections to the vocal score and 415 for Act I only of the full score. Britten came home on the first of June to begin his long convalescence, and though forbidden to attend any rehearsals or performances he kept in close touch with the progress of the opera at Snape. He agreed to the one musical cut which was requested of him at a point which had already been considerably revised earlier in the year: between figs. 115 and 118 in scene 6 ('The foiled departure') there had seemed to be too much time for Aschenbach in his gondola, travelling between Venice and the Lido hotel. At that date Aschenbach was not singing throughout this passage; the lines beginning 'But where? Where shall I go?' were added later, when the cut passage was restored at the end of the year (see also Mitchell, pp. 10–13 and Plate 3, p. 11).

On 16 June, Britten was at his country cottage at Horham, twenty-five miles away from Aldeburgh, where he had been advised to stay to keep out of the way of the inevitable stresses and strains of the Festival. He found that the temptation to listen to the second performance of the opera, broadcast live from Snape Maltings on 22 June, was too strong to resist, but turning on the radio at a quiet orchestral moment, he heard an inexplicable bass note which worried him very much – so he quickly switched off again. (It turned out to be an electric hum set off by one of the revolving periactoid towers which bore John Piper's superb impressionistic views of Venice.) As a result of that brief experience Britten decided to wait until he was stronger physically before listening to a tape recording of the opera, and it was not until August that the opportunity came, organized by Steuart Bedford, who was naturally anxious that the composer should have the chance of hearing the music right through on its own, before seeing the work on stage. By then plans had been made for an extra performance of the opera to be given at Snape especially for Britten's benefit and on 12 September he saw *Death in Venice* for the first time, with the original cast, and in its original setting. For that performance he had already revised the brass for the off-stage boatload of boys and girls between figs. 51 and 53. After Snape, and with the first London performance in mind, there were some other revisions to be made. Still not happy with 'The Idyll', he made numerous small cuts, and adjustments to the percussion, adding the timpani and percussion ostinato round Aschenbach's 'Hymn' up to fig. 183. Aschenbach's soliloquy on arriving at the hotel was cut between figs. 64 and 65, and two of his recitatives actually needed to have previously-cut passages restored to them in order to clarify the text: these were his last recitative in scene 4 (addition after the penultimate sentence '. . . in a pampering partial love' of ' – just as I indulge myself in these novelist's speculations') and the last one in scene 5, where mention of his widowed state ('you have grown self-sufficient since the death of a wife and marriage of an only daughter') helps to define and illuminate the whole scene.

Attending both the London dress rehearsal, and the première at the Royal Opera House on 18 October, Britten decided that yet more changes must be made before the opera was recorded in April 1974 and before the many performances already scheduled at foreign opera houses actually took place. There was some urgency about these alterations, as a print-run of vocal scores had to be set in hand, and a new, corrected, impression of the libretto prepared well ahead of the American première, planned for October 1974 at the Metropolitan Opera House, New York. (The English Opera Group had received generous financial backing for their original production from the American organization, the Gramma Fisher Foundation of Marshalltown, Iowa; part of the arrangement being that the whole EOG production was to travel to New York. This agreement included the services of the producer, conductor and two principal singers, as well as John Piper's scenery and Charles Knode's costumes, which had to be shipped to New York in time for the Met première. This, of course, limited the availability of the opera, which could not be staged by the EOG while the scenery was in transit. It was, in fact, next remounted at Snape and at Covent Garden in the summer of 1975.)

Early in November 1973 Britten rethought the cut made in June between figs. 115 and 118, reinstating it, but adding new lines for Aschenbach; he adjusted Aschenbach's part at fig. 138 (in fact only a change of text proved necessary), added an extra line for Apollo after fig. 173 (this new passage took the place of the earlier version) and – most fundamental – cut out the 'Apollo and Hyacinth' episode altogether between figs. 150 and 157. That last cut was later reconsidered (the music is there on the Decca recording), but it remains as an option in the published score; a little rewriting was done on the three passages for solo violin within the cut. In December the definitive version ᴐf the text was settled between Britten, Myfanwy Piper and Peter Pea⌐ , here and there in the text an individual word or phrase had changed to and fro – sometimes, it seemed, with great frequency – and a firm decision was welcome.[5] There were also some revised lines which came in at this stage, and final adjustments to the Italian phrases some of which had, from the start, been rather confused.

In addition to the optional cut in scene 7, Britten decided to shorten the first scene by making a cut in Aschenbach's first recitative from one bar before fig. 23 to five before fig. 24. This cut was at first intended to be permanent, and the American edition of the libretto (prepared in January 1974) is printed without the excised passage, which was also not performed on the Decca recording made in April. But when the opera was next staged it was found that without the removed bars there was not enough time for the Traveller to make the quick change necessary to transform him into the Elderly Fop of scene 2 for which a new make-up was also required. This cut, too, was therefore reinstated, and it is now printed as an optional choice in the score. (See also Mitchell, pp. 15–16.)

An interim vocal score was printed in January 1974 to bridge the gap between the first-state dyelines used in 1973 and the eventual printed copy. Rather a hybrid in style, the first seventy pages were engraved and the remainder printed from Colin Matthews' manuscript copy (updated, of course, and with the German text added) which had been used for the original dyelines. The interim scores, in white covers, were issued on hire only, but make an interesting study; of the two big cuts mentioned above, the first one (at fig. 23) is incorporated, with a loose (engraved) insertion, printed later in the year, to be used when the cut is *not* made. Finally, some small additions to the scoring were made at figs. 128, 130, 148, 157 and after 323 – all in time for the Decca recording.

This took place at Snape between 18 and 26 April 1974; Britten was again in a low state of health and unable to be in the Concert Hall during the sessions. He was, however, present in one of the dressing rooms (specially equipped as a listening room) for most of the time, and kept a close watch on the proceedings. Just one more adjustment was to be made to the music, following a suggestion from Donald Mitchell in the autumn, at Horham. This was that the Hotel Porter and Waiter should, when calling in the Hotel Guests to dinner in scene 4, begin to sing one bar sooner than the general hubbub five bars before fig. 73 and not (as in the original version, which may be heard on the recording) make their inviting announcement simultaneously with the Guests' chatter (see also Mitchell, pp. 13–15). The extra bar was inserted at the beginning of October 1974, the alteration reaching Steuart Bedford in New York at the Met on the morning of the dress rehearsal there.

The complete engraved vocal score (entirely the work of one man, Jack Thompson) came out on Britten's birthday in November 1975 – delayed on account of the many corrections and adjustments that had been necessary. That very month Britten had managed to visit Venice once more with the help of good friends, and while there in person had (so to speak) also revisited the opera, for in recalling its music he found just what he needed for the last movement of the Third String Quartet. But he never saw the published full score of the opera; appearing in 1979, it had to be seen through the press without him.

3 The libretto

MYFANWY PIPER

Before the final shots of *Owen Wingrave* were taken at the Maltings, Britten had begun to think about *Death in Venice* seriously (it had been in his mind for years) and one September day, just as I began to think that once again the intense months of working with Britten had come to an end, he asked me if I would consider working with him on a new opera. My first thought when I heard its subject was that it was impossible; the second that if Britten said so, it could be done.

In a letter to Wolfgang Born, an artist who had produced 'graphic fantasies' for his novella *Death in Venice*, Thomas Mann wrote: 'For the writer it is always a flattering and moving experience to have a product of his mind taken up, reproduced, celebrated, glorified by an art that appeals more directly to the senses – graphic art or the theatre, say.' It is interesting that his intellectual generosity should have accepted the possibility of a different dimension to his work, and especially to this one, for which he felt such a deep moral and artistic responsibility. 'Truly, it would be ungrateful if I were to complain', he continued, 'about the degree of sympathetic interest that my story has aroused and continues to arouse in the German public. And yet I have frequently been bothered by an element of sensationalism which attached to this interest and which was connected with the pathological subject matter . . . Pathology can enter the realm of literary art only if it is used as a means for intellectual, poetic, symbolical ends.'[1] In reorganizing Mann's story for music and the stage it was even more important to keep a just balance between the passionate–erotic and the poetic–symbolic. As we worked from the first analysis to the last words and notes it became clear that what we were doing, what indeed we had to do to make this 'celebration' work at all, was to amalgamate the dual hero Aschenbach–Mann: Aschenbach, the imagined casualty of genius, with Mann, the acutely self-conscious young writer. Gustav von

45

Aschenbach had to be a real figure, a distinguished middle-aged writer to whom the events of the story actually happened, but in portraying him Mann's self-knowledge and those personal fears of isolation in the creative life that haunt his early letters and works were crucial. In reply to criticism from a friend he wrote, 'I am an ascetic insofar as my *conscience* directs me toward *achievement* . . . I distrust pleasure, I distrust happiness, which I regard as unproductive . . . I think that nowadays one cannot serve both masters, pleasure and art . . . You say that one of these days, if I am ever to become somebody, I will receive more cool respect than heartfelt affection. Dear friend, that is simply not true.'[2] But he was afraid it might be. In the autobiographical short story *Tonio Kröger*, Tonio–Mann cries, 'I tell you I am sick to death of depicting humanity without having any part or lot in it.' Behind all this is the passionate interest of the romantic German philosophers (which Mann inherited) in the nature of genius. The dilemma of Tonio Kröger's life and also of Aschenbach's aptly illustrates Nietzsche's words in *Zur Genealogie der Moral* (1887): 'The perfect artist is forever shut off from reality. But on the other hand it is sometimes understandable that the artist should tire to the point of desperation of the eternal non-reality and falseness of his inner existence and try to venture into the most forbidden territory, the real, try in fact to exist in earnest.'

It took a little over two and a half years from our first conversation to the first night at Snape (16 June 1973) and although we were not working on it all the time during those months, I do not think it was ever out of our thoughts, nor did we cease to discuss it. The intention had been to produce the work in eighteen months and so we had to make our first analysis without very much preliminary research. This, I now think, was an advantage since we were forced to use the text to solve its own problems; to make ourselves so familiar with the symbolism and the reality, the realism and fantasy, with all their cross-references and echoes that even if we had not Mann's rich *prolegomena*, his *kind* of dramatic thinking became natural to us in the course of composition. So that when, for instance, we decided to make the Hotel Manager into one of the Death–Hermes characters, although he had little or nothing to say in the story, it was easy to provide him with the kind of allusive remark, both obsequious and knowing, that would once more underline the strangeness and the inevitability of Aschenbach's adventure. He does not manipulate, he merely takes verbal advantage, and presses home, like the others, his edgy insinuations. The discoveries that we made were afterwards corroborated, and often (necessarily) elucidated by further reading in Mann's own works and in books about him and his background, but that first exploration of his dense and disturbing text was the basis of all that followed.

In Mann's story the order of events is essential: everything depends upon what went before, from the first walk in Munich to the last sighing breath upon the sands of the Lido. Tempting as it was to simplify for the sake of theatrical neatness we decided to keep this order with very few omissions or rearrangement. We did omit the false start of his holiday (on the Adriatic coast) because although it underlines the interplay of chance and fate it adds nothing essential and its inclusion would not have justified the delay in the action. The most difficult problem in planning was that set by Tadzio and his family. Aschenbach has no communication with his own kind and although we know everything that he thought about Tadzio we know nothing of Tadzio's thoughts about him. The implication is that, unlike the Ghosts in *The Turn of the Screw*, what he thought or said would have been of no interest to us. Here what needed to be underlined was not communication, but the lack, indeed the impossibility, of it. The decision to formalize this separateness into dance was neither an arbitrary, nor yet entirely an aesthetic one. It arose out of the nature of theatrical performance. Only dancers find it natural to be on the stage for any length of time in silence and only dancers can express the trivialities and pleasures of human behaviour without speech. By extending the number of dancers to include the children of the Hotel Guests and the beach attendants we were able to organize the children's games in the two beach scenes into ballets and so externalize Aschenbach's habit of poeticizing the events in which he could not partake.

When Aschenbach walked out into the street in Munich on that spring evening, frustrated and ill at ease, he had already set in train the events that were to end in tragedy. He soon encountered the first of the characters who play a double role – the realistic one that their names imply – the Traveller, the Young Old Man (or Elderly Fop), the Old Gondolier, the Leader of the Strolling Players – and a symbolic one. They are the figures who, albeit by their ordinary actions, lead him on his journey towards his fate. Nowhere does Mann suggest that they have supernatural powers, or that they are one and the same person, but he links them by endowing each with the snub nose and grin of Death and the broad-brimmed hat and staff of Hermes, the conductor of the dead across the Styx. The first description of the Traveller, too, seemed to me to have a specific reference to the posture given to representations of Death in medieval German woodcuts as well as the traditional pose of Hermes. 'In his right hand, slantwise to the ground, he held an iron-shod stick, and braced himself against its crrok, with his legs crossed.' To make the symbolic point dramatically it made sense to think of these four characters, who never appear together, being sung by one person. And there seemed very good dramatic reasons why the list should be extended to include the Hotel Manager and the Barber who, by their ordinary actions, also were instrumental in his death. One other voice was eventually added, that of Dionysus, the stranger god. If these seven characters were to be sung by one singer it would make it possible to have a performer capable of creating an impressive role that contrasted and supported the long and taxing one of Aschenbach who, it seemed, would scarcely ever be off the stage. It would also occasionally add to the mystery of verbal and musical echoes that of gesture and of glance.

One of the first difficulties in making a libretto from *Death in Venice* was how to reconcile the comparative austerity of language required by the composer with the extreme wordiness of the text. And all those words of Thomas Mann at first seemed necessary for our full understanding. We need them to know what kind of a person Aschenbach was (only to such a person could the events of the story have happened). The action which is so often only intellectual re-action has to be described in words. Many of the words have several meanings – the obvious meaning within the terms of the action, a symbolic one in terms of the loaded story, and a literary, evocative one.

Some people have wondered why we did not use the device of a narrator who could have told us more about Aschenbach and at the same time have reduced the burden of the part. But Mann is God, the all-knowing of the novella, and he is also Aschenbach, and therefore there is nothing that he knows that Aschenbach does not know too. The division is a matter of style and approach; of irony, self-parody, exhortation on the one hand, and on the other, the awkward taciturnity of a man unaccustomed to ordinary intercourse alternating with the spontaneous flow of poetical musing. The essence of the method and also of the tragedy is that we should be aware of Aschenbach's self-knowledge and also aware, as he is, that he will not profit by it.

There were three kinds of language used. The short rapid early recitative of the exchanges between Aschenbach and another or others; a lengthened measured line, which sometimes becomes verse; and the straight rather literary prose of the ironic comment. This last posed a great problem for Britten. From several points of view he would have liked to have these passages spoken. It would have underlined the dryness and the isolation of the incorrigible writer; it would have provided a rest from singing for Aschenbach and it would have done what we had in mind to do at the outset, create a music-drama in which speech, music and dance all had an integral place. Further it would have made it easier to get across the facts of Aschenbach's past and the working of his mind to an audience who might not be familiar with the book. But it did not work. The change of projection from singing to speaking voice, its relation to the piano accompaniment, the licence to proliferate words because the singer did not have to be considered, the drop in dramatic tone all made Britten change his mind. In the end the Aschenbach of the notebook, the detached comment, came to play a very positive dramatic role. As Aschenbach, the protagonist, became less detached and more fatally involved in events the comments became fewer and less frequent – like Apollo's, 'I go, I go now', in the dream, the voice of his literary sanity fades away.

Not only this but no words or action are used in isolation; they all have back- and cross-references. Of course this is the essence of the musical score – but that needs direction and underlining from the script. So, again unlike *The Turn of the Screw* where I often had to search in the text for some hint that could be expanded, here I had to look for what could be left out. I had to concentrate upon what was essential in a given situation – and if more seemed essential than I could use in one place it had to be saved for another and that place be made appropriate to receive it. For the prose passage at the end of the first scene for example, I had originally used much more of Mann's first chapter in the attempt to plant the hero. But it was turgid and held up the action and so these bits of information about his moral and literary attitudes to life and living were inserted later, only to come back at the very end, just before the last Phaedrus song.

If my problem with the prose comments was selection, the other kinds of language were difficult in a different way. In *Death in Venice* there is a great deal of description, mingled with philosophic musing – it cannot be ignored since it is part of Aschenbach's relation to life as well as to events. Some passages were lyrical acceptance of the event which they follow: for example, the passage that begins,

'Mysterious gondola . . .'. It is a matter of selection (once again) and balance. But what about Aschenbach's reaction to the beauties of Venice and his pleasure at being there again? 'City of Lion and Saint' is all very well in Mann's literary prose but I needed something much more immediate. Aschenbach–Mann had a positive relationship with Venice. When he first sets eyes on it after his journey all his mixed feelings as well as his love of the place need expression. Eventually I found what I wanted in a letter of 1932 from Mann to his children Erika and Klaus who were then staying at the Hotel des Bains on the Lido. 'In spirit I am with you leading that unique life between the warm sea in the morning and the "ambiguous" city in the afternoon. Ambiguous is really the humblest adjective that can be applied . . . , but it is wonderfully relevant in all its meanings, and for all the city's modern silliness and corruptness . . . this musical magic of ambiguity still lives or at least has hours in which it is victorious. . . . For certain people there is a special melancholia associated with the name of Venice. It is full of the home atmosphere – nowadays a spiritually rather corrupt and staled atmosphere, I grant . . . ; but still my heart would be pounding were I there again!'[3] I tried hard to get this pounding heart into the verse, but it refused to fit.

For the last scene of Act I we had to translate a chapter of very elaborate poetic prose into the terms of the stage. When Aschenbach returns to the Lido after his abortive departure he enjoys a brief period of untroubled bliss. He sees the world around him as a Hellenic idyll and expresses this vision in language that reaches extraordinary heights of neo-classical parody. Britten wrote to me just before the Aldeburgh Festival of 1972 (on 12 May): 'I am sure that my decision to put D in V in the safe till after it's all over was the right one, and I'm sticking to it. But I can't stop thinking about it, and I have come to a conclusion . . . The scene in which I came to a grinding halt as you know, is the big final one of Act I, the idyllic one. I couldn't get the tone right, *relaxed* enough, after all that to-ing and fro-ing to Venice, and before the final climax; and *abstract* enough (a word you used in suggesting the naked boys), as if in Aschenbach's mind; and I wanted to save Aschenbach before the big set piece. What would your reaction be to having the "interpretations" of the boys' dances sung by the chorus as kind of madrigals (again, your word)?'[4] He then goes on to describe how he sees it visually. When writing the words of this scene I had not felt familiar enough with the German classical revival to attempt to imitate the

style in English and yet it needed to be removed from the style of the
rest of the work so as to give it the abstract quality that we had discussed. So I went to Elizabethan neo-platonic verse for inspiration.
What I had already written for Aschenbach could be adapted for the
chorus and the musical result did have the required formal abstrac-
tion that Britten looked for.

The most embarrassing task was to have to précis bits from Plato
in the Phaedrus song and its tragic recapitulation in the last act.
Mann was fascinated by the Dialogue and dwells at length on it. I cut
his passage unmercifully short in an attempt to get a dignified simplicity that was not philosophically unthinkable. Incidentally the
last line of the second Phaedrus song provides an example of how a
strong verbal line may be a weak musical one and vice versa. I originally wrote:

> The senses lead to passion Phaedrus,
> And passion to the pit.

but the alliterative p was awkward and ugly to sing and so it became:

> And passion to the abyss.

It was when we were discussing the 'Idyll' scene that the idea of
introducing the voice of Apollo occurred. At first I had thought of a
boy's voice and then, after a concert where James Bowman, the male
alto, was singing, I became entranced by the idea of introducing this
extraordinary sound into the scene. Peter Pears had suggested a
counter-tenor to Britten almost at the same time. Once having
introduced Apollo into this scene the problem of the dream in the
second act, which we had been shirking, had a possible solution:

That night he had a fearful dream – if dream be the right word for a mental
and physical experience which did indeed befall him in deep sleep, as a thing
quite apart and real to his senses, yet without his seeing himself as present in
it. Rather its theatre seemed to be his own soul, and the events burst in from
outside, violently overcoming the profound resistance of his spirit; passed
him through and left him, left the whole cultural structure of a life-time
trampled on, ravaged, and destroyed.

Reading this, and what followed, again and again and reading also
The Bacchae of Euripides, it seemed, to me, that however the
producer and choreographer decided to stage the dream, the dialogue must be between the two sides of Aschenbach's nature; the
Apollonian and the Dionysiac. I was very much helped in sorting out
my ideas about this whole aspect of the story (which I had arrived at

in an uninformed and rather muddled way) by the introduction and
notes to a new German edition of *Death in Venice* edited by T.J.
Reed[5] and by subsequent conversations with him. (See also T.J.
Reed, pp. 163–7.)

Although *Death in Venice* is full of strong visual excitement it
seemed to be essentially a work to be read. But, working on the
libretto, it was surprising to discover how theatrical much of it is.
The events, the series of twists of the tale, of which it is built up, all
have a sharp extrovert front, behind which the mysterious mental
processes seethe. One of the scenes that was, of course, a gift to the
opera was the Players' scene. Brilliant, sinister, embarrassing, it
serves to contrast more strongly than ever Aschenbach's inability to
take part in ordinary pleasures with the easy conviviality and laughter of the Hotel Guests. Mann tells us very little about the songs: the
first was a sentimental duet, the second popular and suggestive, the
third 'a rowdy air, with words in impossible dialect. It had a
laughing-refrain in which the other three artists joined at the top of
their lungs. The refrain had neither words nor accompaniment, it
was nothing but rhythmical, modulated, natural laughter . . .' *O mia
carina* the first song I used was an early popular number that had
been rediscovered (and so it gave us a lot of copyright trouble: see
also Strode, p. 38). It seemed particularly suitable with its suggestion
of love pushed beyond the bounds of good behaviour. I wrote a new
verse translation from a literal one and added a third verse which
I was able to make appropriate for the listening Aschenbach: 'For
you forgotten honour, work and duty'. The second song I rewrote in
a rather raffish style from another popular joke song. The real facer
was the laughing song. What language could it be written in?
Though incomprehensible, words here and there ought to be understood. I toyed with macaronics, using Italian, French and English or
German perhaps, but my Italian was not good enough to play about
with, my German almost nonexistent and there seemed no excuse for
French. I thought of nonsense verse but even if it had been possible,
the Englishness of it would have been unacceptable. At last it
occurred to me that the Venetian dialect would have been incomprehensible to the Hotel Guests, Aschenbach included, and that it
would also be incomprehensible in whatever language the opera
might be translated. So with the help of a book of old Venetian
ballads and nursery songs, having decided with Britten what rhythmic shape was needed, I wrote a version of what was eventually used.
It had no grammar and was all wrong but it said more or less what I

7 A page from the draft libretto in Myfanwy Piper's hand, Act II scene 10, showing pencil modifications and additions by Britten (The Britten-Pears Library and Archive)

wanted to say – then I showed it to a friendly professor of Italian (who wished to remain anonymous). He was amazed at and amused by my unscholarly efforts, but saw what I was after, rewrote it in proper dialect and added the brilliant and suggestive last verse himself.

Anyone who worked with Britten knew his gift for getting work and ideas out of people they did not know they were capable of. From the first conversation about *The Turn of the Screw* to Aschenbach's last cry in *Death in Venice* I could rely on his committed encouragement; whether it was to produce a whole scene or a small alteration for which he would often wait patiently while I gnawed my pen. Perhaps even more important for the final work was his sure dramatic instinct operating through his musical needs. Again and again he made me expand the text with a liveliness that my too-slavish attention to the original might have failed to do. Alterations or modifications were always evoked, never dictated. There was positive and continuing pleasure and pride in working with him and I am grateful to have enjoyed it.

4　*The Venice sketchbook*

COLIN MATTHEWS

Britten kept two kinds of notebook for work in progress, much the more important of these being used for drafts and outlines of texts and librettos, with hardly any musical notations. In the Britten–Pears Library there are only three purely musical sketchbooks which pre-date the one for *Death in Venice*. The earliest of these – a very home-made affair – contains workings for 'Go play, boy, play' (the string quartet suite of 1933)[1] and *A Boy was Born*, and so dates from 1932–3. The second is an 'American' notebook with sketches for *Paul Bunyan*, the *Michelangelo Sonnets*, *Sinfonia da Requiem*, First String Quartet, *Diversions*, a *Partita* for orchestra (not composed), and the *Sonatina Romantica* (1940)[2]. The third is a loose-leaf block from the 1960s and early 1970s which includes *The Prodigal Son*, Mozart cadenzas, Cello Suites, *Owen Wingrave*, *Journey of the Magi* and *Children's Crusade*.

All these works, with one exception, are represented by the barest of outlines, as if mere jottings or reminders. The exception is *Owen Wingrave*, for which there are seven pages of sketches encapsulating a great deal of the opera in a remarkably short space. Though this is a pointer towards the way Britten was to use the Venice notebook, it is hardly a precedent. Nor are there extended sketches for any other works prior to *Death in Venice*, although there are a number of single sheets with workings similar to those in the notebooks. Since Britten tended to keep everything that he wrote, however fragmentary, it is clear that sketching a work in advance was not part of Britten's normal working method.[3]

In an interview given in 1961[4] Britten said, 'Usually I have the music complete in my mind before putting pencil to paper. That doesn't mean that every note has been composed, perhaps not one has, but I have worked out questions of form, texture, character, and so forth, in a very precise way so that I know exactly what effects I want and how I am going to achieve them.' In the *Death in Venice* sketchbook, for the only time, we are able to see Britten working out the 'questions of form, texture and character' on paper.

On the cover of the sketchbook is written 'D in V BB Venice 1971'. He acquired it when he and Peter Pears, together with John and Myfanwy Piper, visited Venice in the autumn of 1971, although it is likely that only the first three pages derive from that trip. It contains sixty pages of eight-stave manuscript paper: the first thirty are devoted to *Death in Venice*, there are a few sketches for *The Death of St Narcissus*, and the last page contains two Venetian folk songs.[5] The rest is blank, but there are also a few loose sheets of paper inserted. In all there are just over one hundred individual sketches relating to the opera.

The sketchbook follows, approximately, the chronological sequence of the opera, with a few displacements and some notable omissions. It is not possible to say with certainty how many of the entries were made before the composition sketch itself was started, although the sketchbook is clearly contemporary with Britten's working copy of the libretto. Many entries must be more or less contemporary with the composition, but it is impossible to define the relationship exactly.

Nearly all the entries are short – usually no more than three or four bars, establishing a thematic idea without necessarily developing it. Harmony is usually sketched together with melody, although this is less often the case if the melody is a vocal line. There are several entries concerned with defining a particular harmonic area, sometimes in association with simp!e twelve-note workings. The three pages which are transcribed complete here are not entirely typical, since they have been chosen for their particular interest, but there is scarcely an entry in the book which was not to be of value for the opera.

The very first entry is the all-important 'Serenissima' theme (Ex. 1), here sketched with a (rejected) alternative rhythm; both are crossed out, and the definitive form, with its barcarolle figuration, is found on page 2. (A loose six-stave sheet of paper, marked 'Venice', contains the same material and may pre-date the sketchbook.) Also on page 1 is an outline of Aschenbach's opening vocal line, 'My mind beats on', a fourth lower than it appears in the opera, and 'St Mark's Bells' (the music four bars after fig. 43), a semitone lower. At the top of page 2 the so-called 'view' theme is sketched (Ex. 2), next only in importance to 'Serenissima'.[6] Page 3 is devoted entirely to notations of gondoliers' calls, while page 4 contains plainsong workings for the brass music at fig. 43 (Britten derived this from the litanies of St Mark in the *Liber Usualis*). On page 5 there is a list of the (mainly percussion) scoring of the gamelan music from *The Prince of the*

Ex. 2

Pagodas, obviously a reminder for the beach scenes. (See also Cooke, Plate 20, p. 118.)

With page 6 the motivic working starts in earnest, beginning with the Traveller's 'No boundaries hold you' (see Ex. 9) (the rushing string figures which introduce him are sketched on the back of the loose sheet mentioned above) and continuing with several twelve-note workings – for the string figuration at fig. 6 and the offstage chorus at fig. 9. There is a jump ahead to Aschenbach's words as he is rowed to the Lido, 'Where should I come but to you to soothe and revive me?',[7] and on page 7 a further jump to fig. 54, marked 'Hp acc to Gondola song – low sustained string chords'. On the same page is the chorus song 'We'll meet in the Piazza' (fig. 29) and then a return to Aschenbach's vocal line at fig. 6, which appears in four versions. There is also a sequence of six two-note chords, discussed further in the next paragraph.

Page 8 is reproduced here in full (Ex. 3). At the top, Britten sketched the rhythm of Aschenbach's vocal line, combined with the Old Gondolier's mutterings – the two bars before fig. 51. The three chains of six two-note chords below this are twelve-note derivatives of the 'Serenissima' harmony, which itself appears, marked 'Fl', above a bustling bass figure. (In the full score this is used virtually note for note eleven bars after fig. 53, but scored for oboes and clarinets, above bassoons.) The bass figure is to become part of the music for the Hotel Guests after fig. 68; but the sketch here marked 'Hotel Guests', an attempt to work the 'Serenissima' music, is one of the few entries not to be used.

Ex. 3

The 'chord chain' is significant not so much in itself but for its role in determining a great deal of the harmonic development of the opera. Its thematic significance is rather puzzling: its first appearance is at fig. 31, an exact retrograde of the first 'chain' sketched on this page, where it represents Aschenbach's shock at seeing the Elderly Fop. It ends the first scene, opening out into D major for the Overture, and it pervades the little scene with the Boatman and Porter. Its only other appearance in this specific form is at fig. 176, as Tadzio is crowned victor of the games. As an important influence on harmonic movement elsewhere it differs from most of Britten's twelve-note ideas in this opera, which usually serve a purely local purpose, that of filling out a small area of musical space.

On page 10, transcribed as Ex. 4 (see also J. Evans, Plate 19, p. 110),
we can see the twelve-note workings fulfilling their most important
function in the opera. But first, at the top of the page, is a sketch of
the transition from figs. 62 to 63, its instrumentation already clearly
defined: this is the only indication in the sketchbook of the important 'I, Aschenbach' figuration which first appeared at fig. 3. It is
followed by a variant of the 'view' theme as it appears at fig. 65,
where it leads to the Hotel Guests, who are now sketched here in their

Ex. 4

correct form together with the bustling figure from page 8. At each appearance in the scene of this six-note figure there is a seven-note *bisbigliando* chord in the harp above it (the two elements do not, though, consistently use all twelve notes between them). At its last appearance (Ex. 5 – the extended bar of 'recitative', five bars before

Ex. 5

fig. 73) the upper chord is identical with the one sketched on the bottom stave of page 10. The chord next to it is most likely a possible (but unused) progression from it, then the chord is written out a second time. This is followed by the noteheads of a chromatic scale – Britten's usual *aide-mémoire* to ensure that he was using all twelve notes. All the notes are crossed out, but it may be assumed that Britten first crossed through the seven notes present in the chord to find the remaining five, which were then also crossed through. These remaining notes appear as semibreves at the end of the bottom stave, and a line from these goes to the end result: Tadzio's theme. (The nine-note figure above this seems to be an elaboration of the six-note figure, but it serves no apparent purpose.) Tadzio's theme is further elaborated on page 11. (See also Mitchell, pp. 3–4 and J. Evans, Ex. 13 and pp. 110–11.)

Thus far it has been possible to describe the sketchbook in some detail, and it is clear that a great deal of the material for the opera is already present. The following pages are concerned for the most part with the beach music of scene 5 (there are only three entries for scene 6) and 'The Games of Apollo' (scene 7). This scene is the most comprehensively sketched of any part of the opera with eight pages devoted to it, and the sketchbook clearly reflects Britten's difficulties with the scene (see Rosamund Strode's account on pp. 33–4). Of these pages the last two are the most significant, with page 19 introducing what is to become the passacaglia theme of Act II ('So longing[8] passes back and forth' at fig. 186) and page 20, transcribed as Ex. 6, rounding off Act I and containing important elements for Act II. (See also p. 65 for some details of page 16 of the sketchbook.)

Ex. 6

At the top left of page 20 (see Plate 8) the lower of the two scales
(a modified version of the other) is the harmonic and melodic basis
of the climactic rising passage at fig. 188.[9] Just after it, but barely
noticeable, is one of the most important entries in the book, the outline of 'I love you', with the two unbeamed quavers giving away its
vocal origins. (Note also the double bar-line, although at this stage
the division between Acts I and II did not exist.) Below this, and also
on the right-hand side of the page, the Hotel Barber appears. The

8   The Venice sketchbook, p. 20 (The Britten–Pears Library
and Archive)

four-note chords sketched above him on the top stave are ambiguous, both foreshadowing the Barber's scissors and echoing the
harmony of the end of Act I: thus it is no coincidence that his
platitudinous 'Va bene signore' is closely related to 'I love you'.
Beneath these sketches is the definitive form of the passacaglia
theme, whose outlines had appeared on the previous page. Its chordal accompaniment on the line below is here rather crude; on the
next page it acquires its definitive Tadzio-associated harmony.
Finally there is a 'Serenissima' working at the pitch-level of the
beginning of scene 9, inappropriately marked 'Chorus' (although the
chorus of Citizens is just about to appear).

The final third of the notebook continues its way through the
second act, although the entries are more sporadic. The most
detailed workings are for the individual numbers of the Players'
scene (scene 10 – three pages in all). The only notation for scene 11 is
a line for 'One moment if you please', which is neither rhythmically
nor melodically the same as it appears in the opera. On page 26 a
small fragment is marked 'arrival of Mama' (Ex. 7), the only appearance of her theme in the sketchbook as well as of the agitated
figuration first used in the Street Vendors' scene in Act I. This sketch

Ex. 7

is for scene 12, as are also the outlines of the chorus of Followers of Dionysus sketched on the same page.

On page 27 the powerful statement of the 'view' theme at fig. 311 is marked 'last Fugato'; but it appears before rather than after the Phaedrus aria, which is sketched on page 28. On this page are five bars of the music at fig. 320, marked 'last scene – sea – v. slow', as well as the final bars of the 'last fugato' leading into scene 17. The latter can clearly be seen as a development of the former (both are in C minor), rather than as a continuation from the previous page. The final page (page 29)[10] contains two sketches only. One is for the Hotel Manager's 'No doubt the Signore' in two versions, with accompanying chords (not those used). The other is marked 'End of fight' and is a rough draft of the music from Aschenbach's cry of 'Ah, no!' to his final 'Tadziù!' – twelve bars of sketch, expanded to twenty-two in the opera. (See also Mitchell, pp. 17–20.) This is the longest entry in the book.

Almost as significant as what is in the sketchbook is what is not in it. The Traveller, in his first and other guises, makes hardly any appearance: indeed although his characteristic vocal line is sketched several times, beginning with 'No boundaries hold you', there is no accompanying music sketched specifically for him except for the Barber's scene. Most surprising of all is the complete absence of the so-called 'plague' motive which he introduces in scene 1 (Ex. 8) and which commentators have rightly seen as playing a crucial role in the opera's musical development.

Ex. 8

(Mar - vels un - fold)

Yet the motive, with its minor third enfolded within a major third, is already implicit in the very first notebook entry, 'Serenissima', as it is too in the version of 'No boundaries hold you' sketched on page 6 (Ex. 9) – rhythmically but not melodically as it appears in the opera:

Ex. 9

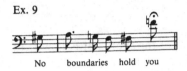

No   boundaries hold you

here the melody is very clearly derived from 'Serenissima'. And of course 'I love you' contains the same combination of intervals. Only once is the 'plague' motive itself sketched and this is not in the sketchbook but on one of the loose sheets inserted in it (Ex. 10). This is for scene 6, where the agitated Aschenbach sings the same melodic shape no less than six times (though never at this pitch level). In Ex. 10 Britten has picked out the motive, and turned it into a four-

Ex. 10

Whilst this si - roc - – – co blows nothing delights me

note chord: the chord accompanies Aschenbach each time he sings the phrase (on tremolo woodwind), and only at the end of the scene is the motive itself played instrumentally (on the brass, three bars before fig. 114). This single instance of the ubiquitous motive being sketched seems to imply that its emergence came about more by accident than design: or perhaps that Britten did not see it so much as a motive in itself, but as only one amongst the many derivatives of 'Serenissima' that pervade the opera.

Such accidental, or instinctive, working towards large-scale design is also evident in the similarity of Apollo's and Tadzio's music. The Voice of Apollo is sketched on pages 15 and 16 to the melody of the

First Delphic Hymn (the most extensive piece of ancient Greek music known: it dates from the second century BC). On page 15 it is written out in F major; transposed into a modal D major on page 16 (Ex. 11) the notes have become identical with Tadzio's. Yet this is

Ex. 11

surely fortuitous, since Tadzio's theme had been sketched ten pages before, and that too had come about by chance, as is evident from the sketches (and as acknowledged by Britten in conversation).

In the example above the key signature is A major, but the melody is notated in D major when it appears at this pitch and with these words at fig. 161. At Apollo's first appearance, at fig. 143, the Hymn is in a modal E major, although notated in A. These two keys, A major and E major, are the ones associated throughout the opera with, respectively, Tadzio and Aschenbach. But they are not prominent in the sketchbook: for example, Aschenbach's radiant A major hymn at the end of Act I was sketched in C major (although the quintuplet figuration which dominates the music *was* sketched in A). E major appears as a key signature only in the sketch for the café music in scene 9 (which is in fact in A major!).

Mention of the café music draws attention to another oddity of the sketchbook, since nearly a whole page is devoted to this tiny episode. The only other sections of the opera where the sketches are relatively disproportionate are 'The Games of Apollo' and the Players' scene. All these share a lightness of touch which one would imagine might have come easily to Britten. The evidence of the sketchbook implies that it did not.

Other absences from the sketchbook have already been noted –

Mama's theme and the Street Vendors' figuration are essentially
absent in spite of Ex. 7, since this sketch is rather remote from the
real thing (Mama's theme is, understandably, closely related to
Tadzio's in its definitive form). Most notable of the 'Traveller' omissions is, perhaps, the absence of the rather complex chords which
accompany him in the role of Hotel Manager. These, for once, are
not derived from 'Serenissima', although they do have a link with the
'Gondola song' sketched on page 7. Although many of Aschenbach's
vocal lines are sketched, none of his recitatives appear; probably an
indication that Britten knew in advance exactly what he was going
to do. (See, however, Mitchell, pp. 4–5.)

While this sketchbook is a unique document, it does not essentially
alter our perception of Britten's working methods. The only question that remains is that of the relationship between the sketchbook
and the composition sketch (see n. 3, p. 210). It is certainly not the
case that the sketchbook as a whole pre-dates the composition, since
we know that in several places (notably 'The Games of Apollo')
Britten became stuck for long periods. It seems most likely that the
sketchbook kept a little in advance of the composition, an *aide-
mémoire* as Britten's mind raced ahead of what he was composing.
But ambiguities remain – especially where pitch is concerned, since
sketchbook entries are frequently at widely differing pitches from
their final form. This is unexpected and puzzling.

Yet more remarkable is the sheer amount of material crammed
into a tiny space – 30 pages of sketchbook, representing 249 pages of
composition sketch, in turn to become 723 pages of full score; the
wonder is that prior to this Britten had been able to keep so much in
his head before committing himself to paper. That for this one composition he changed a lifetime's working methods is evidence of the
importance he attached to *Death in Venice*.

5 *The first production*[1]

COLIN GRAHAM

Owen Wingrave had been conceived for a television performance but paradoxically the libretto of *Death in Venice* reads even more like a film script than its predecessor and makes greater 'cinematic' demands on the staging. Britten managed to keep the early discussions of *Death in Venice* under wraps for some time. He had mentioned the idea from time to time and, a few weeks after the filming of *Owen Wingrave*, I presented him with a scenario to suggest how Thomas Mann's novella might be adapted as an opera for the stage. He gave me a funny look, and it turned out that he had already discussed the idea with Myfanwy Piper, whose libretto is a masterly achievement of a very difficult task.

The forces of the opera are unusual. The orchestra, apart from a large percussion section, is standard. (It is similar to that of *Owen Wingrave*, which was the first full-scale opera, orchestrally, since *Gloriana*, eighteen years its senior.) There are three principal protagonists: Aschenbach, the author; the ambiguous Traveller who recurs in seven different guises during the course of the opera; and Tadzio, the Polish boy. The Traveller is a fate-figure represented by all the characters in the story who are responsible for turning Aschenbach towards Venice and eventually to his death. In the book many of these have features in common – a certain shape of hat, a skull-like aspect, bad teeth – and to them the librettist has added the enigmatic Hotel Manager who becomes Aschenbach's principal antagonist. This role was written especially for John Shirley-Quirk, who provided a *tour de force*. Tadzio was not as easy to find: not only had he to be 'perfect', but also a good dancer.

The dance aspect was crucial. All of us who had seen Visconti's film found the relationship between Tadzio and Aschenbach too sentimental and salacious. (See also P. Reed, pp. 178–83.) Britten, who did not see it, was nevertheless certain that a convention had to be found which would keep these protagonists separated on different

Saturday 16 June

The Royal Opera House, Covent Garden Limited, presents
The English Opera Group in the first performance of

8.15 pm in the Maltings,
Snape

DEATH IN VENICE An opera in two acts

Music *by* BENJAMIN BRITTEN
Libretto *by* MYFANWY PIPER, after the story by Thomas Mann

Conducted by STEUART BEDFORD   *Scenery designed by* JOHN PIPER
Produced by COLIN GRAHAM   *Costumes designed by* CHARLES KNODE
Choreography by FREDERICK ASHTON *Lighting designed by* JOHN B. READ

Gustav von Aschenbach, a novelist   PETER PEARS

The Traveller   JOHN SHIRLEY-QUIRK
The Elderly Fop   The Hotel Barber
The Old Gondolier   The Leader of the Players
The Hotel Manager   Dionysus

Voice of Apollo   JAMES BOWMAN

The Polish Mother   DEANNE BERGSMA

Tadzio, her son   ROBERT HUGUENIN
Her two Daughters   ELIZABETH GRIFFITHS   MELANIE PHILLIPS

Their Governess   SHEILA HUMPHRLYS
Jaschiu, Tadzio's friend   NICHOLAS KIRBY

Hotel porter   THOMAS EDMONDS   Glass-maker   STEPHEN JAMES ADAMS
Lido boatman   MICHAEL BAUER   Lace-seller   ALEXANDRA BROWNING
Hotel waiter   STUART HARLING   Beggar-woman   ANNE WILKENS
Strawberry-seller   IRIS SAUNDERS   Newspaper-seller   SHEILA BRAND
Guide   ROBERT CARPENTER TURNER
Strolling Players   NEVILLE WILLIAMS   PENELOPE MACKAY
English clerk in a travel bureau   PETER LEEMING
Two acrobats   MICHAEL VROOMAN   VICTOR KRAVCHENKO

Venetians and Hotel Guests from many countries:
HELEN ATTFIELD   ANGELA VERNON-BATES
and   ROBIN BELL   ANNE CONOLEY   JANICE HOOPER-ROE
WENDY PASHLEY   KATHLEEN SMALES   ANNA VINCENT   MICHAEL FOLLIS
KEITH JONES   ARNOST KOPECKY   NORMAN LLOYD-MILLER
RONALD MURDOCK   WYNDHAM PARFITT

Polish, Russian and German children, Beggars: ANGELA COX
MARK SEWELL   MATTHEW HAWKINS   ANDRIS PLUCIS
MARK WELFORD   ASHLEY WHEATER

THE ENGLISH CHAMBER ORCHESTRA   *Leader* KENNETH SILLITO

Assistant Conductor   *Répétiteurs*   *Dance Notator and Assistant*
ROGER VIGNOLES   STEPHEN RALLS   *to the Choreographer*
ALISTAIR DAWES   FAITH WORTH
Assistant Producer   BRIAN STANBOROUGH
RICHARD GREGSON

Ballet Mistress
SHEILA HUMPHREYS

9, 10   The first performance of the opera at the Aldeburgh Festival, 1973
(from the Festival Programme Book)

69

The action takes place in 1911

planes. One of the more poignant aspects of the story is that Aschenbach finds it impossible to make contact with the boy.

Britten had wanted to work with Sir Frederick Ashton again ever since he [Ashton] had directed the première of *Albert Herring* (in 1947). Now he approached him to explore the possibility of containing Tadzio's world in dance and stylized movement. Tadzio, his Mother – the Lady of the Pearls – and the rest of his family and friends all became dancers. It was important to find someone with the right qualities of personality and looks for Tadzio. Eventually Ashton discovered Robert Huguenin in the ranks of the Royal Ballet, and Deanne Bergsma performed the role of the Lady of the Pearls to perfection. The cast is completed by an ensemble of twenty-seven young soloists who fill all the other roles, large and small, of the citizens of Venice and her foreign visitors, and also act as 'chorus' when necessary.

Britten had been growing away from conventional forms of staging ever since *Gloriana*, and he was at first particularly keen on finding an unconventional way to stage *Death in Venice*. The filmic approach to the libretto made it difficult for John Piper and me to find the right convention. Britten had first to be persuaded that no scene needed to be presented in a literal way; there had to be some expressionistic form of stylization. This was compounded by the use of dance.

Snape seemed to lend itself to various unconventional shapes of stage, which were suggested, but eventually and inevitably it was the musical convention that dictated our final solution. We set the whole in a black box like the inside of a camera whose shutter opened to reveal the constantly shifting pattern of colour and images of Aschenbach's mind. The recitatives were placed in a sharp horizontal shaft of white light which isolated and lifted Aschenbach from the black recesses of his mind. The dance sections were presented in a different colour-quality of light or against a gleaming white background to highlight the Greek classical aspect. These walls could also change to John Piper's depiction of Venice during the author's visits to La Serenissima. His striking paintings were complemented by Charles Knode's evocative costumes and the lighting of John B. Read, which played a more important, complementary part in the design than is usual in opera.

The first act of *Death in Venice* takes Aschenbach to the city and to 'the warm and lovely South' where, against his better nature, he becomes involved with Tadzio. The act is not without its problems, not least in the many extended recitatives. In the second act these are fewer, shorter, and more subjective. It is significant that the Overture ('Venice') is heard after the Prologue, some twenty minutes after the beginning of the opera. The long dance sequence which ends the act – 'The Games of Apollo' – set a series of problems once the composer and librettist had decided to base the scene on a pentathlon. Although set to some exquisite music, five events are too many and dilute the impression made by Tadzio in Ashton's choreography. Even Ashton was somewhat stumped when confronted by long-jumps and sprinting races. When Britten eventually saw the opera at a special performance at Snape some months after the première, he was dissatisfied with the shape of this scene. He made small cuts, but I feel he might have reconsidered its shape more drastically had he been able to be present at rehearsals; it would not have been the first occasion that he found subsequent alterations necessary. He nearly always had one sticking point; the scores of *The Rape of Lucretia* and *Billy Budd* were considerably revised after their first production, and the climax of *Curlew River* was rewritten five times during rehearsals before he was satisfied.[2]

To say that we missed the composer during rehearsals would be an understatement. He was always a remarkable colleague on these occasions, and his interpreters were here trying to realize what was perhaps the most difficult assignment he had ever set them. Peter Pears was working on the most arduous and personally-involving role of his career at the same time that Britten was under surgery in hospital; his professional devotion and application had never been greater. In spite of the strain, perhaps because of it, Aschenbach was arguably his finest interpretation.

It was typical of Britten that, at the special performance when he saw his opera for the first time, he was more nervous on his colleagues' behalf than on his own, knowing how we would have felt had he not liked it. Since the designs were completed he had seen and heard nothing, and he can have had no idea how he would find his own work when presented with it so objectively. Happily he made only a few minor adjustments – mostly involved with 'The Games of Apollo'. (See, however, Strode, pp. 41–3 and Mitchell, pp. 9–16.)

[Revised 1984]

11 Act I scene 2: On the boat to Venice. John Shirley-Quirk as the Elderly Fop, Peter Pears as Aschenbach

12 The Hotel Guests assemble for dinner, Act I scene 4: The first evening at the hotel

13 Victor of the Pentathlon, Act I scene 7: 'The Games of Apollo'.
Robert Huguenin as Tadzio

14 Barber: 'Now the Signore can fall in love with a good grace.' Act II
scene 15: the Hotel Barbershop (ii). John Shirley-Quirk as the Hotel
Barber, Peter Pears as Aschenbach

15 One of John Piper's sketches for *Death in Venice*. (The Britten–Pears
    Library and Archive)

16 Act II scene 13: 'The dream'. Peter Pears as Aschenbach, Robert Huguenin as Tadzio

6 *Synopsis: the story, the music not excluded*[1]
PETER EVANS

Like Mann's novella, Britten's opera compels the attention simply as a span of cumulatively dramatic incident, but, as our acquaintance grows, reveals networks of connections which confirm a profundity we may at first only sense. The music is clearly among Britten's most economical in texture, but the extent to which it derives from a few motivic sources will be less immediately apparent, for the composer's mastery of aptly illustrative detail has not been jettisoned. None the less, it is this unremitting concentration upon certain fundamental note-shapes which gives to the opera that sense of mounting obsession which so faithfully mirrors the original story.

Mann's narrative records Aschenbach's thoughts, visions and dreams far more than his conversation; indeed, it is his total inability to speak at a crucial moment which isolates him within the morbid emotional atmosphere that thickens throughout the second act, and, on one level, brings about his destruction. As Mann writes, 'a solitary, unused to speaking of what he sees and feels, has mental experiences which are at once more intense and less articulate than those of a gregarious man'. But the dominating character of an opera must be articulate, even if chiefly in soliloquy. Aschenbach's role thrusts a burden on the singer far more exclusive than that borne by any other Britten operatic character, yet for long stretches this huge part represents an entirely inward debate.

Act I

Scene 1: This habitual self-examination is made clear from the opening of the opera. We see Aschenbach, the much-honoured writer, thwarted in that disciplined search after beauty on which he has prided himself: the mental activity that still throbs relentlessly now yields no fruit in his parched imagination. The trumpet rhythms which symbolize the famous public figure are thus ironic even on

76

their first appearance. His walk through the suburbs of Munich brings him to a graveyard, the texts (chorally evoked) on its chapel façade creating bleak resonances in his mind. But his attention is caught by a foreign-looking figure on the chapel steps, and the vision this Traveller conjures up, of an alluringly exotic, swampy landscape, is conveyed in an extended bass-baritone solo, 'Marvels unfold' (see Ex. 1a and its coda, Ex. 1b). The technique of closely superimposing melody notes to form accompaniments, adapted from Britten's Church Parables, fashions a fitting symbol for the 'fearful growth', while successive phrases fantastically permute the shape of Ex. 1a.

Ex. 1a

Ex. 1b

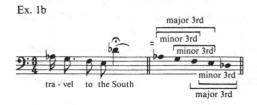

Ex. 1c

In this one figure, containing within a major third a minor third (a recurrent Britten symbol of the 'canker') and both tone and semitone steps, are the seeds of innumerable later developments. Ex. 1a itself is to become explicitly a motive, commonly in the tuba, representing the advance of the plague (how that relates to this oriental vision is forcefully revealed later). But the plague is only one, albeit physically the decisive one, of the agencies of a fate that is to destroy Aschenbach. The Traveller, whose appearance, and inexplicable disappearance, rouse in Aschenbach the urge to travel, is the first; following some clear leads from Mann, Britten has assigned many of the subsequent roles to the same bass-baritone. This thrusts home their single function of conducting Aschenbach towards a preordained end, and, together with the common origin of much of their material in the Ex. 1a and the derived Ex. 1b shapes, heightens the impression of an unfolding myth.

Scene 2: The decision to leave Munich is reached only after characteristic self-analysis, but the aspiring string phrases are telling and, at a great blast of the siren, we discover Aschenbach on board ship for Venice. His travelling companions, a party of callow youths, are seen off by their girl friends, and the boat's engines (see Palmer, Ex. 1, p. 132) provide a vivid accompaniment to the voyage. The tension of this remarkable scene, mirroring Aschenbach's uneasiness, stems musically from the contrasts between the inane chatter of an Elderly Fop (the bass-baritone, reaching into *falsetto* at times) and the youths, and the faint snatches of their song, 'Serenissima'. Venice, the city that draws Aschenbach so powerfully, is inevitably symbolized by a variant form of the intervallic cell (see Ex. 1c). Though the song's nostalgia reflects a popular sentimentality, the opera's most haunting refrain is its transformation into an orchestral barcarolle that accompanies, and implicitly suggests the emotional inflections of, Aschenbach's many journeys by gondola; a sound-picture of Venice on his arrival punctuates this with liturgical strains and bells (the Overture).

Scene 3: Then we see him being rowed to the Lido – contrary to his intentions. The surly Gondolier, a Charon-like figure (and, of course, the original bass-baritone, evoking the Ex. 1b shape) disregards his protests; 'Serenissima' is heard again as a boatload of young people passes. But on his disembarking at the Lido, the Gondolier disappears as mysteriously as did the Munich Traveller, leaving Aschenbach to apostrophize in a short aria the gondola as a symbol of death.

Scene 4: The obsequious Hotel Manager, in another bass-baritone solo (its melodic lines deriving from the Traveller's Ex. 1b), conducts him to his room and reveals its splendid view of the beach, depicted musically by Ex. 2, an opulent orchestral theme of falling-third chains.[2] Left alone, the public figure (trumpet theme) gives way to the ironic self-analyst as Aschenbach reflects on his journey and its motivation.

As the hour for dinner nears, Hotel Guests of many nationalities

Ex. 2

assemble; the hubbub of their polyglot smalltalk fades as they move
into the dining room. Aschenbach, remaining behind, finds he is not
alone: attended by their governess, three Polish children, two girls
and a boy, are also waiting. A soundworld entirely unlike anything
heard so far[3] is opened up as Aschenbach responds to the boy's perfect, classical beauty; the theme (Ex. 3a), spanning a major seventh,
is supported on harmony compounded of its melody notes, and its
oddly disembodied effect is intensified by the colour of the vibraphone. This symbol of the boy Tadzio is essentially inert (merely by

Ex. 3a

Ex. 3b

Ex. 3c

being he exercises the spell) but in varied forms it pervades all that relates to him – the delicately bright percussive music of his friends no less than the stately orchestral harmonization of an Ex. 3a variant that marks his mother's presence (see Ex. 3b). As these characters execute their roles not through singing but through balletic mime, their musical depiction reflects Aschenbach's idealized view of them, and a highly distinctive orchestral treatment reinforces this 'otherness'. Mama joins the children and with their departure Aschenbach ponders on the incidence of beauty and his artist's predilection towards it.

Scene 5: An interlude develops the 'view' theme, Ex. 2, into which a new calling figure (see Ex. 3c) is introduced. On the beach, a languid Aschenbach is troubled by the grey skies and the heavy, stagnant atmosphere, but the games of children (percussion and Ex. 3a derivatives) offer some distraction; he buys some strawberries from a passing seller, gazes at the sea and decides to stay. The Polish boy appears (to an Ex. 3a form), registering in dumbshow his hatred of some Russian guests he has to pass. As he sits down with his family, friends call to him across the beach (Ex. 3c); the call acquires a strong allure for Aschenbach, the more so since at first the name of the godlike boy, still unknown to him, comes over as a mystifying 'Adziù'. Tadzio's music achieves a resonant climax as the children salute him as their leader; the boy takes this, and the admiration of his mother's friends to whom he is introduced, as his due, while Aschenbach looks on approvingly at this masterpiece he could wish to have created.

Scene 6: The barcarolle form of Ex. 1c accompanies Aschenbach to Venice where, to new, urgent orchestral figurations, he shrugs off importunate traders but cannot fight off the oppressive mood the sirocco and the foul air have induced; quotations and harmonic conflations of Ex. 1a mark these foreshadowings of the plague's corruption. In panic he resolves to leave the city and is rowed back to the hotel, where the Manager bids a farewell no less silky than was his welcome. A glimpse of Tadzio before he leaves for the station helps to intensify the regret with which Aschenbach on his gondola journey views all he is renouncing, so the Hotel Porter's officious consignment of his luggage to the wrong train provides a pretext for returning to the Lido; how eagerly he seizes on this is heard in the warm swell of the barcarolle as the gondola sets off yet again. Such vacillation is disturbing to an orderly mind and Aschenbach fastidiously examines his motives. But one factor is left out of account:

only when the Hotel Manager has again led him to his room and its celebrated view does he acknowledge this, for playing on the beach is Tadzio. With a gesture of acceptance, Aschenbach makes the fateful decision: 'So be it. Here I will stay, here dedicate my days to the sun, and Apollo himself'.

Scene 7: By innumerable nuances of language Mann filled out the picture of these blissful days in which, under the stimulus of Tadzio's proximity, Aschenbach's imagination flowers again, transporting him back to the world of classical mythology. Britten creates the Elysian atmosphere by other means. An orchestral prelude prefigures the simple choral harmony (of an arresting beauty that recalls early Britten) which ushers in a series of choral dances. In the theatre we see, on a beach ablaze with sunlight, Tadzio and his friends competing in games and athletic feats. But the chorus tells us of the vision into which Aschenbach, a silent spectator, translates the scene. These are rites in praise of Apollo, whose voice (counter-tenor) is heard in acknowledgement of the tribute. They depict Phoebus 'driving his horses through the azure sky'; Hyacinthus killed by the jealous Zephyr; and, after a digression on the nature of beauty as expounded by Socrates to Phaedrus, the pentathlon (race, long-jump, discus, javelin, wrestling). Tadzio is the hero or the victor in every tableau; in each his theme can be traced in the orchestra, a unifying thread through the diverse choral textures. Apollo's commendation of this 'very essence of beauty' rouses the excited Aschenbach to a solemn resolve: feeling shall be translated into thought, Eros celebrated in the word. Though this hymn begins by expanding the shape of Apollo's own phrases, it is founded on Tadzio's harmony, and the climactic phrase ennobles Tadzio's theme.

But this is not quite the end of Act I.[4] Aschenbach experiences a sudden panic that thwarts his intention of speaking at last to the godlike boy. He attributes it to the heat of the sun, but the recurrence of Ex. 1a shapes in the orchestral bass is ominous, and they are prominent too in a new 'yearning' theme, Ex. 4. Leaving the beach with his Mama, Tadzio passes Aschenbach and smiles at him ('Ah! don't smile like that! No one should be smiled at like that'). The unnerving moment of self-discovery in which Aschenbach recognizes his reaction to this is captured in the phrase that ends the act – 'I love you'. It follows a great crescendo, which reworks the string texture in which the longing to visit Venice formed itself, under the pervasive influence of the Ex. 1a shape, and the vocal phrase which the brass have been so insistently prompting proves to be com-

Ex. 4

pounded from the fateful note-cell. So the 'canker' motive that on the physical level symbolizes the plague has here entered Aschenbach's emotional world.

Act II

The prelude resumes from the closing sound of Act I (see n. 4, p. 211). It takes up the 'love' motive again, which constantly checks the flow of ardent string lines. We discover Aschenbach rationalizing an experience he can now see to be 'ridiculous yet sacred too, but not dishonourable'.

Scene 8: This takes place in the shop of the Hotel Barber, another bass-baritone character. His music, though a witty portrayal, is based on an inversion of Ex. 1b, for it is from his unguarded remark that Aschenbach first learns of the 'sickness' spreading through Venice; Ex. 1a looms up here in the tuba – its 'plague' form.

Scene 9: Troubled by what he has heard, Aschenbach crosses to the city to find that warning, if noncommittal, notices have been posted. To the orchestral figure of his earlier uneasiness (cf. scene 6) he makes enquiries, but only when he buys a German paper does he find clear evidence that a cholera epidemic is developing. The appearance of the Polish family brings a new anxiety – they must not hear the news, lest they leave Venice. To a ground bass of the 'plague' motive (Ex. 1a, reordered here as a straight ascent, has become more openly threatening), and with conflations of Tadzio's theme sighing above it, the 'yearning' theme (Ex. 4) marks a frenzied pursuit to keep the boy in sight – to a café in the Piazza (where even the little band reflects Tadzio's presence in its distortion of his music), through the crowded Merceria (where he momentarily comes face to face with the Polish family) and into a gondola to follow the one taken by his quarry. Finally, wholly given up to the 'bliss of madness', he follows the boy even to his bedroom door; the Act II prelude music recurs here. Back in his own room, he struggles to reconcile his public persona, his self-denial in the cause of his art, with this voluptuous frenzy; the precedents of antiquity still offer some reassurance.

Scene 10: The Hotel Guests assemble to watch a team of Strolling Players. Aschenbach, arriving during their sentimental opening duet, sees that Tadzio is also present. After the Leader of the Players (a bass-baritone character) has sung a comic song, Aschenbach draws him aside to ask for news of the epidemic; Ex. 1a inevitably punctuates this. The man's answers are evasive – to the satisfaction of the Hotel Porter, who questions him when he has left Aschenbach. Back with his team, the Leader sings a nightmarish little laughing song, vacuous yet oddly sinister, against a wheezing concertina-like accompaniment. Aschenbach notes with approval that Tadzio, perhaps following his own example, does not share the audience's mirth; when all have left, he reflects, in a rare stillness, on the inexorable passing of time that he now knows may be short.

Scene 11: In a travel bureau, surrounded by Hotel Guests clamouring for tickets to leave Venice, the young English clerk on duty is driven to close his counter, but Aschenbach engages him in conversation that leads to his account of the plague – from its origins in the Ganges delta to the toll it is exacting in Venice. The whole of this narrative takes place above the slow unwinding in the orchestral bass of the Munich Traveller's solo: the exotic, swampy landscape is identified, its marvels are unfolding.

Scene 12: Resuming his agitated walk, Aschenbach rehearses how he will break the news to Tadzio's mother, and so save the boy's life. Her theme, Ex. 3b, in the orchestra signals her approach, but at the crucial moment Aschenbach remains silent. He falls back on a self-examination that throws up the motive for his failure – 'What if all were dead, and only we two left alive'; the Ex. 1a shape is potently at work here, while the orchestral interlude muses on phrases from the love music of the prelude.

Scene 13: A choral dream sequence balances the choral visionary sequence of scene 7, but the white Apollonian idyll has now become a black Dionysiac orgy. As Aschenbach sleeps, the voices of the 'stranger god', Dionysus (the last of the bass-baritone parts), and of Apollo (counter-tenor) are heard, pressing on him their conflicting claims; the former prevails and his followers invade the scene. Their bestial cries horribly distort the music of Tadzio (Ex. 3c, then 3a), whose figure is seen at the climax of the dance; and the roar of a goaded animal that punctuates it is the motive of corruption in its 'plague' form (tuba). Waking from this terrible dream, Aschenbach recognizes his betrayal of lifelong ideals, and abandons himself to the gods' whims.

Scene 14: Pale echoes of the sunlit harmony of scene 7 and of the related 'view' theme (Ex. 2) introduce a sombre scene on the almost deserted beach, where Tadzio and his friends execute a desultory dance (xylophone). Aschenbach, watching from his chair, is confirmed in his surrender.

Scene 15 shows him, all restraint and shame cast aside, attempting a winning rejuvenation at the Hotel Barber's, and it ironically recalls the Elderly Fop he found so disgusting on the voyage (scene 2).

Scene 16: Aschenbach even plays on the parallel, quoting with a frenzied abandon from the youths' songs. Anguished counterpoints of the 'yearning' theme (Ex. 4), Tadzio's harmony (Ex. 3a) and permutations of Ex. 1a attend his distracted pursuit of the Polish family; this time Tadzio lingers and looks full at him, a climactic moment that leaves Aschenbach drained. The strawberry seller of scene 5 reappears, but the fruit he buys is rotten. Exhausted, he sits down by a well-head, pitiably recalls the wish that tempted him in scene 12, and to the trumpet figure (cf. scene 1) soberly views the ruin of the famous writer. As in Mann, this leads to a beautifully still moment when he traces his path to the abyss in Socrates' words to Phaedrus – a little strophic piece accompanied by warm harp and cold piano, and founded on harmonies that conflate the C major/minor implicit in Ex. 1a. A broad orchestral interlude salutes the quest of beauty that was once his, developing grandly the 'view' theme, Ex. 2.

Scene 17: The Hotel Manager and Porter exchange comments on the hasty departure of their guests. Aschenbach enters, to a wearied version of Ex. 4, and ascertains that the Polish family is about to leave; on this final appearance the Manager's smooth manner has given way to overt, and sinister, echoes of the Munich Traveller – the task of fate's messengers is almost completed. On the beach (Ex. 2 theme in the flute, Ex. 1 forms in double-basses) Tadzio still plays with a few friends. But no longer is his domination supreme, and to an orchestral crescendo he is brought down and humiliated. The tuba's 'plague' motive emerges with unprecedented savagery, and Aschenbach cries out in a vain attempt to help Tadzio. His tormentor runs off and Tadzio slowly picks himself up, walking off towards the sea, oblivious to the forlorn calls of his friends. Aschenbach gently echoes the call (Ex. 3c) and, as the boy seems to beckon to him, he collapses in his chair. The figure of Tadzio recedes, and an orchestral postlude (see Plate 17) washes away the corruption that has festered throughout this second act, recalling the ideal of beauty celebrated in the Hymn to Apollo, counterpointed by Tadzio's alluringly bright music.

[Revised 1985]

17 The beginning of the orchestral postlude in the composition sketch (at fig. 325) (The Britten–Pears Library and Archive)

7 Tonal ambiguity in 'Death in Venice': a symphonic view

ERIC ROSEBERRY

> The whole movement is based on a premonition of death, which is constantly recurring. All earthly dreams up to this peak; that is why the tenderest passages are followed by tremendous climaxes like new eruptions of a volcano. This, of course, is most obvious of all in the place where the premonition of death becomes certain knowledge, where in the most profound and anguished love of life death appears 'mit höchster Gewalt' [with the utmost force] . . . Against that there is no resistance left, and I see what follows as a sort of resignation.
>
> Alban Berg on the first movement of Mahler's Ninth Symphony.
> Letter to his wife, autumn 1912[1]

The fluid continuity – as scene dissolves, flows into scene, as Act II begins its yearning reflections on the confessional 'I love you' wrung out of Aschenbach at the end of Act I, as the whole 'weight of musical experience' (to use Myfanwy Piper's phrase)[2] gathers into a sweeping torrent that ultimately disperses in the calm open sea of the final apotheosis – this quality above all must strike the listener coming to Britten's *Death in Venice* for the first time. It is essentially a continuity of *line*, a stylistic renewal on Britten's part via the primal current of recitative, whose historical source may be traced back to Monteverdi and the origins of opera itself in the *stile rappresentativo*. (In this sense the opera is Britten's double tribute to Peter Pears and to the great Venetian father of opera who was, no less fittingly for the subject in hand, a Platonist.)[3] A notable feature of this continuity of line (evident from Aschenbach's very first utterance) is what is known as 'linkage technique': the carrying over of pitches from the end of one segment or scene to form the beginning of the next – one of the most natural and comprehensible means of continuity available to the composer (see Ex. 1).[4]

Stepwise motion, whether of melody or harmony (in a Debussy-like revival of the principle of organum) creates the fluctuating, tonally ambiguous movement of *Death in Venice*. Chains of arpeggiated thirds (see also Britten's tonal analogue for the lapping of the

86

Ex. 1

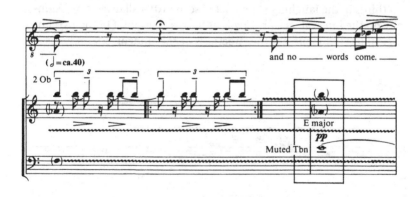

Ex. 1 (*cont.*)

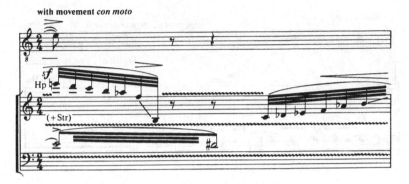

waves in *Grimes*) expand these steps, as, for example, in the 'view' theme (Ex. 2).

The third is indeed the opera's leading interval, the basic leitmotif which – whether in vertical or horizontal guise – sounds through each significant theme and musical configuration. Throughout, from the opening twelve-note musings of Aschenbach in Munich to the transfigured calm of 'The departure' (Act II scene 17) this interval haunts the ear. Even the 'outer' realistic characterizations – ship's siren, popular serenade ('Serenissima'), church bells, the calls of the gondoliers, the sinister, wheezy drone of the piano accordion's piled-up thirds in the laughing song (Act II scene 10) – all dwell obsessionally on the interval, confirming it as a tonal symbol. On the psychological level, it expresses the sweetness of the 'Tadziù' cry and – as if

Ex. 2

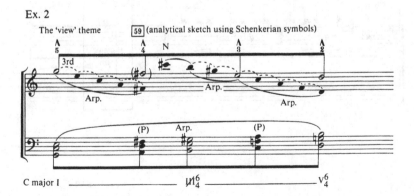

Key to symbols used:

Λ = scalic degree
N = neighbour note
P = passing note (or harmony)
Arp. = arpeggiation

Beamed notes using open note heads indicate an interpretation of the main linear descent (the hypothetical structural background) and, in the lower stave, the 'structural' harmonies. Stemmed black notes and notes without stems indicate foreground detail – the smaller the note value, the less structural weight it carries. The bracketed fourth degree of the linear descent is a hypothetical registral transfer of the lower F sharp'.

by reflection – Aschenbach's startled self-confession of love at the end of Act I. The 'natural' third of sweetness and serenity is poisoned by its 'dissonant' minor inflection[5] in the 'plague' motive whose major/minor ambiguity is cast in the symbolic key of C which, as the opera unfolds, comes to rank in importance with Aschenbach's E major and Tadzio's A major. (The memorable 'view' theme quoted above (Ex. 2) is a highly significant C major–E major event.) C major/minor is the mediant link between E and A major, which three third-related key areas create what may be heard as the tidal ebb and flow (we cannot speak of an unequivocal key *centre*) of this opera. Tonality remains a characterizing, subtly referential agent, and the pull between these three leading keys, their frequently ambiguous fusion of identity, is never completely resolved. As early as scene 1, E major and C major/minor are fused in the inflections of the Traveller's fluttering scales – as if Aschenbach's fate were already sealed. This symbolic fusion creates a memorable timpani figure in an extension of the Traveller's original motive (Ex. 3) which is reflected by inversion in the much later motto phrase of Act II.

Ex. 3

Broad (♩.= 72) *Largamente*

Ex. 4

By the end of Act I Tadzio's A major has established itself as the third main field in the larger symbolic interplay of tonal regions. Once A major is in view it becomes the sun of Act I, the Apollonian key centre of the final scene. Indeed, so strong is this A major 'sun' that it may well seem a more strongly affirmed tonal presence than that of Aschenbach's original E major, and therefore an alternative 'tonic', to which Aschenbach's E major functions as a kind of 'dominant' preparation. (If to speak now of a 'tonic' appears to contradict the above-expressed view of E–C–A as the tonal field of gravity then let it stand in order to draw attention to the perplexing tonal ambiguity of the opera.)

Our knowledge of Britten's characteristic mastery of *transition*, whether in opera, song cycle, variation or suite, could hardly have prepared us for its heightened significance as a leading principle in *Death in Venice*.[6] For this, uniquely in Britten's *oeuvre*, is an opera worked out exclusively in terms of a musicalization of the 'stream of consciousness' of its protagonist. Only at the end is there a radical shift of perspective from the expression of Aschenbach's 'I' to a presentation of events through the eye of the outsider. The (C major!) luminous aria 'Does beauty lead to wisdom, Phaedrus?' (fig. 308) is Aschenbach's last connected (if not wholly coherent) statement. After this memorable farewell we are to hear no more than a few pitiful ejaculations from the 'flabby, rouged lips' of a degraded hero cast in the soliloquizing mould of Hamlet, whose musing incapacity for direct speech and resolute action is the cause of his degradation. As death closes in on him it is we, the audience, who now become the observers. This crucial change of perspective is marked by the great brass interlude (a fugato on the 'view' theme, Ex. 2) leading to the final scene. Its context and climactic strength suggest a parallel with Berg's D minor Adagio before the final scene of *Wozzeck* – the opera which surely remained archetypal for Britten in the composition of both *Grimes* and *Death in Venice*.[7]

In an opera which is obsessively concerned with the progress of a disintegrating consciousness and its attendant, well-nigh expressionistic horrors and strange beauties, Britten's musical objectivity of genre[8] (whether 'straight' or parodistic) and underlying structure can be as reassuring a pathway through the emotional labyrinth as was Berg's explicitly 'classical' substructure in *Wozzeck*. Now although Britten's escape from the sonata aesthetic was almost complete (Donald Mitchell has disclosed that Britten regarded his Third Quartet as a significant achievement in this respect)[9] yet the classically trained ear can sense in the opera a sonata-like scheme comprising exposition (Act I), development (Act II scenes 8–13) overlapping with a telescoped recapitulation/coda (scenes 13–17). Sonata style as a metaphor for the unfolding of a Greek tragedy, its three stages standing for protasis, epitasis and catastrophe! Although, as has already been suggested, key is best understood as locally characterizing and long-range cross-referential rather than a form-building element in this opera, yet the overriding significance of E–C–A as a tonal field of gravity enables the ear to sense a larger interaction and goal orientation, as in a classical sonata scheme. Thus if E major– C major/minor are taken as the point of departure in scene 1, then Tadzio's A major in scene 4 can carry, to the sonata-conditioned ear, the expressive connotation and structural weight of a 'second subject' in the tonal continuum. And although the first act closes in Aschenbach's 're-discovery' of his own E major[10] (the startled confession of love is wrung, as it were, out of a harrowing linear conflict which negates key sense) there is, none the less, sufficient emphasis on A major in 'The Games of Apollo' to enable us to experience that key as a point of arrival, a structural downbeat in Act I which is even more solidly established than E major itself. The firm E major Adagio that begins the second act establishes immediate tonal continuity with the preceding act and (in a manner not unlike the introduction of the ballad at the beginning of Act II in *Owen Wingrave*) provides an important new 'boost' that will be transformed in brief but emotionally intensifying episodes (see especially fig. 279 before 'The dream') as the action develops. This placing of E major suggests another structural analogue with the sonata tradition; it is a vestige of the convention of the repeat of the exposition, a stabilizing reference back to the 'tonic' key before embarking on tonal instability – a procedure which will be familiar to readers acquainted with Beethoven (Op. 59, No. 1, first movement), Mahler (Symphony No. 4, first movement) or Schoenberg (First Chamber Symphony). All this, however, is based on the somewhat questionable assumption of E major as the 'tonic' key (see also J. Evans, pp. 107-9 and Plate 18, p. 108): as we have already seen, Tadzio's A major is a strong rival candidate – and from a symbolic point of view Aschenbach has become totally dependent on the boy, a 'dominant' to his 'tonic', as it were.

The 'development' achieves its own climactic points of tonal 'arrival' – in the clerk's warning of the arrival of the plague (C minor) and in Aschenbach's dream (A major–C major/minor), both transformations of material from Act I. Tadzio's A major, however, recurs periodically as an inescapable obsession, and in this connection we should note the pathetic A major echo of the E major Adagio prelude at fig. 233. The extraordinarily unified sweep of the first stage of the development as it plunges restlessly forward is attained through Britten's deployment of an extended passacaglia which is interrupted at cadential points by a series of pauses – temporary stations of arrival in Aschenbach's pursuit of his A major goal. This leads to the ironic central interlude of the development – the Players' scene (scene 10) – which begins with an ironic A major waltz transformation of the terminal pitches a'–g sharp" of Tadzio's theme – before development is resumed in a second stage: the clerk's explanation (scene 11: a transformation of 'Marvels unfold', scene 1), the 'Lady of the Pearls' (scene 12: corresponding with the tonally restless 'foiled departure' of Act I scene 6), and the main climax of 'The dream' (the 'brutalized' theme which is that of Tadzio: see also Palmer, pp. 150-2) in A major, superimposed over the plague's C major/minor tuba motive and a percussion ostinato based on that of the Traveller (see scene 1). Here we are confronted with a musico-dramatic situation familiar in sonata movements by Mahler (Symphony No. 4, first movement) and Shostakovich (Symphony No. 5, first movement), but stemming ultimately from the first movement of Beethoven's Ninth – the climactic overlap of development with recapitulation, in which a recognizable tonal–thematic return is transformed by means of the developmental thrust which has brought it about. (If we prefer to regard E major as the tonic key of the opera, then here is an analogue to one of Schubert's favourite devices – recapitulation in the subdominant.) From this point on, the final scenes present us with a (still developing!) conflation of recapitulation and coda in a continuity which encompasses Aschenbach's ultimate descent into the abyss, his death and transfiguration. In this final stretch Aschenbach's E major becomes sufficiently a foreground key to justify a sense of return to the tonic in the manner of a sonata movement cast in arch form. But such a view does not completely answer the case. A more realistic tonal perspective would be to view this section as a recapitulatory fusion of E–C–A, which complex of mediant related tonal regions has already been designated as the tidal 'ebb and flow' of the opera. This is, moreover, recapitulatory in effect, because it tightens the proximity of key relationships which were initially experienced in looser temporal succession.

Like Berg's *Wozzeck*, Britten's *Death in Venice* is conceived in terms of multiple correspondences, of mirror images more or less remotely transformed. The principle operates at all levels – whether in the interplay of surface relationships (motive, phrase, local harmonic movement) or hidden in the deeper groundswell of conflicting tonal currents. In scene 1, for example, Britten's scalic twelve-note melodic line extends through four-note cellular correspondences and larger balancing mirror forms (see also J. Evans, pp. 100–2), with heterophonically derived harmonies of a bitonal, whole tone or (as in the case of the Traveller) even purely tonal nature. This heterophony is a harmony which 'reflects' line; the vertical corresponds to the horizontal. And such a state is paradigmatic for the whole work, operating as it does in the relationship between whole scenes and the two acts. Take Britten's characteristic repeated verse and cadenza refrain technique which has a long, memorable lineage in his *oeuvre*, stretching back, for example, to the sparkling 'Marine' of *Les Illuminations*. From the very first notes of the opera, we may observe this Brittenish formal convention at the foreground level in *Death in Venice*; a little later, both 'Marvels unfold' with its expanding percussion cadenzas derived from the Traveller's timpani motive, and the Hotel Manager's ironic chorale welcome, with its Stygian A minor chord pauses (referring back to Aschenbach's canal journey) at the close of each phrase are further manifestations of this pervasive technique. But how powerfully the same idea works on the *large* scale in 'The pursuit' of Act II scene 9, where each stage of the restless passacaglia, with its successively rising key levels (E–A–F–G–B) in the bass, is punctuated by a new static port of call or temporary haven, so to speak. This is indeed a symphonic opera, which is shaped into what resembles a vastly extended movement in the manner of Mahler. As in Mahler's symphonies (and, one might add, Schubert's song cycles) key operates with expressive connotations that can override the classical unities. It is the structural and expressive ambiguity of Mahler's symphonic style in general and, perhaps, that of the first movement of his Ninth Symphony in particular (with its enlargement of the sonata principle by means of rondo-like episodic elements, its tonal freedom, its principle of constant development, its multiple climaxes and ambiguity of recapitulation) which, I would suggest, offer the closest historical parallel to the total effect of *Death in Venice*. And the Mahlerian structural expressive model is reinforced in gestural detail not only by the continuous play of musical irony – which was, after all, Mahler's very special province – but by what are almost direct allusions to his manner. I am thinking here of the appoggiatura-laden, 'yearning' string Adagio (shades of the Adagietto from Symphony No. 5!) which begins Act II, or the work's conclusion, with its extraordinarily close reminiscence of the ending of the Ninth Symphony's first movement (much admired by Berg). The textural dissolution, the insistent major third (how like Britten's evocative Tadziù cry are Mahler's falling thirds in the horns!), the upward resolution of the falling appoggiature on to the high violin and glockenspiel a'''', the whole spiritual effect of such Alpine purity of transformation after so much emotional turmoil here unite two great twentieth-century musical farewells.

I want to round off this 'symphonic' view of the opera with a concise 'foreground' commentary on the events of its recapitulation/coda in relation to the total 'symphonic' context. This works largely in terms of a transformed restatement of scenes (or parts of scenes) that have been crucial to the opera's unfolding, but – in keeping with Britten's Mahlerian aesthetic of constantly developing variation – there is much that is apparently new. If, in this final section, I concentrate mainly on line and harmony it is not to deny the significance of instrumental timbre and texture in an opera where sheer beauty of orchestral colour has its own symbolic role to play. Far from it. But there is a not inapt Platonic implication here; an irony of interpretation that would see the orchestral colours of sensory perception as but a reflection of the musical essence that can be reproduced in black and white on the piano. In this respect Britten remains a composer in the traditional, 'absolute' mould.

'The dream', then – led into by a searching transformation of the Mahlerian Adagio which began Act I – is a temporal proximation (in highly charged transformation) of what were originally disparate musical elements in Act I. (This Mahlerian reshuffling of material is characteristic of *Death in Venice*.) Aschenbach's E major soft dreaming string scales are loaded with a preludial high tension through an increasingly abrupt shortening and acceleration; they discharge violently into a choral version of Tadzio's A major motive (here Aschenbach's E major serves as functional dominant) that is set against the tuba's obscene C major/minor 'plague' motive in conjunction with a brutal ostinato of percussion (note the dotted rhythm, referring back once more to the Traveller's original timpani motive). This is the opera's climax of destruction which counterbalances Aschenbach's ecstatic climax of exultation ('Then Eros is in the word') at the end of Act I. The climactic imagery is in the Mahler–Berg tradition: we can hear in it an echo of the 'destruction of innocence' climax in Berg's Violin Concerto or the famous crescendo on the note B in *Wozzeck*.

Once again, psychological collapse follows. The sense of frustration that accompanied Aschenbach's inability to speak and congratulate the boy is now replaced by a sense of degradation in the wake of the dream's physical wish-fulfilment. In the mediant shifts and 'false relations' of the tonal configurations of the ensuing recitative and beach scene we may already experience a confirmation of that symbolic converging of Aschenbach's plague-ridden E major–C major/minor and Tadzio's innocent A major which characterized the dream and intensifies these closing scenes. Indeed, in the beach scene, what was originally presented in a bright Lydian-inflected A major (cf. scene 7) has now become a desultory C minor. In the second encounter with the Hotel Barber, C major has become a 'falsely bright' key (it is shortly to acquire a more poignant irony) as Aschenbach is transformed by the Barber's cosmetic art into a resemblance of the very Fop by whom he was repelled on the way to Venice. Observe the subtlety of the backward referring tonal symbolism here. In the F sharp scalic seconds which pirouette into the C major tonality of this scene we encounter both the shape of the original Traveller's 'Go, travel to the South' *and* the key in which we first encountered the old Fop. *Death in Venice* abounds in such subtle, minute references which use key characterization in a thematic, referential manner (Ex. 5).

A grotesquely transformed 'Serenissima' brings back the music originally associated with the boat trip to Venice, with its breezily vulgar band tune now lewdly distorted by Aschenbach into the Tadzio motive ('all hail to my beauty'). (See Cooke, Ex. 13, pp. 126–7.) Via a labyrinthine précis of the developmental pursuit (the music now seems to be totally in control of Aschenbach's helpless situation) he is led to his last fatal encounter with the strawberry seller whose tonally ambiguous cry is tainted with the symbolic associations of the dominant thirteenth chords of the piano accordion which accompanied the laughing song in the scene of the Players.

Ex. 5

(It is interesting to notice that the 'missing' G' and B' notes of this chord are now transferred to the extreme registers of orchestral double basses and solo violin harmonic.) In the context of so much ironic transformation, Aschenbach's broken return to E major (originally a proud fanfare of affirmation) strikes the ear as a parody whose bitterness of disillusion is underlined through its formal, i.e. recapitulatory significance. The heavy despair carried in the rise and fall of the phrase 'O perilous sweetness/the wisdom poets crave' carries a weight of musical experience – so reminiscent is this pregnantly simple phrase of other memorable shapes in the opera. It echoes and transforms the 'view' theme, the Traveller's scalic motive, and Aschenbach's original parched cry 'O tender leaves and tardy spring refresh me!'; its falling thirds 'contain' the Tadzio theme; its C major purity of expression is a supreme tonal irony. It was an inspiration of Britten and his librettist to reshape Mann's account of Aschenbach's deranged self-communings into the classical purity of an aria which now becomes a still, held moment, a climax of quietness. The emotional climax of *Peter Grimes* was a mad scene also, but there Grimes disjointedly dredged up snatches of hope, despair, accusation from the past; Aschenbach, in contrast, attains a strange spiritual serenity by means of a subtler process of transformation. The recitative phrase 'O perilous sweetness' now becomes the starting point of the aria, accompanied by the opposed timbre of piano and harp, whose bitonal arpeggios constitute a direct allusion to Tadzio's formal solo dance in 'The Games of Apollo' (see fig. 158). Consistent with

Britten's characteristic 'linkage technique', the last two pitches of Aschenbach's phrase 'then you go too' (E flat–F) become the point of departure for a massive build-up of successive entries of the 'view' theme in a 'broad and strong' brass fanfare. It heralds the climactic arrival of C minor and the 'view' theme in string octaves, moving to F sharp minor for the farewell scene at the hotel. This grand transitional interlude makes weighty recapitulatory reference to the third-related tonal complex of C minor, E major and A major before 'arriving' at the C minor–F sharp minor tonal sweep of the 'view' theme and, for the last time, the hotel.

In an opera which handles so many genre elements with consummate mastery, Britten's ironic handling of the chorale and chorale four-part harmony (Bach/Stravinsky!) as a vehicle for presenting the Hotel Manager's ritualistic role (F sharp minor) is yet a further stylistic resource that works admirably. Punctuating each of three verses of this chorale like a comic refrain is the 'business' of the Hotel Porter as he trots in and out with the baggage of the departing guests. His 'First one goes, then another goes' replaces the original dark A minor chords of the Stygian journey across the lagoon (see fig. 57 *et seq.*). Britten's ironic substitution of the *opera buffa* genre for what was formerly a stark hint of the abyss is a sinister and, for this opera, typically laconic stroke. (*Death in Venice* is a masterly synthesis of techniques taken from earlier operas of Britten: here the ritualistic spareness of gesture in *Death in Venice* – yet a further genre element! – springs directly from *Curlew River* and the Noh play conventions.) A tired resumé of the passacaglia 'pursuit' theme (still in F sharp minor) marks Aschenbach's entrance, underpinning his faint, broken conversation with the Manager. The Hotel Manager's chorale is resumed: in a brutal climactic transition to E major Aschenbach is, as it were, dismissed. Tonally, this is the 'official' ending of the opera.

But there is the final apotheosis. When Aschenbach goes out to the deserted beach the inflection is once more towards an ambiguous C major/minor, in the desultory 'view' music with its cadenza-like percussion interpolations that present Aschenbach with his last view of Tadzio and his playmates. As the game becomes rough the 'plague' motive on the tuba confirms C major/minor as the tonality. By a natural extension of Aschenbach's cry 'Ah, no!' (now transformed into the distant cry of 'Adziù' – a reflection of scene 5 in Act I) the music rises stepwise to Aschenbach's dying cry of 'Tadziù' and the 'goal' of A major (Ex. 6).

Ex. 6

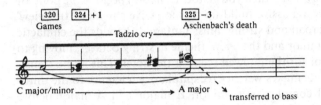

The transfigured restatement of Aschenbach's 'When thought becomes feeling' – which was itself a transformation of the 'Hymn to the Sun' (how faithfully Britten's operatic sense kept to the Verdian idea of 'the big tune!') – signifies A major as the 'epitaph' key. Though 'resolution' would be too strong a word yet it does symbolize – in keeping with the manifold ambiguities of this work – a kind of peace, a dissolution which finds its exact musical image in Aschenbach's fading G sharp in the bass (G sharp, we may remember, was the starting note of Tadzio's A major motive) resolving upwardly and remotely to that single high, clear A.

8 Twelve-note structures and tonal polarity

JOHN EVANS

Britten's very personal brand of eclectic conservatism embraced a wide range of musical resources, and this is perhaps nowhere better in evidence than in his last opera *Death in Venice*. Twelve-note devices, a recurrent tension between tonal clarity and tonal ambivalence, textures and techniques derived from the Balinese gamelan and the Japanese Noh play, an intricate system of motivic interrelationships, recitatives that owe their particular quality of melodic precision and rhythmic freedom to the example of Schütz: all these resources contribute to the work's rich tapestry of musical languages. As Arnold Whittall has observed: 'Like *Owen Wingrave*, *Death in Venice* "modulates" from an initial twelve-note proposition to a modal "resolution" which seems both ambiguous and inevitable.'[1] If one is tempted to conclude that the twelve-note proposition and the modal resolution are unrelated strands of an eclectic score, one would be mistaken. Though the resolution is 'ambiguous' it is also 'inevitable', as Whittall points out, and the concept of *modulation* between the twelve-note proposition of the opening scene and the modal resolution of the opera's postlude acknowledges an extraordinary symphonic logic that permeates the score.

The strength of Britten's eclecticism lies in the fact that he was able to absorb diverse musical resources (and even diverse musical languages), make them his own and, more importantly, make them function within the parameters of any work. In *The Turn of the Screw* it is the turning action of the perpetual rising fourth and falling third and the 'white'/'black' key juxtapositions of the twelve-note *Theme* that actually control the thematic and tonal processes of the score; in *Owen Wingrave* it is the diminished triad (that arises from the four three-note chords of the opera's robust twelve-note proposition) that infiltrates every level of the opera and is subsequently echoed in no less than seven further series employed throughout the score. Similarly, the opening twelve-note proposition

99

in *Death in Venice*, while encapsulating the dramatic image of intellectual sterility within Aschenbach ('My mind beats on, and no words come'), initiates the central major/minor third motivic cell of the score and, as I hope to demonstrate, highlights the tonal polarities that place the Apollonian/Dionysiac conflict in context throughout the opera.

The very opening of *Death in Venice* is one of the most subtle yet graphic responses to a text in Britten's entire output. Aschenbach's brooding monologue establishes at the outset the image of a beating, throbbing mind leading nowhere, achieving nothing. This is precisely what Britten gives us in three hesitantly repetitive unison wind duets freely aligned in a rhythmic texture of great complexity. The diminished triads (cf. *Wingrave*) and consequent highlighting of tritones arising from the piling up of minor thirds in this texture underpin Aschenbach's monologue (see Ex. 1), the melodic setting of which is derived from a twelve-note series (Ex. 2) that compounds the tonal ambiguity of the instrumental texture, juxtaposing the *major* third against the omnipresent *minor*. This circumscribed major/minor ambivalence is the single most exploited idea in the entire score.

Ex. 1

Ex. 2

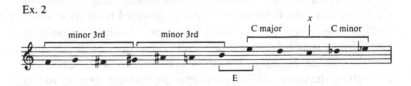

The rising shape of the vocal line in Ex. 1 from a low F to a high E flat should be noted. However, the minor seventh is soon resolved on to the major seventh with the first flourishes of the harp in the ensuing *con moto* bridge passage. This E natural/E flat juxtaposition is derived from the second hexachord of the series above (*x* in Ex. 2), but this resolution is by no means stable. While the diminished triads are sustained in the wind, the trombone perpetuates the E/E flat (now spelt D sharp) juxtaposition and the upward *glissandi* in the harp are similarly ambivalent.

There are a further four statements of this twelve-note idea in the first sixty-three bars of scene 1, two in its primary state (as in Ex. 2) and two in alternative free retrograde inversions. In the second sentence of scene 1 (fig. 1, bars 10–17) the twelve-note proposition and its diminished triad underpinning are freely inverted and the series spelt in retrograde. The woodwind duets start on a high E flat on two piccolos and expand downwards through the texture (with the same octave displacements as in Ex. 1) through C and A. The vocal line ('Taxing, tiring') is similarly drawn from a high E flat (two octaves lower than the piccolos) moving down towards F, the second hexachord of the series strongly suggesting first E major (*x*) then F minor (*y*) (Ex. 3). This E major/F minor juxtaposition is now transferred to the tuba tremolo that supports the bridge passage for the piano. The climax of this sentence (one bar before fig. 2) draws together these disparate elements with the E major/F minor juxtaposition sustained by the tuba at the bottom of the texture; a resolution on to F^7 derived from the second hexachord of Ex. 2; and the continued presence of the woodwinds' diminished triad (A–C–E flat) which, supported by the root, F, establishes a major mode juxtaposition with the F *minor* of Ex. 3.

The third sentence (at fig. 2) begins as though to recapitulate the opening proposition. But in this statement the second hexachord reaffirms the *major* seventh (E natural), introducing it by tonal stepwise motion from the dominant (B) and through an auxiliary-note

Ex. 3

pattern of flattened sixth and seventh introduces a new minor/major conflict in relation to E, taking both C sharp and C natural in its path. Again the major/minor third, major/minor seventh and the E/F juxtaposition are being stressed through the fluctuating horizontal and vertical tensions arising from the series. This is high-lighted still further in the tonal structure of Aschenbach's 'identity' aria between figs. 3 and 5. Over punctuating flourishes in the strings and a fanfare-like trumpet underpinning, Aschenbach's line is poised at first on repeated high Es. The fanfares soon attempt an extension of their unison octaves to the lower ninth (D) but this is only temporary. Rather, Aschenbach redirects the passage up by step, though not on to F sharp (a logical move in the context of E major) but on to F *natural* major. Thus the E/F juxtaposition is sustained in an emphatically convincing way. The ensuing bridge passage that links with the refrain is equally skilful. Six bars after fig. 4 the trumpet octaves begin to contract to a minor seventh, with the crucial E flat in first trumpet. The final descending phrase passes from a high F and E flat via both A flat and A natural (the minor *and* major third), but its last dying fall resists any attempt to resolve on to F, remaining on G.

A reprise of the twelve-note refrain in its original state leads to the climax of this first paragraph of scene 1 (at fig. 6). Now the inner tensions of this man of discipline and order become more apparent and the preliminary conflicts of this scene are expanded. Each of Aschenbach's four phrases derives its impetus from a high melodic juxtaposition of E and F and the first three phrases come to rest on F sharp major.[2] Aschenbach's fourth phrase ('And delight in fastidious choice') now ascends from a low E/F juxtaposition rising towards a high D sharp (= E flat, the initial pitch of the reprise of the refrain that follows). This final statement of the refrain is in free retrograde inversion (E flat–F) and the ambivalent swing of tonal regions in Aschenbach's penultimate phrase ('O tender leaves and tardy spring refresh me!') moves from F minor to E major to accom-modate the orchestral reprise of the 'identity' aria, only to move characteristically back to F at fig. 9.

The choral evocation of the texts on the façade of the mortuary chapel (at fig. 9) is also derived from a twelve-note series, each hex-achord of which constitutes a whole-tone scale – the first upward rising from F, the second descending from E. The series, an early form of which was worked out in Britten's sketchbook for *Death in Venice*, is shown in Ex. 4.

Ex. 4

whole - tone scale   whole - tone scale

After the brass take up the whole-tone scales in stretto, the strings
derive fragmentary whole-tone shapes from this texture over a pedal
C to prepare for the arrival of the mysterious Traveller at fig. 9. The
motive that announces this sudden manifestation of the first of the
Messengers of Death has a strong rhythmic thrust and is derived
from the now well-established major/minor ambivalence accorded
to F (Ex. 5).

Ex. 5

On the third of its statements, between figs. 13 and 14, Ex. 5 alludes
to the E flat/E juxtaposition of Ex. 2 and it influences Aschenbach's
melodic line by the same token (Ex. 6).

Ex. 6

At fig. 14 the Traveller introduces his own version of the major/
minor tension of this first scene. The pedal C of fig. 12 is here established as a tonal point of departure for the Traveller's extended
scena. The setting of 'Marvels unfold' (see Ex. 7) spans a major third
but also highlights the minor (E flat spelt as D sharp).

Ex. 7

C major   C minor

So, what conclusions can be drawn from this analysis of the exposi-
tionary Prologue to this first scene? Tensions established between the
major and minor modes (particularly in relation to the intervals of a
third and a seventh) and between the adjacent pitches of F and E
derive from the fundamental properties of the initial twelve-note
proposition. While F, as a linear pitch, is constantly reaffirmed as a
point of departure for successive statements, and as a goal for those
in retrograde inversion, at the beginning of the second hexachord of
Ex. 2 the leap of a fourth from B to E brings the juxtaposition into
question. Even within the ambiguous texture of diminished triads
that underpin these twelve-note statements a feeling of the centrality
of F is fairly strong. By more recognizable tonal gestures E major is
affirmed at fig. 3 (a prime case of a triadically enforced tonality being
juxtaposed with a tonality of single notes) and at fig. 4 the tonal
'centre' of F is also asserted. A further twelve-note juxtaposition of
F and E is highlighted in the two hexachordal whole-tone scales at
fig. 9.

Two scenes of crucial musico-dramatic importance reflect these
harmonic tensions and tonal juxtapositions from scene 1: 'The
Games of Apollo' (Act I scene 7), particularly Aschenbach's Hymn
to Apollo at the end of the scene; and 'The dream' (Act II scene 13)
where the Apollo/Dionysus conflict is brought to a head.

The prominence of A major in relation to Tadzio throughout the
choral dances and the pentathlon at the end of Act I reaches its
zenith when Tadzio is proclaimed victor. As Aschenbach yields to
the force of beauty, his Hymn to Apollo (in Tadzio's tonal region and
in the melodic shapes of his music) celebrates beauty as 'the mirror

of the spirit'. Deriving also from Apollo's Delphic Hymn and over a
sustained conflation of Tadzio's theme in the strings, Aschenbach's
Lydian song exposes the strong polarity between his music and
Tadzio's (Ex. 8).

Ex. 8

Having failed to speak to Tadzio and place their relationship on a
saner footing, Aschenbach's crisis begins: bassoons and violas
embroider the major/minor figure of the 'plague' motive (Ex. 7) in
C major/minor at fig. 185+6, and at fig. 186 Tadzio's A major is
abandoned and the three-sharp key signature cancelled. The transition of yearning from the Apollonian to the Dionysiac planes has
begun; and the infestation of the cankerous major/minor third
manifests itself in both Tadzio's and Aschenbach's music. The tonal
scheme begins a cycle of fifths with the entrance of Tadzio's mother
(fig. 186+5) moving from B to E, and finally to A *minor* two bars
before fig. 187. Against this minor mode, Tadzio's smile stimulates a
new motive that juxtaposes the major third degree and reinstates the
Lydian fourth that links with Aschenbach's E major (Ex. 9). This
major/minor deviation of Tadzio's A is sustained over nine bars. It
releases a dense chromatic elaboration of the blurred alignment
of scales[3] that accompanied Aschenbach's urge to 'travel to the
South' in the coda to scene 1 (fig. 20) and at the point of self-
discovery, Aschenbach's E major likewise embraces the minor third
(Ex. 10). This major/minor third juxtaposition in Aschenbach's
music is a reflection of the fundamental flaw in this sudden awareness of 'love'.

Ex. 9

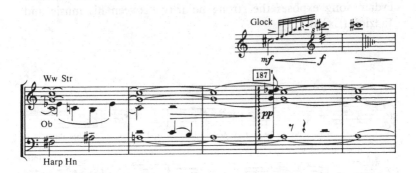

ASCHENBACH

Ah!   don't smile   like   that!

Ex. 10

(realising the truth at last.)

ASCHENBACH

I _____   love you.

The major/minor tension now present in both tonal regions confirms the point of crisis, establishing Tadzio in the role of Summoner for the rest of the drama (linking him with the Messengers of Death) and it indicates Aschenbach's surrender to Dionysus long before 'The dream' in Act II. That this conclusion to Act I, in terms of its motivic and tonal gestures, is the direct result of the tensions within the twelve-note proposition of the opera is entirely confirmed by Britten's composition sketch. The end of Act I (building to the climax at Aschenbach's 'I love you') and the orchestral prelude to Act II were composed as a continuous sequence of music – the division of the acts came at a later stage. In its final form this is in E major. But this complete sequence, from fig. 188 to the recitative at fig. 191, was first sketched by Britten a semitone higher in *F major* (see Plate 18). It is probable, I feel, that Britten came to the conclusion that the colder, brighter Apollonian F major at this crucial point in the opera was not what was required. The move to the warmer, richer tone of E major is relevant to the crisis here. E major was the tonality of Aschenbach's sudden urge to 'travel to the South', it will also be the tonality of the darker side of his persona in 'The dream' in Act II. But it is clear that Britten felt that he had only two options open to him in this scene: he could either set it in F or in E, and Aschenbach's home key of E major was the more appropriate for this moment of self-discovery.

It is in 'The dream' in Act II that the Apollo/Dionysus polarity is most clearly and profoundly expressed. Out of the blurred string scales of Aschenbach's E major the Voice of Dionysus emerges, poised on Tadzio's A major. The Voice of Apollo also attempts this assertion of Tadzio's A, but is undermined by an F major/minor juxtaposition in bell and woodwind flourishes. Soon Apollo's vocal line, too, asserts F in place of A. Meanwhile Dionysus has exploited the major/minor ambivalence now present in Tadzio's A since the end of Act I. The exchange between the gods is at first distinguished by alternating four-sharp and one-flat key signatures. As the conflict comes to a head, the two regions come into closer bitonal conflict, the voices now in duet. But E major is triumphant and as Apollo fades away, his final phrases, punctuated by tolling bell clusters, surrender to the major/minor ambivalences now accorded to the region of A (Ex. 11).

108

18 A discarded sketch page showing the end of Act I (and what proved to be the opening of Act II) in F, with the composer's indication that the passage was to be transposed down a semitone (Collection: HRH The Princess of Hesse and the Rhine/The Britten–Pears Library and Archive)

Ex. 11

When the followers of Dionysus appear the rising seventh (A–G sharp) of Tadzio's theme abounds in various transpositions across the chorus and as the climax is reached (announced by the 'plague' motive in the tuba at fig. 284) Dionysus asserts his supremacy on a rising fourth (A–D natural), which is extended by the chorus as the sopranos reach the high G sharp of Tadzio's theme for the first time. The conflict between the Dionysiac E and the Apollonian F which was first resolved in favour of E, now achieves a shattering resolution in A major as Aschenbach receives the sacrifice of Tadzio at the climax of the Dionysiac orgy.

In retrospect one can identify the cold resolution of the twelve-note statements of scene 1 on to F, and the terrible irony of Aschenbach's 'successful, honoured' E major resolving on to F major for 'self-discipline my strength', as encapsulating the very crisis of the drama. F major in relation to A could be interpreted as expressing the Apollonian ideal of perfection of form and physical beauty as a reflection of the divine spirit. E major, with its ready link to Tadzio's A, is the more sensuous tonal region exploited by Dionysus and is associated with Aschenbach from the very start.

A further three elements in the score are unified by twelve-note structures. For instance, twelve-note textures of a very different order from that of the opening statement of scene 1 abound in the piano accompaniments to the interior monologue recitatives. These very often arise from the alignment of complementary whole-tone scales or adjacent 'white-note'/'black-note' combinations. Ex. 12 is but one short example, taken from the very first recitative in the coda to scene 1.

Ex. 12

It will be noted that in Ex. 12 the piano right hand covers the 'white-note' pitches while the left hand covers the 'black-note' pitches. This sort of construction was carefully calculated throughout the score, as Britten's sketchbook will confirm. Linking these recitatives with the musical language of the opening monologue was clearly intended to reflect what Peter Evans has described as 'Aschenbach's intellectualizing propensity'.[4] The remaining two elements united by twelve-note ordering relate to Tadzio, however. The first, and perhaps the most suprising of all, is the very theme associated with Tadzio himself. In fact, the derivation of Tadzio's motive – seemingly spontaneous and lyrically haunting – is achieved by the most precise and technical of means. In Britten's sketchbook for *Death in Venice* (see Plate 19 and C. Matthews, Ex. 4, p. 59) the series from

19   The Venice sketchbook, p. 10 (The Britten–Pears Library and Archive)

which Tadzio's theme is derived is spelt out, while, of the pitches of the series, the first seven are deleted as Britten exploits them for the sustained chord that supports Aschenbach's observation of the Hotel Guests as they move into the dining room: 'United in their formal ways, in the ease that wide horizons bring. Well-mannered murmurs of a large hotel.' The five pitches that remain of the series – A, G sharp, F sharp, D, C sharp – then form the basis for the preliminary sketch for Tadzio's theme (see Ex. 13).

Ex. 13

But perhaps the twelve-note derivation of this theme is not so suprising after all. It is drawn from the chromatic texture that supports Aschenbach's line and thereafter Tadzio is the subject of all his most personal thoughts, whether expressed in the context of a fully drawn scene or an intimate soliloquy. As Aschenbach himself says: 'I could have created him', and he is indeed created – sculpted – out of Aschenbach's music.[5]

The only other instance of twelve-note ordering is a curious cadential-like figure of two-note chords described by Peter Evans as a 'Bergian series of intervals'.[6] A prominent version of this twelve-note construction coincides with the sudden disappearance of the Old Gondolier on Aschenbach's arrival at the Lido in scene 3 (Ex. 14).

Ex. 14

It has been adumbrated in scene 2 when the Elderly Fop first addresses Aschenbach (fig. 31), and it accompanies the Fop's suggestive, leering parting words to Aschenbach,[7] now resolving on to D major to prepare for the Overture (Ex. 15). Peter Evans points out that, unlike other twelve-note material in the opera, this figure 'does not relate to Aschenbach's intellectualizing propensity'. Like him, I find it difficult to identify a clear role for this figure, though it achieves prominence at the beginning of Aschenbach's Hymn to Apollo (Ex. 16) when the writer recognizes a possible source of artistic inspiration in Tadzio. Taking into account the twelve-note initiation of Tadzio's theme, perhaps this further development of Ex. 14 is fully justified. It was perhaps designed to indicate a link between Tadzio and certain of the Messengers of Death and to anticipate his function as the *final* Messenger of Death.

Ex. 15

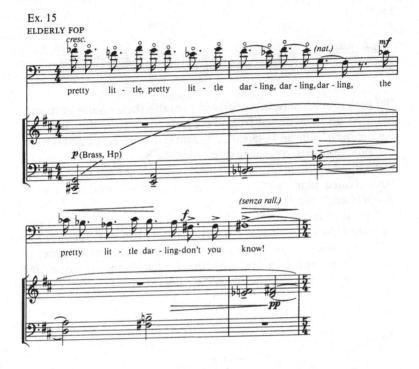

It further compounds the irony of Aschenbach's 'parched creativity', as Peter Evans has put it,[8] that the musical idiom associated with the writer's incessant intellectualizing should be employed to generate both Tadzio's theme and Aschenbach's own ecstatic celebration of Tadzio as a force of divine inspiration in the Hymn to Apollo. By linking these elements to the twelve-note idiom of Aschenbach's self-conscious soliloquies, Britten surely attempted to sustain the detached quality of the writer's Apollonian appreciation of Tadzio's god-like beauty until the point, at the end of Act I, when the Dionysiac force first manifests itself. Aschenbach then becomes disconcertingly aware that the feeling he harbours for the boy is no longer that of the artist's preoccupation with beauty and form, but that of 'love': 'So longing passes back and forth between life and the mind.' The 'just balance between the passionate–erotic and the poetic–symbolic'[9] that Myfanwy Piper strove to achieve is sustained musically by Britten's selective exploitation of a twelve-note idiom within the perspective of a more immediate, expressive musical

Ex. 16

[Chorus omitted]

language. This balance is maintained throughout Act I, but as the Dionysiac defeats the Apollonian in Act II the detached expression of the twelve-note idiom is almost entirely absent and the interior monologues, which now alone sustain the 'detached' musical idiom are fewer and briefer as Aschenbach loses self-possession and surrenders to fate. After the triumphant resolution on A major at the climax of 'The dream', the E/F tensions of Act I are resolved in favour of the Locrian modality arising from Tadzio's motive. Just as the adjacent pitches of E and F assumed importance from the span of the opening twelve-note proposition of the opera, so now the adjacent pitches of A and G sharp (derived from the span of Tadzio's motive) supersede the E/F conflict of Act I as Aschenbach is no longer in control of his own destiny and Tadzio assumes the role of Summoner. The 'modulation' from the twelve-note proposition to the modal postlude is achieved in scene 13 ('The dream'). At the very end of the opera the A–G sharp tension of Tadzio's motive is inverted, with the G sharp at the very bottom of the texture and Tadzio's theme and Aschenbach's Hymn to Apollo uniting on a high A. This is an exact mirror of the E/F tensions of Aschenbach's music at the start, and, as I hope to have shown, even this modal resolution is in part the result of the initiating twelve-note idea which forms Ex. 1.

9 Britten and the gamelan: Balinese influences in 'Death in Venice'

MERVYN COOKE

Death in Venice marks the culmination of Britten's long involvement with Balinese gamelan music and represents a notable development from the composer's earlier experimentation with oriental material in *The Prince of the Pagodas*. Balinese influences are clearly felt not only in the highly original percussion writing which accompanies the children's beach games but also in the distinctive music associated with Tadzio. Perhaps more importantly, techniques characteristic of gamelan music are encountered throughout the opera as a natural feature of Britten's style (nowhere more evidently than in the heterophonic orchestral prelude to Act II) and Britten's deliberate integration of the Balinese-inspired material into the musical fabric of the opera as a whole creates a complex and extremely subtle network of musico-dramatic symbolism.

The choice of a percussion ensemble as the accompanying medium for the opera's balletic sections is highly significant. During his visit to Java and Bali in January 1956 Britten had been particularly struck by a gamelan composed entirely of adolescent boys[1] which he described enthusiastically in a letter to Roger Duncan on 8 February: 'Jolly good they were too, and enjoying it like fun!' If, as seems likely, this incident served as the initial stimulus for the adolescent 'gamelan' in *Death in Venice*, the idea was doubly apposite in view of Britten's earlier use of tuned percussion as a symbol of powerful attraction. The concept of an allure of the kind that Tadzio has for Aschenbach (specifically one which will ultimately lead to corruption and death) had already achieved an accomplished realization in *The Turn of the Screw* where Quint's celesta and Miss Jessel's gong suggest the power of attraction the ghosts have over the imaginative children. Tuned percussion is again used to characterize the supernatural elements in *A Midsummer Night's Dream*, and the trend is continued in *Owen Wingrave* where the gamelan sonorities implied in the accompaniment to Owen's peace aria suggest both the attrac-

115

tiveness and remoteness of the perfect peace he seeks. This example appears to make an extremely subtle aural reference to the earlier martial music which had also been characterized by percussion scoring. Owen's aria may therefore be interpreted as a rather disturbing illustration of his predicament, and it is significant that his soliloquy is interrupted by the appearance of the two ghosts who will bring about his death. The closest precursor of the similar procedures in *Death in Venice* is, of course, the 'gamelan' music of *Pagodas* which accompanies the fantastic elements in Pagoda-land and depicts their attraction for Belle Rose.

Music is inextricably linked with dance in Balinese society and Britten's use of a gamelan style for the opera's balletic sections reveals the composer's own awareness of this essential concept. Britten had witnessed Balinese dancing at first hand in 1956 and was evidently captivated by the beauty and precision of its gestural language. Although not the first of Britten's dramatic works to incorporate a dance element,[2] *Death in Venice* is the first real illustration of an approach to the medium which exactly mirrors the Balinese aesthetic. In their pioneering work *Dance and Drama in Bali* Beryl de Zoete and Walter Spies discuss this cultural phenomenon with great relevance to the present context:

Watching dancing is not for the Balinese a matter of such concentrated attention as with us. It is almost a state of being, a feeling rather than an action. We gaze and gaze with an earnestness of purpose which fatigues us long before the dance is over. The Balinese, like other orientals, enters into the atmosphere of the dance and remains there as in a familiar landscape . . . His attitude towards the performance at which we gaze with such rapt and fatiguing attention must be a good deal like that of the fashionable world who had their boxes in the Italian opera; noticing now and then, criticizing technical points, enjoying the improvisations and topical jokes of the clowns, admiring pretty girls on the stage and off, flirting, talking to their friends, and then watching again.[3]

The parallel with *Death in Venice* is striking: Aschenbach watches the dancing Tadzio with a 'rapt and fatiguing attention' quite unique to him. The dancing reflects his own lyrical reaction to the Poles and is a vivid representation of Mann's constant observation in the novel that Aschenbach's conception of Tadzio's perfection is nothing more than an illusion.

The gamelan passages in *Death in Venice* differ from those in *Pagodas* in several important respects. In the ballet a percussion group had been given music which clearly attempted a direct reconstruction of specific Balinese prototypes: in contrast, there appear to be no such obvious models for the 'oriental' sections in the opera. Britten's empathy with Balinese techniques now enabled him to compose in his own synthetic gamelan idiom, characterized by a more flexible attitude towards the distinctive Balinese modes he had employed in *Pagodas* with authentic strictness, and concentrating less emphatically on capturing the gamelan sound in every detail. Although Britten drew up an *aide-mémoire* for the scoring of the gamelan effects in *Pagodas* in his preliminary sketchbook for the opera (Plate 20) and compiled a more detailed set of notes which clearly refer to Act II of the ballet (Plate 21), the final result is very different from the sonorities achieved in the earlier work. This is largely due to the new emphasis on wooden tuned percussion (large and small xylophones and marimba) which suggests the influence of the Balinese *gamelan gambang*[4] and *gamelan pejogedan*[5] (both of which Britten had witnessed in Bali) rather than the metallic instruments of the *gamelan gong* which had served as the model for the percussion ensemble in *Pagodas*.

In spite of this prominent difference in scoring, the principal influence on Britten's gamelan idiom remains that of the *kebiar* style which he had emulated in the earlier ballet. This school of composition had evolved in the early twentieth century and combined spectacular virtuosity with a wide range of dynamic contrast and rhythmic vitality. Significantly, it remains the only genre of Balinese music to involve the creative composition of a new performing repertory and Britten's contribution is therefore wholly within the spirit of the style. Two features of the *kebiar* idiom are particularly prominent in *Death in Venice*: the first consists of a free tremolo with unmeasured *accelerando* or *rallentando* (notated by Britten with the symbols ⁖⁖⁖⁖ and ⁖⁖⁖⁖ first introduced in the *War Requiem*),[6] and the second comprises a distinctive chordal effect in which several dissonant notes of a mode are sounded simultaneously. The passage at fig. 99 illustrates Britten's combined use of both techniques at the climactic moment of scene 5 when Tadzio is acknowledged as the children's leader. (See Strode, Plate 6, p. 39.)

Britten's appropriation of the gamelan style may best be demonstrated by an extract from the first set of beach games in the same scene (Ex. 1), the passage in which the debt to *Pagodas* is most obvious. (Cf. *Pagodas*, Act II, fig. 72.) Here each of the contrasting layers of a typical gamelan texture are faithfully reproduced. At the lowest level the piano, gong and double-bass provide a scheme of colotomic

20 The Venice sketchbook, p. 5 (The Britten–Pears Library and Archive)

21 Notes on the use of the percussion group (The Britten–Pears Library and Archive)

Ex. 1

punctuation at nine-beat intervals. Above this the reiterated C natural on timpano piccolo and cello pizzicato imitates the small pulse-keeping gong known as a *kempli*. There are two further levels, comprising the xylophone ostinato and the extraordinary presentation of the strawberry seller's theme by glockenspiel and violin harmonics (a sonority probably intended to imitate the flautato tone of Balinese *sulings*).[7] In the second important gamelan passage (Ex. 2) the function of the *kempli* is taken by the marimba and the colotomic punctuation provided by a small gong tuned to G. The lively syncopations prominent throughout this section exactly capture the vitality of the *kebiar* style.

Tadzio is primarily characterized by a solo vibraphone played without fans which imitates the melodic role of the Balinese *trompong*[8] in the same fashion as it had in the scoring of *Pagodas*. Tadzio's theme itself (see Ex. 8) has the exact improvisatory quality of a *trompong* solo and passages such as at fig. 214 are remarkably close to the original Balinese style. The other instruments most closely associated with the gamelan style in *Death in Venice* are the three tomtoms and four gongs. The tomtoms function as substitutes for the Balinese *kendangs* and are frequently doubled by pizzicato notes in a manner which once more recalls *Pagodas*;[9] the gamelan

Ex. 2

debt is particularly evident in Ex. 3 where each phrase is punctuated by a gong stroke. Elsewhere in the opera (notably at fig. 95) Britten employs two gongs of different pitches in a scheme of double punctuation reflecting the influence of the two large gongs in the gamelan.[10] This technique again derives from *Pagodas* where the composer had employed a similar pair of gongs in the ostinato underlying the lengthy crescendo heralding the appearance of the Pagoda Palace in Act III.

Britten's sketches for the opera reveal the process by which the composer arrived at the synthetic gamelan style eventually employed

Ex. 3

in the work. Before fig. 161 in 'The Games of Apollo' Britten originally planned a long vibraphone solo in the *trompong* style to accompany a stage direction which reads 'Tadzio wanders out of sight'. Two versions of this passage are deleted in the composition sketch, and Britten decided to replace this idea with a much more daring passage for the full percussion group. This is preserved on a discarded sketch page (Plate 22) and takes the form of a collage of

22 A discarded sketch for the percussion group intended for Act I scene 7: 'The Games of Apollo' (The Britten–Pears Library and Archive)

independent percussion motives freely superimposed in the nonalignment technique Britten had developed in the Church Parables. This entire section was ultimately abandoned but it provides an intriguing glimpse of the possibilities with which Britten was experimenting during the process of composition. A page from the composer's preliminary sketchbook contains thematic material for the opera's gamelan passages sketched in a purely diatonic idiom; Exx. 4a and 4b show how Britten subsequently transformed these ideas by presenting them in characteristic Balinese modes.

In *Pagodas* Britten had employed one of the most distinctive Balinese modes at the pitch levels illustrated in Ex. 5. This scale (the variant of the *saih pitu* mode known as *selisir gong*) is encountered in *Death in Venice* in the opening phrase of the first beach game (Ex. 6)

Ex. 4a

Ex. 4b

Ex. 5

Ex. 6

and during 'The Games of Apollo'. It is particularly prominent in an earlier version of the latter written before the decision to include the chorus was taken (Ex. 7: cf. Act I fig. 144). Tadzio's theme is constructed from a *selisir* variant closely related to Ex. 5b (see Ex. 8) and to two sketches Britten made in Bali in 1956 (Exx. 9a and 9b). Ex. 9b

Ex. 7

Ex. 8

Ex. 9

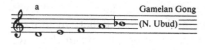

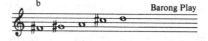

occurs at the pitch level with which Tadzio is always associated, the
implication of A major symbolizing innocence and purity as so
often in Britten's work. Three further motives are derived from this
mode: two are harmonic conflations (the dyads employed in the calls
of 'Adziù' and the *kebiar* chord discussed above) and the third com-

prises the theme representing Tadzio's mother. The latter derivation
is only made clear as Aschenbach pursues the Polish family in Act II
(fig. 211) and it is this version of the theme which appears in Britten's
sketchbook (Ex. 10). Appropriately enough, the mode also makes
several very obvious appearances in Apollo's vocal lines during 'The
Games of Apollo'. (See especially two bars before fig. 162.) The
unusual scale Britten eventually used at fig. 93 (cf. Ex. 4a) is essentially the same as another mode the composer jotted down during his
stay in Bali (Ex. 11).

Ex. 10

Ex. 11

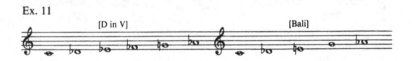

Britten's application of these Balinese modes is highly flexible. His
approach is exemplified in the first gamelan passage (fig. 80 to fig. 87)
which employs a number of different oriental scales in contrasting
transpositions, a procedure very different from the rigorous application of a single mode in the more overtly authentic gamelan music in
Pagodas. This tonal freedom is carefully controlled to create a vivid
method of musical symbolism which involves extensive reference to
the Balinese material throughout the opera as a whole. At the same
time, it permits the composer to achieve a far greater degree of stylistic synthesis than was possible in the earlier ballet: memorable
moments such as the music for the children playing in the waves
(fig. 95) and the passage quoted in Ex. 3 openly acknowledge their
debt to the gamelan but inhabit a soundworld quite characteristic of
Britten's own idiomatic style.

Britten's treatment of the scale associated with Tadzio is particularly impressive. The frequent occurrence of his mode on instruments not associated with the gamelan and in Aschenbach's vocal
lines and piano accompaniments ensures that Tadzio's influence is
felt not merely as an isolated phenomenon but as a feature which
infuses the musical fabric of the entire opera.[11] The initial twelve-
note derivation of Tadzio's theme at his first appearance[12] is a *locus*

classicus of Britten's tonal symbolism: when Aschenbach first catches sight of the boy he perceives him in the context of a large group of people and Tadzio's mode is therefore accompanied by the seven notes *not* in his scale, a chord conflated from the preceding 'chatter' recitative and representing the other Hotel Guests; but once Aschenbach has admitted that the boy is a 'beautiful young creature' the vibraphone theme returns in a much more expansive form and is now accompanied by a chord derived exclusively from Tadzio's own five-note mode. This is an extremely telling reflection of the process by which Aschenbach becomes totally immersed in the appearance of the boy and completely loses touch with his surroundings.

Aschenbach's own use of Tadzio's mode varies according to the relevant dramatic situation. During their first encounter Aschenbach stresses the note E which represents himself and is significantly absent from Tadzio's scale; this note is therefore conspicuously avoided by the vibraphone in a subtle depiction of the essential incompatibility of the two central characters (Ex. 12). Whenever Aschenbach notices that his conception of Tadzio's perfection is being threatened he corrupts the mode by introducing F natural (or E sharp): this may be seen during Tadzio's pantomime of hatred

Ex. 12

for the Russians ('He is human after all' and 'There is a dark side to perfection': see the vocal score, p. 82) and when he fears the Polish family will leave Venice on account of the plague ('They must receive no hint': see the vocal score, p. 178). A brilliantly ironic transformation occurs as Aschenbach stumbles from his gondola after his pitiful rejuvenation by the Hotel Barber and sings the song associated with the Elderly Fop's retinue. His rendering of the lines 'all hail to my beauty, "the pretty little darling don't you know"' is significantly accompanied by a chord derived directly from Tadzio's mode. When he sees Tadzio, however, the *kebiar* chord representing the boy and consisting of a conflation of all the notes of his scale abruptly appears in a number of different transpositions (Ex. 13). This is the only point in the opera where Tadzio's scale does not appear at its original pitch level, a striking symbol of both Aschenbach's dementia and the alienation of the two characters. The most dramatic

Ex. 13

Aschenbach sees the Polish family walking in front of him and starts distractedly following them.

transformation of the Tadzio material is found in Aschenbach's Dionysiac nightmare in which a frenzied version of the boy's theme in the full chorus and orchestra (see also Palmer, pp. 150–2) subsides to leave Aschenbach moaning in his sleep to a distorted form of the theme as it had appeared in his earlier Hymn to Apollo.

In conclusion, it is evident that the use of material derived from Balinese sources in *Death in Venice* is not restricted to the passages written in an overtly gamelanesque style and is therefore of more than local interest. The gamelan passages themselves are conceived in a style far more flexible than that of the Balinese reconstructions in *Pagodas*, and Britten's novel treatment of certain Balinese modes is tailored to the interests of musico-dramatic symbolism. The final gamelan passage, in which the modality becomes increasingly distorted as Jaschiu violently dominates Tadzio, is one of many possible illustrations of Britten's effective application of this new flexibility.[13] The musical style of *Death in Venice* is a remarkably original synthesis of western and oriental compositional procedures and the score stands as an eloquent monument to the profundity of its composer's involvement with Balinese music.

10   Britten's Venice orchestra
CHRISTOPHER PALMER

However critical reaction to Britten's music *per se* may vary – and few composers seem to inflame such extremities of passion, not only of love or hate, but also of that extremely complex and highly combustible emotion known as love-hate – few have impugned his sheer technical prowess as a composer, and no one (to the best of my knowledge) has ever suggested that he was anything but a complete master of instrumentation. His particular type of orchestrational professionalism had a distinguished precedent in the work of Elgar, a composer to whom Britten seemed to warm only in the last years of his life. Yet they have a curious amount in common, not least a virtuosic brilliance of instrumentation-technique – the extending of instrumentalists to the outer limits of, but never beyond, their capacities – which derives both from a secure practical knowledge of instruments and how they are played, and from an ingrained exhibitionistic impulse. This in its turn was almost certainly rooted in a profound insecurity. They *had* to succeed, *had* to show the world that they were as good as, indeed better than, the next man – and, by Heaven, show it they would – and did.

We can press the parallel further and land ourselves a neat little paradox. In terms of orchestration Elgar loved to give, Britten to take away. Elgar's preferred medium was the full, rich panoply of the late-romantic symphony orchestra with all its massed and massive effects of sonority and bloom, every voice doubled *ad infinitum* (though rarely *ad nauseam* as can happen in Strauss). By contrast, Britten's was essentially a chamber-music mentality; he favoured spareness and economy of texture, a soloistic approach to instrumentation (interesting precedents for this aspect of Britten's art are to be found in Holst, though it was almost certainly Mahler who was the leading influence here). Yet once we start to examine in detail the orchestration of a work like *The Dream of Gerontius* (which Britten recorded[1]) we find ourselves tempted to put the case for a basic

129

affinity of mind even more strongly. Follow the bassoon parts through the score: you will find them scarcely ever doing what is expected of them either in a conventional tutti or anywhere else: their part is imagined, as it were, soloistically. And imagine dropping an instrument, or doubling. In Strauss you would more than likely get away with it; in Elgar – as in Britten – you would feel the loss immediately. In other words, I think one can make a case for a proto-Brittenian chamber-music concept operating within an apparently full-orchestra symphonic framework.[2]

I do not wish to make untenable claims for an Elgar–Britten connection, merely to suggest that Britten may have drawn more (no doubt unconsciously) from his English environment than has often been critically conceded.[3] It is a point worth making, particularly in connection with *Death in Venice*, which is so thoroughly steeped in Mahlerisms as to compel an almost exaggerated amount of attention to its Mahler sources. The latter could easily form the subject of a study in its own right. *Death in Venice*: its heterophonic textures, its oriental–pentatonic colourations, its consistently featured antitheses between rigid formality and unformal freedom – all these, it seems to me, are intimately related to, have blossomed from, seed long since sown in the great 'Abschied' in *Das Lied von der Erde*,[4] which Britten is known to have admired profoundly.[5] However this is no legitimate concern of mine here. What I must first and foremost emphasize, as at least in part Mahler-inspired, is that the instrumentational principle of diversity-in-unity which informed so many of Britten's scores over the years, reaches in *Death in Venice* – its last manifestation – an apogee of perfection. 'Shine out, fair sun, with all your heat', entreats the anonymous medieval poet Britten sets in the introduction to the *Spring Symphony*, 'show all your thousand-coloured light!' Britten is adept at showing us the 'thousand colours' of the modern orchestra in an infinite variety of combinations; but never in such a way as to negate its heat and light. Which is probably no more than a fancy way of describing his ability to create novelty within a framework of tradition, instrumentally as in all other departments.

With one important exception, the orchestra in *Death in Venice* is traditional enough, and is of similar size and constitution to those Britten had earlier employed in *A Midsummer Night's Dream* and *Owen Wingrave*. The exception is the large percussion ensemble associated with Tadzio and his family. Here again the instruments themselves are (sundry exotica like the small Chinese drum and bell-tree apart) fairly standard – tuned (vibraphone, glockenspiel, xylophone, marimba, chimes) and un-tuned (cymbals, gongs, drums, whips, wood block). What is *un*-standard is the use to which Britten puts them. Inasmuch as this is the most immediately striking feature of the *Death in Venice* orchestra, let it receive priority comment.

Britten's interest in gamelan music and its overmastering influence on *The Prince of the Pagodas* and *Death in Venice* has already been documented;[6] the discussion has brought to the fore the percussion's function as sound-symbol of Tadzio's world, exotic, remote, the acme of inaccessibility as far as Aschenbach is concerned. There is moreover a complex of overtones (the term is peculiarly appropriate in this context). The tuned percussion (and Tadzio's preferred instruments are the vibraphone and glockenspiel) play tunes, but mechanically, un-expressively, un-emotionally, un-humanly. These two – vibraphone and glockenspiel – have a kind of brittle glamour, a prettiness, a 'sweetish medicinal cleanliness' – like Tadzio. Of the two the vibraphone is the one first and most consistently associated with Tadzio. In fact *Death in Venice* is a kind of apotheosis of the vibraphone: there are few contemporary scores outside jazz in which it plays so prominent a role. The instrument itself (because of the way its sounds are electronically after-rung) has a certain equivocal, mysterious quality entirely suited to the purpose; Britten legitimately pairs it with the glockenspiel since it is a kind of reverberant, lower-pitched, mellow-toned relation of the latter (Percy Grainger called it the 'bass glockenspiel').

We can make a broad division of categories: if the tuned percussion represent the bright side of beauty, its sweet, smiling face (Tadzio's fatal smile – the smile which causes Aschenbach finally to realize the truth – is marked by a soft glockenspiel glissando (fig. 187)), the un-tuned percussion – the drums (I include the timpani in this category even though they play precise pitches) – sound the way to the abyss. This is the dark side of passion, the swamp, the black beast. In *The Turn of the Screw* the Governess journeys to Bly to a drum-ostinato which nominally suggests merely the rhythm of the coach. But these are also jungle-drums, presaging the eruption of God knows what primitive forces and passions. So too here. Aschenbach becomes aware of Tadzio and hears the silvery bells of the glockenspiel, the sound of Mercury the Winged Messenger, who is also the Angel of Death; likewise, he becomes aware of the Traveller and hears the *Ur*-sound of drums, beating as if in preparation for some ritual sacrifice – his own. Note the remarkably *Screw*-like antithesis of high and low sonorities, heaven and hell – Quint's celesta/Miss Jessel's gong: Tadzio's vibraphone or glockenspiel/the Traveller's drums. Quint and Miss Jessel are as one: their object is to destroy the children and/or the Governess. Tadzio on the one hand; the Traveller/Elderly Fop/Gondolier/Hotel Manager/Barber/Leader of the Players on the other: all are (wittingly or unwittingly) mortal enemies of Aschenbach, even though the one be apparently Heaven-sent, the others emissaries of Hell. Further to the *Screw*: note well that *there is no celesta* in *Death in Venice*, though one might most reasonably have expected there to be, and the combination of glockenspiel and piano often suggests in fact that there is one. The celesta was Quint's instrument; but the affinity (the tempter!) of sound remains.

As for the jungle drums, the timpani is leader – and gradually gathers his retinue about him (tomtoms of different pitches and bass drum) all *agents évocateurs* of hallucination and longing, always in an undertone, stealthy, sinister.

The next time we are prominently aware of percussion is on the boat to Venice. I mentioned the Governess' journey to Bly and the drum-ostinato which had both a realistic and symbolic import. The same applies here. The sacrificial drums throb here also, this time in the guise of ship's engines (see Ex. 1). It is on the boat in fact that Aschenbach encounters the Elderly Fop, the 'young-old horror', the second Messenger of Death, or rather the second incarnation of the same persona or symbol.

Ex. 1

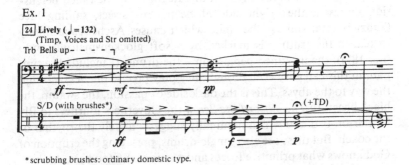

24 Lively (♩ = 132)
(Timp, Voices and Str omitted)

*scrubbing brushes: ordinary domestic type.

The next time we hear the drums is in the first children's game on the beach; watching this game Aschenbach decides to stay, despite the enervating west wind and the stagnant smell from the lagoons. It is also the first of the many beautifully crafted percussion ensembles that are a particular feature of *Death in Venice*. (See Cooke, Ex. 1 p. 119.) It is 'The Games of Apollo' that really put Britten's inventiveness to the test, since he must devise a different percussion combination for each. First, Tadzio executes a formal slow dance (the 'Hyacinth' dance) as the chorus sings of Socrates discoursing with Phaedrus on the nature of beauty. The dominant sound here is that of the tomtoms – refined, disciplined, hypercivilized in their present setting, but incontrovertibly barbaric, primeval, in implication. Jungle-drums. For Phaedrus learned – as we discover later – that beauty leads ultimately to the abyss. Then, the contests themselves:

    (i) *Running*: small bass drum, chimes;
    (ii) *Long Jump*: glockenspiel, marimba, small gong, timpani;
    (iii) *Discus throwing*: timpani;
    (iv) *Javelin throwing*: silvery, graceful with bell-tree, glockenspiel, crotales, vibraphone, small cymbals;
    (v) *Wrestling*: wind-machine, side drum.

Tadzio is victor in all, and timpani and drums beat excitedly and forcefully (heart-poundingly?) throughout Aschenbach's subsequent monologue: he embraces the ecstatic moment, announces his intention of 'leaving contemplation for one moment of reality'. Alas, too late: the jungle lies in wait for him, the drums sound a warning which he will not, cannot heed. Signs and omens attend his every step: the Leader of the Players, whose horrible laughing song (pitchless voices and percussion) is the sheerest animal sound – raw, inarticulate, as it were the sound of first matter, reminiscent of the would-be mutiny-chorus after the hanging of Billy in *Billy Budd* (Ex. 2).

Ex. 2

The climax of Aschenbach's dream-dance – a Dionysiac orgy culminating (implicitly) in the rape of Tadzio – is goaded on by the drums, rolling at first, then erupting in *fortissimo* rhythmic abandon. After this, Aschenbach is lost. He can no longer contain himself, even when Tadzio's percussion-cluster assumes the aspect – visual (i.e. the actual sight of the notes on the page!) as well as aural – of a danger-signal (see figs. 302, 307 and Ex. 3).

Ex. 3

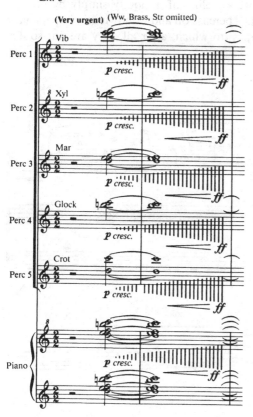

Primitive man not only beat on drums, he also blew on reeds; and it cannot be coincidental that the woodwinds are also potent and consistent symbols of primordial chaos and sickness in *Death in Venice*. As long ago as 1936 they were carriers of pestilence in the

'Rats away!' movement of *Our Hunting Fathers*; and in the Cook's
travel bureau (scene 11) the clerk tells Aschenbach that Venice is in
the grip of Asiatic cholera, spread from the delta of the Ganges
(almost certainly transmitted by rats on board ship). Throughout the
scene the solo woodwinds are featured (particularly the bass clarinet), their quasi-improvised music full of Eastern threat rather than
promise; and the flutes are particularly noxious in their extreme
low register (see the fourth and fifth bars after fig. 266). Elsewhere in
the flute parts we find intimations of Pan-pipes, a clear indication of
Britten's desire to create a feeling of antiquity simply by making
present-day instruments – percussion and woodwinds – impersonate
their primitive prototypes (to which, after all, they are not so dis-
tantly related).

Ex. 4a

Ex. 4b

It is no coincidence that Aschenbach's first vision of the abyss –
the scene with the Traveller – is beset primarily by woodwind
arabesques similar in character to Exx. 4a and 4b. Nor can it be coincidence that when the insane truth about his infatuation finally
strikes Aschenbach ('I love you', four bars before fig. 189) the

orchestra responds with one of the most primitive sounds of all – the drone. A drone is generally sustained by some kind of wind instrument.[7] (See Strode, Plate 5, p. 37.)

The sirocco-motive is a two-part woodwind trill; but perhaps the most chilling woodwind sound of all is the simplest and quietest – the little chord sequence for muted horns and bass clarinet which accompanies the Hotel Manager's innocent – oh, so innocent! – enquiry: 'No doubt the Signore will be leaving us soon? We must all lose what we think to enjoy the most.' (Ex. 5.)

Ex. 5

One other wind instrument needs to be discussed in connection with the woodwind, for it is of crucial importance throughout: the tuba. There is a certain ambivalence about the tuba; it is more legitimately a bass for the *horns* rather than for the trombones and trumpets, and the horns belong partly to the brass, partly to the woodwind. At all events, the tuba in *Death in Venice* has the same connotations of pestilence as the verminous woodwind; and, in the tuba's case also, these connotations originated (in 1936!) in the 'Rats away!' movement of *Our Hunting Fathers*.[8] From the start the tuba imposes itself; muted, it contributes a trilled bass to part of Aschenbach's opening monologue (in itself an unorthodox effect). (Ex. 6.)

Ex. 6

Again, the sound of the low horns holding the 'drone' which links Acts I and II is more closely linked to that of the tuba than to that of the bassoons with which they alternate. Observe also Aschenbach's 'the heat of the sun must have made me ill' where the bass stirs or heaves in horns and tuba in octaves; and note the bassoons' quasi-obbligato (Ex. 7).

Ex. 7

We do not hear the tuba in the Traveller's scene, although we *do* very much hear the related sonority of muted horns. It is characteristic of the tuba's increasing omnipresence that it often intrudes in unexpected contexts, like some monster reptile or beast of prey dogging our footsteps and lying in wait for us (the tuba somehow *does* sound like that: it has an unwieldiness and lethargy which suggest immense size, and an oily smoothness of quality which to my ears is definitely reptilian). For the tuba to serve as bass to the chords in Ex. 8 the upper voices would normally be given to trombones; instead Britten entrusts them to the much less powerful bassoons, thereby focusing attention on the tuba at the root.

Ex. 8

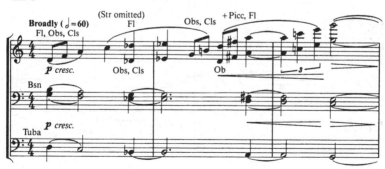

Ex. 8 (*cont.*)

That the 'plague' theme is primarily the tuba's prerogative is most strongly affirmed in the orgy scene and during Tadzio's final tussle with Jaschiu; on both of which occasions the instrument rears and lunges in its middle register, its most menacing and dangerous (its normal habitat is deep below the staff, where its characteristic

Ex. 9

*Bow freely

sonority is less pronounced). We soon come to associate its very colour with the 'plague' motive, so that we do not always even need to hear the motive complete (see the tuba's first appearance in the first scene with the Hotel Barber, fig. 196). However, Britten is not mechanical or doctrinaire with what one might term his *Leitfarben*, his 'leading colours'. We do not *always* hear the woodwinds or tuba when the plague is referred to or implied. On one memorable occasion the solo double-bass – a low, lean, mean, predatory sound – substitutes for the tuba (when Aschenbach buys the infected strawberries).

Generally (and indeed it is a broad, though not so broad as to be invalid, generalization), the strings tend to concern themselves not so much with inimical forces of nature – the plague – as with man (i.e. Aschenbach), his human feelings and responses, and man-in-nature. Aschenbach's yearning for the South-beyond-the-mountains, with only impulse as his guide: the soft, sensuous muted-string texture (fig. 20 *et. seq.*), all edges blurred in a quasi-impressionistic heterophonic haze,[9] perfectly articulates a change of mind. On the journey to Venice Britten enlists a similar textural pattern to evoke the

ever-changing sameness of sea and sky (Ex. 9). Notice the direction
to bow freely, in the interests of imprecision; for nature in her
immensities is never well-defined, never measured. The solo cello
perfectly embodies the melancholia of Aschenbach's farewell to
Tadzio prior to the foiled departure. Note the confrontation between
Aschenbach's strings and Tadzio's percussion (see fig. 124 *et seq.*).

It is surely significant that the two occasions on which the strings
come most intensely, eloquently, expressively, *emotively* into their
own are (a) the prelude to Act II (over the wind drone), which has to
do with the dawning of Aschenbach's self-realization and with his
struggle to come to terms with it and (b) the epilogue for orchestra
alone, his *Liebestod* on the beach, within sight of, and as it were at
the behest of, the Beloved. Aschenbach slumps dead in his chair,
Tadzio continues his walk out to sea; and the opera's apotheosis is a
tender dialogue, *molto tranquillo*, between Tadzio's (non-human)
vibraphone (passing in its higher reaches to glockenspiel) and
Aschenbach's (all-too-human) strings (see Plate 23). Violins and

23   The end of the opera in its final version in the composition sketch (The Britten–Pears Library and Archive)

glockenspiel climb ever higher, the void between high treble and low bass grows ever wider, until finally (with the persistent pedal G sharp at last relinquished) the topmost A of the first violins' harmonic meets with the topmost A of the glockenspiel – so ethereal as to be barely perceptible. It is a logical confluence, for very high string harmonics are frequently reinforced by triangle or glockenspiel, the two highest-pitched instruments in the percussion.

There is, I say, nothing unusual about this combination; what is profoundly unusual is the way Britten employs it in an attempt symbolically to express the inexpressible, i.e. some mystic, ineffable union of the Lover and the Beloved. Earlier, Aschenbach invokes a long-departed Lover taking leave of *his* Beloved, namely Socrates and Phaedrus; and the mention of Socrates' name – and the immemorial truths he calls to remembrance – is responsible for a sound that is perhaps best described as perfection, ideally beautiful, a moment of pure tranquility, pure concentration (Ex. 10).

Ex. 10

Strings again, fastidiously voiced; and observe: each note a *natural* harmonic on the open string (hence the need for the double-basses to be sounding *above* the cellos, that A below middle C being unavailable as a natural harmonic on any other instrument).

So much for the principles which govern much of Britten's basic thinking about the *Death in Venice* instrumentation. Certain features now call for more specific comment. First, the poetic use of voices as part of the timbral complex. There is evocative magic in the hazy, floating sounds of the distant boat-chorus, as it were diffused in the air and over the water, which disturbs Aschenbach yet echoes, realizes, his all-but-unformed thoughts and longings as the Old Gondolier rows him to the Lido. On the beach the women are heard calling to Tadzio, and the sound has a seductive, siren-like quality: but it is Aschenbach who is being seduced – drawn into the chain of events that will lead to his destruction – not Tadzio.[10]

Ex. 11

Ex. 11 shows the Gondoliers' cries, marvellously recreated by Britten from authentic Venetian sources (see Strode, p. 30, and C. Matthews, p. 56) not for their meaning (they have none anyway) but for their sound. Here is another Mahler reminiscence: for Donald Mitchell has noted how in the 'Abschied' of *Das Lied von der Erde* Mahler repeats the key-word 'allüberall' as much for its sound as for its meaning. 'If one examines Mahler's projection of it as a vocal shape . . . it is clear how, through the inspired and unnatural prolongation of the syllables, the component sounds of the word, *above all the isolated vowel 'ü'*, are used as part of the orchestration, to contribute to the making of the sound of the ecstatic moment . . . at this particular juncture in *Das Lied*, it is not the sense that one is most aware of, but rather the sound, in which it is intended that one should lose oneself.' (My italics.)[11] *Mutatis*

mutandis this is the exact state of affairs in *Death in Venice*. Donald Mitchell goes on to find a meaningful parallel with Wagnerian practice, especially with the 'ecstatic moments' in *Tristan* where the sound of the words makes a far more significant contribution than their sense.[12] In the case of the Gondoliers' cries this sound is doubly significant, for the oft-repeated 'Aou'!' is surely intended to invoke for Aschenbach the soft-drawn 'ü' sound of Tadzio's name, as discussed above. Note also the curious fact that the Gondoliers' cries tend to slide upwards through a minor third, exactly like Mahler's favourite *Naturlaut*, the nightbird's oboe in the Third Symphony and *Das Lied*. And when the Hotel Porter appropriates the call in instructing a Gondolier to convey Aschenbach back to the Lido, Britten leaves a huge empty space between the airy, high-register tenor and the watery depths of *tremolo* cellos and basses (sustaining the same minor third as the notes of the call). The impact is brief but stunning. The voice shoots out over the water and into the atmosphere (Ex. 12).

Ex. 12

The role of the piano is ambiguous in an archetypal Death-in-Venetian manner. Soloistically it accompanies Aschenbach's recitative-like monologues. Fine; the keyboard traditionally accompanies recitatives. But in this case the actual *sound* of the piano – black-and-white, matter-of-fact, cold, brittle, clipped and dry – is also symptomatic of Aschenbach's arid, exhausted emotional state. We *see* him each time with his notebook, symbol of his novelist's trade; we *hear* each time a sound-symbol of the condition to which this trade has reduced him. Only once in this context is another instrument admitted, in the Socrates (Aschenbach) Phaedrus

(Tadzio) dialogue excerpt, where Phaedrus is represented by the harp – an instrument which essentially complements the piano (and its music here – arpeggios and chords – tends to mirror-image or invert the piano's) but has warmth and colour, opposes youth to age.

Britten's well-practised touch for pungent, instrumental characterization and imaginative, sophisticated 'realism' has lost none of its sureness here. Witness the bassoons' muttering semiquavers (marked with Britten's favourite and most useful *heavy* staccato, a wedge-shaped mark which should not be confused – though it often is, not only by copyists but also by performing musicians – with the dot which signifies the *light* staccato) to represent the Gondolier (Ex. 13).

Ex. 13

This type of bassoon writing always carries a suggestion of the comic or grotesque and intimates here thereby that the old man poses no immediate threat to Aschenbach. Not so the Hotel Manager, who turns out to be a figure of cosmic omnipotence, in fact master-mind of the novelist's fate. There is an aura of ceremony and formality about him, faithfully reflected in a kind of brass chorale; while the string pizzicati give something of an edge to his *manières* (see fig. 57 *et seq*.). That there *is* something sinister about the Hotel Manager we know from the start through the frequent, almost surrealistic flashbacks to Aschenbach's 'Mysterious gondola' aria (see the sixth bar after fig. 57) which punctuate all the Manager's appearances, intimately linking him with the dark Charon-like figure which Aschenbach has fashioned from the Old Gondolier. Here is one of Britten's most extraordinary flights of timbral imagination: the deep, ominous, black-water sound of bass drum and *divisi* cellos and basses, close-voiced in their lowest register; the harp *solo* in the centre; while up aloft, suspended in the void, the bright but quiet combination of oboe and two piccolos (the piccolos being employed precisely because they *can* play both quietly and brightly in an upper register) (Ex. 14).

Ex. 14

Britten does the Hotel Barber's empty chatter and fussy scissors by combining oboes and muted horns at an octave's remove (oboes only really blend well with horns when the latter are muted, so that their sonority – much blander when unmuted – more nearly approaches the oboes' acidity). There is unctuousness in the three-part string chords, mostly triads; but notice the absence of violins, and the wide space between the two lower voices, cello and bass. This gives the sound of the latter a particular prominence which, knowing what we do of the double-bass as a kind of surrogate tuba in this score, is most probably intentional on Britten's part (Ex. 15).

As for 'realism' or 'naturalism': John Evans remarks on the trial-and-error process (reminiscent of Britten's pre-war days as composer-in-residence of the GPO Film Unit) whereby the throb of the boat's engines came to be impersonated by a rhythmic ostinato on the side-drum played with scrubbing brushes (Ex. 1). Evans describes the sound of trombones, alias the boat's siren (see Mitchell, n. 17,

Ex. 15

p. 207), as 'hard-edged'.[13] Even more, to my ears, it has definite alarmist overtones; again bearing in mind the way in which Britten in the 'Dance of Death' movement, the wild hunt, in *Our Hunting Fathers*, and consistently in *Billy Budd*, uses essentially the same type of peremptory, ejaculatory, comminatory trombone-summonses or calls-to-order, they are I am sure (albeit subconsciously) intentional.

Ned Rorem, in 1978, made impressive claims for Britten's 'metaphoric' naturalism in *Death in Venice* (see pp. 186–7). 'In giving nonvocal music a recognizable meaning beyond its "abstract" meaning Britten becomes . . . a metaphorist rather than a similist. This he manages through orchestrational *tours de force* and through obsessional rhythmic patterns . . . his brushed drums *are* what you hear – not *like* what you hear – from vaporetto motors; his dipping viola patterns *are* what you hear from dripping gondola paddles.' (Ex. 16.)

Ex. 16

This gondola-music is curiously grey in its mixture of timbres (woodwind/strings/piano); the expected 'watery' harp, which would have provided a contrasting 'splash' of colour, is intentionally absent. Then – is it again not so much *like* what we hear as *what* we hear? – the bells of St Mark's, two peals in alternation.

Britten's bell-ringing techniques repay some attention. Notice in Ex. 17a the heterophony (non-alignment of voices), and cymbal strokes, both realistically creating the confused yet vaguely euphonious tangle-and-hum of bell harmonics; and in Ex. 17b a totally different texture (woodwind, chant-like, on the tune, strings, gong and actual chimes prolonging the reverberations, organum-like parallel fourths between the voices, the chant varied rhythmically from one bar to the next) but one no less authentically bell-like.

Although I have here perforce concentrated for the most part on Britten's way of treating colour particles as individual units, either isolating them as soloists or combining them in families, none the less the doubling process in *Death in Venice* is as great a force for clarity and expression as in any other Britten score. This, however, is something the reader, armed with a full score, can easily study for himself, noting such subtleties as Ex. 18, the theme of 'The pursuit'. This theme is nearly always given to cellos doubled by bassoons – the former causing the feeling of compulsive chase, the latter muddying or darkening its colour.

On only three significant occasions is the full orchestra used as a tutti: and they all conspire at edging the drama to its climax. The first is released in the dream-orgy (fig. 289) which causes Aschenbach to abandon all further show of self-discipline. The second is the great stretto which begins in the brass (after Socrates' 'And now, Phaedrus, I will go; but you stay here') and leads up to the start of the finale, 'The departure'; the third, and last, is the climactic confronta-

Ex. 17a

Ex. 17b

Ex. 18

tion (though nothing happens in actuality, only in the music) between Aschenbach and the Hotel Manager ('Yes, Signor von Aschenbach, the season comes to an end, our work is nearly done'). It begins with the Manager's familiar brass/pizzicato chords but gradually crescendos, accelerates rhythmically and at length involves every member of the orchestra. It is the means by which Aschenbach's death sentence is pronounced.[14]

Oliver Knussen, who has made his own study of the tuttis in *Death in Venice*, has pointed out another and singular bona fide tutti, again placed at a critical juncture. This occurs on the last quaver of the fourth bar after fig. 323, on which Mr Knussen comments: 'however, the strings are pizz. and the horns, trumpets, and trombones mute just for that one note, so that this only other fraction-of-a-second unleashing of the orchestral mass is strangled at the point where Aschenbach has – one presumes – his fatal attack'. Mr Knussen is surely right: this most abbreviated of tuttis represents the blow that stops Aschenbach's heart beating. Mr Knussen notes one other tutti; he refers to fig. 188 *et seq.*: 'A real tutti, but without keyboard, harp, or any percussion'. Britten's planning of the tuttis in *Death in Venice*, in short, is an important part of the *dramatic* architecture of the work.

I do not have the space to touch on certain important aspects of Britten's orchestration – for example the evolution of the *Death in Venice* orchestral texture from precedents in Britten's own chamber operas, the Church Parables, *A Midsummer Night's Dream* and *Owen Wingrave*. Much too remains to be explored in the wider genealogy of Britten's scoring; the influence not only of Mahler but also of Mahler's disciples, Shostakovich and Berg (see Roseberry, pp. 90–5 and n. 4, p. 211). But, as in other contexts, his supreme achievement as an orchestrator is the amount of new wine he seems able to pour into the old familiar bottles. He uses traditional instruments in a traditional manner – even Tadzio's percussion ensemble draws for the most part on conventional instruments, the requirements being less recherché in fact than those of the Church Parables – and yet creates his own individual soundworld. Nor are we ever aware of this soundworld as an end in itself: it is all part and parcel of a total concept. In a sense it is as idle, and as impertinent, to praise Britten for his instrumentation as it is to praise Bach or Mozart for theirs; which is not to say that we cannot draw a distinction between composers like Beethoven, Brahms, Bruckner and Shostakovich, who use the orchestra primarily as a vehicle for ideas, and Mozart, Tchaikovsky, Britten and Prokofiev, who are more attuned to it for its own sake. If I should ever realize my ambition to compile an orchestration handbook which draws its examples solely from the works of Britten, I can guarantee that *Death in Venice* will have to be awarded a disproportionate (or, rather, proportionate) number of pages. The score represents a unique achievement in his own *oeuvre* and in the history of orchestration in the twentieth century.

11 'Death in Venice' and the Third String Quartet

DAVID MATTHEWS

The recitative introduction to the passacaglia finale of Britten's Third String Quartet contains five quotations from *Death in Venice*. These are: the Venice Overture motive (Ex. 1a), played in the quartet by the cello (Ex. 1b); the motive associated with Aschenbach's pursuit of Tadzio in Act II (Ex. 1c), on the second violin (Ex. 1d); the harp phrase from the Phaedrus aria (Ex. 1e), on the first violin, pizzicato (Ex. 1f); the agitated motive which appears in the scene of Aschenbach's persecution by street vendors and beggars in Act I (Ex. 1g), on the viola (Ex. 1h); and finally Aschenbach's 'I love you' from the end of Act I (Ex. 1i), played by all four instruments (Ex. 1j).

Ex. 1a

Ex. 1b

Ex. 1c

154

Ex. 1d

Ex. 1e

Ex. 1f

Ex. 1g

Ex. 1h

recit.

Ex. 1i

Ex. 1j

Why are these quotations here? The finale's subtitle, 'La Serenissima' (see Plate 24), gives one explanation. Britten composed the movement in Venice on his last visit there, in November 1975, and he intended it as a tribute to the city he loved above all others. The passacaglia bass, on which the movement is built, he derived from the sound of Venetian bells. Quotations from *Death in Venice* were also appropriate; and the first of the quotations, the Venice Overture motive, is based on the notes to which the chorus repeatedly sing 'Serenissima' in the preceding boat journey scene. But this is certainly not the whole explanation nor the only link between opera and quartet. It is clear that Britten identified with Aschenbach, more

24 The composition sketch of the opening of the last movement of the Third String Quartet (The British Library Add.MS.No. 60620, f. 13/The Britten–Pears Library and Archive)

closely, I suspect, than with any other of his operatic protagonists.[1]
One wonders if, when he was composing *Death in Venice*, Britten
imagined that he would share Aschenbach's fate. What is probable is
that he hastened his own death by postponing his heart operation
until he had finished the score – the operation from which, when he
eventually underwent it, he made only a partial recovery. The Third
Quartet, the *chef-d'oeuvre* of the works he wrote in the four years
between *Death in Venice* and his own death, is, I would suggest,
Aschenbach's quartet; it continues, on a purely musical level, his
quest for transcendence, whose symbol in the opera is Tadzio and, in
the Quartet, Venice herself.

At the end of *Death in Venice* Aschenbach dies a broken and defeated man, believing that his pursuit of ideal beauty in the real world has led him, in Socrates' words which he quotes, 'to the abyss'. But the music of these closing pages tells us otherwise. Immediately after the Phaedrus aria – the passage in which Aschenbach unequivocally condemns himself – comes the fullest statement of the 'view' motive. In its context and in its character this passage is comparable to the D minor interlude in Berg's *Wozzeck*: in both passages the composer, as it were, steps on to the stage to plead for his hero. The warmth and indeed nobility of Britten's music here serve to purge Aschenbach of much of his accumulated guilt. The orchestral postlude after Aschenbach's death takes this redemptive process a stage further. Over a deep, tolling bass, the strings gently restate Aschenbach's Hymn to Apollo, which he had sung exultantly at the end of Act I; the Hymn rises yearningly upwards towards Tadzio's theme which is suspended above it on the glockenspiel, the two themes reaching a high unison A in the very last bar.

The exotic sonority of Tadzio's music had always emphasized his remoteness from Aschenbach, though its tonality, an unvarying pentatonic A major, is close to Aschenbach's own E major – E is its dominant, in fact. When Aschenbach sings his exultant Hymn to Apollo after watching Tadzio's victory in the games it is in Tadzio's key of A; the music then moves to the dominant for Aschenbach's climactic 'I love you' and the subsequent prelude to Act II.[2] Though the association of E major with Aschenbach was made at the outset with 'I, Aschenbach, famous as a master writer', this is the first time E major has been firmly established, and the fact that it appears here as the dominant to Tadzio's key contributes to its security. It is a short-lived security, however; suspicion of his motives soon begins to undermine Aschenbach's idealism. Tadzio's theme disappears and A major becomes the key associated with Aschenbach's relentless pursuit of Tadzio through the streets of Venice (beginning at fig. 211); while the stability of E major collapses as Aschenbach gradually loses his self-control. In the climactic dream scene – the vision of a Dionysiac orgy – Aschenbach's E major is finally overwhelmed by the shattering reappearance of Tadzio's theme, in its original A major but now cruelly overladen with dissonance. (See also Palmer, pp. 150–2.) As the vision fades and the still sleeping Aschenbach takes up the Tadzio theme and distorts it, the theme becomes, quite literally, perverted.

The feeble stuttering of the 'I, Aschenbach' motive at fig. 307 indicates how thoroughly Aschenbach's key has been destroyed. But this passage, showing him at his lowest ebb, turns out to be the prelude to his partial redemption. The orchestral postlude (fig. 325) rehabilitates A major and restores Tadzio's music to its original purity. The trilling bass pedal on the leading note, G sharp, however, makes the tonality uneasy until the very last bar, when the pedal lifts off. One of the advantages of a tonal composer is the subtlety of expression he can achieve: the precariousness of the affirmation that Britten wants to make here is precisely expressed by this last-minute resolution.

The ambiguity still present in this ending is underlined by the fact that Aschenbach's E major has not been reaffirmed. For this we must turn to the Third Quartet, and here E major is achieved only after a long and complex process.[3] The first movement begins with a motive (Ex. 2a) related, as Peter Evans has pointed out,[4] to the music of Aschenbach's unhappy wanderings through Venice (cf. Ex. 2b). In

Ex. 2a

Ex. 2b

addition, the figure marked *x* in Ex. 2a happens to be a retrograde of the opera's 'I love you' motive at the same pitch that it is presented in the introduction to the passacaglia (cf. Ex. 1j). It is impossible to say whether this is conscious or unconscious. The two-flat key signature of this movement would seem to imply B flat, which is at the furthest tonal remove (an augmented fourth away) from the quartet's E major goal. But the tonality is not defined; this is the least tonal movement of the quartet and consequently the least stable. (See also Roseberry, n. 9, p. 212.) The quartet is about the rediscovery of stability, and it begins at a point which corresponds to Aschenbach's psychological condition at his death.

Stability is first sought in the key of C major and that key is serenely achieved in the slow movement. The fourth movement, which is called 'Burlesque', begins in A minor, the relative minor of C. So E major is once again approached through A, though this A, both minor and (after the trio) major, is worlds apart from Tadzio's pure pentatonic A. The music of the 'Burlesque' is hard, satirical, the trio deliberately banal – as in Mahler's 'Rondo-Burleske' in his Ninth Symphony, to which it consciously refers. After this movement the finale can hardly begin without a long, tentative introduction, which presents the five quotations mentioned above. The last of these, 'I love you', is stated, appropriately, in C, from which key the music moves smoothly into E major and stays there, for the longest passage of pure diatonic music that Britten allowed himself in his late music. We cannot but feel that the redemption of Aschenbach

Ex. 3a

Ex. 3b

ASCHENBACH

When thought-becomes feel - ing, — feel - ing — thought . . . —

which had begun in *Death in Venice* is completed here, with the radiant resurrection of his true key: this and the obvious derivation of
the main melody (Ex. 3a) from 'I love you', and the reference, in the
second phrase, to the Hymn to Apollo (Ex. 3b; see the notes marked
y in both examples) make Britten's intention clear.

The questioning ending that Britten chose instead of the expected
E major triad (see Ex. 4) opens up a fresh perspective. In *Death in
Venice*, the last bar brought sudden clarification; here too something
is glimpsed, but more mysteriously. What lies beyond death is
beyond the scope of most artists, but Britten, close to his own death,
came as near as anyone to providing a clue.

Ex. 4

25 Act II scene 9: 'The pursuit'. Aschenbach confronts the Polish family. Robert Huguenin as Tadzio and Deanne Bergsma as The Polish Mother

12   Mann and his novella: 'Death in Venice'[1]

T. J. REED

It would have given Thomas Mann singular pleasure to see a work of his made into an opera. In an early letter he wrote that music was 'the art which I pursue with a heart full of yearning and unrequited love'. Later he called his talent 'transposed musicianship' and his works 'good scores'. When he came to write the final reckoning with his own and Germany's past in the novel *Doctor Faustus* (1947), he made his Faust an avant-garde composer and matched point for point the techniques which this involved describing, by literary intricacies of his own. His ambition to emulate music was thus more than the vague aspiration many writers have shared.

The status music had for him certainly owed something to the fascination of Wagner, whose massive works 'goaded his creative instinct' like no one else's. Perhaps it owed something to the highly metaphysical aesthetics of Schopenhauer, who declared that music – unlike all the other arts, which merely represented the surface appearance of things – directly expressed the ultimate reality of the world. But there were more precise reasons too. Behind the desire to emulate lay a sense of literature's natural limitations. Literature has to work with words, the much-worn counters men use in daily communication of every kind. Music, in contrast, has means of expression enviably free from the associations of day-to-day explicitness and unambiguous reference. The writer's problem is to shake off such associations and build up others, of sound and sense, which will add dimensions to the merely literal and eventually convert the linearity of statement into the ambiguous richness of form.

When Mann began to write, this problem was particularly acute. The 1890s were dominated by the literature of Naturalism which analyzed society, heredity, environment, psychology. It strove to rival science and pursued not simply verisimilitude but verifiability. Mann from the first resisted. Though his first novel, *Buddenbrooks* (1901), analyzed the decline of a bourgeois family, it also wove patterns of

163

more than Naturalistic meaning with the aid of a leitmotif technique claiming descent from Wagner. Then, in the decade between *Buddenbrooks* and *Death in Venice*, Mann struggled to 'elevate' prose narrative further and to create poetic meanings which would not be end-stopped by factual reference. He experimented, not very successfully as yet, with allegory. Techniques apart, it was a struggle to refashion the image of the novel, and an uphill struggle. Prose was traditionally assumed inferior to poetry, and in a Germany now reacting against Naturalism and its limiting of the imagination, the novel was tarred with the brush of that movement, scorned as social rather than metaphysical, as analytic, intellectual, unvital, decadent. The ideal now was once more beauty – the unexplicit beauty of full plastic representation, or the spontaneous sensuous beauty (that is how it was seen) of Wagner's music. Only if literature attained such qualities was it 'art'.

These issues of the times are the stuff of Aschenbach's career as Mann sketches it in. They are also a key to his Venice adventure. For it is his enhanced feeling for external beauty that first fixes his gaze on Tadzio. The boy is an aesthetic ideal, an analogue of the artistic form which the mature Aschenbach aspires to create. The text duly evokes Tadzio in the language of sculpture and picture. And when, insidiously, aesthetic admiration becomes passion, it does so the more easily because Aschenbach, once more in tune with his times, has rejected psychological analysis. It is an abyss he is weary of peering into as he did when young. So he will not question his feelings and motives until too late, when Tadzio's apollinian beauty has led him to the abyss of Dionysiac feeling.

Dionysus and Apollo: *Death in Venice* moves between these two deities. It draws on Nietzsche's theory that art conjoins the Dionysiac forces of the depths – unconscious or collective feeling – and the apollinian principle of form, control, individuation. In Aschenbach these elements are not in balance. Through a career of disciplined achievement, control has become repression. When his work reaches the impasse which begins the story, it is a sign that his discipline is exhausted and has exhausted him. Feeling presses to take revenge. His downfall is a psychological collapse, essentially complete before he ever leaves Munich and only fulfilled by the journey to Venice.

Of course, what he dies of is cholera. Yet this physical cause and the psychological cause are not at odds, indeed, they are strangely linked. The epidemic which reached Venice in 1911 came from India.

So, it was thought, did the cult of the alien god Dionysus which once swept like an epidemic through ancient Greece. The physical cause, disease, thus aptly coincided with the psychological explanation, itself stated in terms which bordered on mythology. This was already the beginning of an ambiguity such as Mann aspired to, enriching the anecdote he had brought back from his Venice journey. The bizarre circumstances and encounters of that journey, all of them (Mann assures us) fact not fiction, contributed further. The figures along Aschenbach's route, from the foreigner in Munich who stirs his wanderlust to the gondolier and the street-singer in Venice, all merged readily into an ominous unity. Real at the blandly realistic surface of the narrative, they also embody Hermes, the guide of souls to Hades. It became possible to speak of one thing and yet move on three levels – literal, psychological, mythological.

Tadzio is the final Hermes-figure. Yet he might have guided Aschenbach to something other than death. Deep in the work's conception is the idea that passion – the intoxication of Dionysus – liberates and inspires, and that subconsciously Aschenbach travelled to seek emotional release and literary regeneration. This is how Mann experienced his own meeting with 'Tadzio' in Venice – disturbingly intense and poetically inspiring in a way unfamiliar to the writer of measured prose:

> Remember? Intoxication, a heightened exceptional feeling
> Came over you as well on one occasion and threw you
> Down, your brow in your hands. To hymnic impulse your spirit
> Rose, amid tears your struggling mind pressed urgently upward
> Into song.

This description from a hexameter idyll of 1919 makes the matter plain and it is confirmed by a letter of the following year which gives a detailed interpretation of *Death in Venice*. As Mann there frankly admits, he was no stranger to homosexual feeling. His relationship with the painter Paul Ehrenberg in 1901 gave him a happiness from which up till then he had believed the artist was necessarily cut off. It inspired the delicate recreation of boyhood feeling in *Tonio Kröger* and was still, decades later, intense enough in memory to become a major episode in *Doctor Faustus*, the tragic friendship of the composer-hero Adrian Leverkühn and the violinist Rudi Schwerdtfeger.

Then, by one more of the coincidences which helped shape *Death in Venice*, Mann's attention was drawn to the classic texts on homosexual love – Plato's *Phaedrus* and *Symposium* and Plutarch's *Erotikos*. Reading these placed the emotions of his chance experience in Venice in a larger context and added to an already complex story a new level of philosophical understanding and moral judgement. The Greek texts touched on the noble possibilities and the pitfalls of this mode of feeling: it might inspire or debase, provide the spiritual impetus to see all beauty through a single form or the spiritual limitation of pursuing only beauty's single exemplar. They presented homosexual love as above all a test of the lover. Aschenbach, a man of letters and of the spirit, a lover and creator of form, long aware that his art was a disciplined courtship of a chastely distant reality through the medium of the word – surely he would pass the test?

That was perhaps the first conception, and in Aschenbach's early responses to Tadzio it apparently begins to be realized. Yet it proved an impossible conception to execute. Under Mann's hands, under the influence alike of the puritan streak in him and of the inherent tendency of narrative to cool and objectivize, the hymnic celebration of passion was transformed. It left its traces in the text, but Aschenbach's passion is finally the subject of a moral fable, a warning. Beauty, Plato taught in the *Phaedrus*, was the one absolute which had sensuous existence; hence its ability to mediate between sensuous man and the realm of the spirit. But this dual nature was also its danger. For the artist, able to pursue spirit only through the sensuous reality of the world, being trapped in sense was an ever-present risk. This much Aschenbach understands shortly before he dies. He has pursued not beauty through Tadzio, but only the beautiful Tadzio.

In that original hymnic conception, the tableau with which the story closes might have been a triumph. The boy stands at the water's edge and points out to sea, fulfilling an image which caught Mann's attention in the *Symposium*, where Plato writes that the initiate who has left behind him all particular beautiful forms approaches the 'vast sea of beauty', grows strong 'on that shore' and comes to see the vision of a single ultimate beauty which embraces all he has experienced. But Aschenbach has fallen, failed. The ending is tragic. The sea towards which the boy beckons him and points the way contains only the uncertain promise of death.

Even so, Mann's story is not a total rejection of Aschenbach and his experience. The moral condemnations in the later stages of the text, so emphatic that they surprise a reader who knows Mann's habitual ironic manner, are not the whole and final truth by them-

selves. They restore a balance by exposing Aschenbach's excesses –
his sweating pursuit of Tadzio, his attempt at cosmetic rejuvenation
– just as the yielding of a hymnic conception to a moral fable
restored a balance. The sequence meant that Mann the autobiographical writer and moralist had changed and learned. But the story in
which the sequence is recorded transcends its dual elements and
achieves tragedy: that is, it is a work which constructs a single vision
of impulse and failure, value and loss, beauty and catastrophe.
Aschenbach is not abandoned but understood. Mann had peered
once more into the abyss and bound Dionysus with the spell of
Apollo.

Thomas Mann once compared *Death in Venice* to a crystal. The
image is apt for the remarkable way in which complex issues suddenly, under the pressure of an unexpected emotion, fused into a
near-perfect artefact. It is apt again for a work so rich in facets which
catch reflections from psychology, philosophy and myth. To convey
all these in the briefer span of a libretto is hardly possible. Mann's
verbal score (to return to the other image he used of his writing) is
too intricate. Above all, there are limits to what the protagonist,
largely silent in the story and only gradually coming to understand
his plight and its causes, can be made to tell us about himself. But if
Mann's 'music' cannot be transferred to the stage, Aschenbach now
has another music to speak for him. Thomas Mann, who loved and
envied that other art, would have been more than satisfied with
the exchange.

13 The novella transformed: Thomas Mann as opera

PATRICK CARNEGY

Although we can never know what Thomas Mann would have thought of Britten's transformation of his most celebrated novella into an opera, it seems to be generally agreed that he would have approved both of the idea, and of the opera itself. That is not only the view of the distinguished Mann scholar T.J. Reed (see pp. 163-7) but also of the writer's own family. Britten's letter seeking permission to set the text received a reply from the author's son, Professor Golo Mann, that could not have been more encouraging:

. . . my old mother and I, and everybody concerned would be delighted, would be happy, would be enthused if you could realize this project. . . . a 'Death in Venice'-opera by B.B. would have made the author of 'Death in Venice' happy. (14 September 1970)

Yet at first sight this is rather a surprising response: no less so when Golo Mann adds:

My father, incidentally, used to say, that if it ever came to some musical illustration of his novel, 'Doctor Faustus', you would be the composer to do it.[1]

The music of Adrian Leverkühn, the intensely Germanic, quasi-Schoenbergian hero of *Doctor Faustus*, composed by Britten? There are, I believe, two principal reasons why Golo Mann's reaction gives us pause for thought. The first has to do with the nature of Thomas Mann's art and the second with that of Britten's.

Thomas Mann was, of course, a profoundly musical writer. Music meant a great deal to him and it is both a constant subject in his fiction and a stylistic influence – he deliberately endows his prose with musical qualities, a practice that is specially noticeable in *Death in Venice* and the works leading up to it. But by no means would one think of his books (nor I am sure did their author) as potential libretti – as works which, as has been remarked of Maeterlinck's play *Pelléas and Mélisande*, were not *sui generis* but texts in search of their composer.

168

Mann's 'orchestration' is already fully realized; the literary leit-motifs (consciously modelled on Wagner) are so tightly interwoven that any intending composer would appear to be knocking on a closed door. And Mann the writer was more than a little wary of music's tendency to subjugate literature to its own ends. His love of music, and his indebtedness to it, were balanced by critical caution. In the 'Mind and Art' essay fragments (1909–12),[2] he suggests that music had seized so dominant a hold on the German imagination as to constitute a threat to the other arts, and particularly to literature. The German mind had come to prefer the inchoate, polyphonic feelings engendered by music to the linear lucidity of prose. The hegemony of music was a threat to literature and – perhaps precisely because music meant so much to him – to his own craft as a writer. Mann's solution was to absorb whatever he could of music – whether by way of subject matter or technical emulation – into his stories. It was a way of acknowledging an obsession while keeping it under control. Composers are sometimes accused of subjugating literature in their settings, and of coercing verbal values into musical ones. Here, the reverse happens; for Mann keeps music under control by constructing fictions about its extraordinary powers, as in his description of the eight-year-old Hanno Buddenbrook improvising at the piano – 'an irresistible mounting, a chromatic upward struggle, a wild relentless longing . . . sinking into a gulf of desire'[3] – or in the story 'Wälsungenblut' (Blood of the Volsungs) where a twin brother and sister, rich and pampered, are keyed up by an albeit pitiful performance of *Die Walküre* to round off the evening by re-enacting the conclusion of Act I on a bearskin rug at home. Music can do more, as in the story 'Tristan' where the exertion of Gabriele Klöterjahn's playing through at the piano the so-called 'Liebestod' from Wagner's opera – a forbidden deed urged by her would-be lover – is enough to hasten the heroine's death.

Music, Mann seems to be insisting, is a dangerous, highly subversive force, capable of exacting terrible penalties from those through whose hands and minds it passes. But it is on one branch or stream of the art of music, and on one composer in particular, that we must understand that he is concentrating his admonitions. It is with the music and name of Wagner that Thomas Mann is most concerned, and when he or his characters are supposedly talking about music in a general, non-specific, sense, they usually have in mind that from the Bayreuth Festspielhaus rather than, say, the clear, cool draught of Bach. Although imbued with Tristanesque ethos, *Death in Venice* is less overt in its musical allusions and appropriations than stories like 'Wälsungenblut'. But it needs no special knowledge to see that the novella pays homage to Venice's age-old association with music, and in particular to its connection with Wagner, who wrote much of the second act of *Tristan* there (1858), and died there in the Palazzo Vendramin on 13 February 1883. On arrival at the lagoon, Aschenbach is preoccupied almost as much with the sounds as with the sights of the city, not least 'the martial sound of horns coming across the water from the direction of the Public Gardens'[4] which draws the carousing youths up on deck. As Aschenbach is rowed in his gondola to the Lido, another boat draws alongside, 'full of men and women singing to guitar and mandolin. They rowed persistently bow for bow with the gondola and filled the silence with their lyrical love of gain.' (DVP, p. 28.) Later comes the serenade by the Strolling Players on the terraces of the Hotel des Bains – a musical entertainment for the Guests of course, while at the same time a mockery of them, especially in the valedictory laughing song into which all the Guests, with the pointed exceptions of Aschenbach and Tadzio, are seduced into joining.

Mann's scene-setting description of the Venetian soundscape is a prelude to the play he makes with music as a sweetly dangerous seduction, as that which both charms and disarms. It is a view which is recognizably Platonic: music as a paradigm of perfect beauty and, because it necessarily works through the senses, a potential path to the abyss. So the living music of Venice does not by any means strike Aschenbach as beneficial:

Yes, this was Venice, this the fair frailty that fawned and that betrayed, half fairy-tale, half-snare; the city in whose stagnating air the art of painting once put forth so lusty a growth, and where musicians were moved to accords so weirdly lulling and lascivious. Our adventurer felt his senses wooed by this voluptuousness of sight and sound, tasted his secret knowledge that the city sickened and hid its sickness for love of gain . . . (DVP, p. 63.)

In the Dionysiac horror of Aschenbach's nightmare, it is the *sound* of Tadzio's name – previously so sweet in Aschenbach's ear when called by playmates – which now torments and deranges him:

Night reigned, and his senses were on the alert; he heard loud, confused noises from far away, clamour and hubbub. . . . dominating them all, flute-notes of the cruellest sweetness, deep and cooing, keeping shamelessly on until the listener felt his very entrails bewitched. . . . one and all the mad rout yelled that cry, composed of soft consonants and with a long-drawn *u*-sound at the end, so sweet and wild it was together, and like nothing ever heard before! It would ring through the air like the bellow of a challenging stag, and be given back many-tongued . . . they never let it die. But the deep, beguiling notes of the flute wove in and out and over all. . . . His heart throbbed to the drums, his brain reeled, a blind rage seized him, a whirling lust, he craved with all his soul to join the ring that formed about the obscene symbol of the godhead . . . (DVP, pp. 74–6.)

Plainly, there is more than enough here to excite and inspire a composer.

Effortlessly at home in creating the mimetic Venetian soundscape – both as conjured up by Mann's words, and as experienced by his own ears on many visits – Britten and his librettist, Myfanwy Piper, had a more difficult task in deciding how to 'dramatize' the novella for the stage. Throughout the novella, Aschenbach's infrequent verbal exchanges are more or less exclusively with gondoliers, booking clerks and hotel staff (especially the Manager and solicitous Barber). The only dialogue of any consequence is with himself. But how could an opera be built from the soliloquy of a single principal character? Britten met the challenge head on. Sustained musical monologue could manifest Aschenbach's inner life upon the stage in a way that no conversion of Aschenbach's reflections into direct speech could ever do. Aschenbach need share his secrets only with the audience, avoiding the betrayal of himself to others that would be hard to avoid if anyone were to make a play out of *Death in Venice*. It was for this very reason that Visconti in his passionately 'realistic' film (as films like this nearly always are) minimized Aschenbach's words and himself used music (especially from Mahler's Third and Fifth Symphonies) to suggest what was passing through Aschenbach's heart and mind without compelling him to be verbally articulate.

But soliloquy still needs words. At the very beginning of the opera, Britten's Aschenbach complains that 'no words come . . . I reject the words called forth by passion'. This utterance itself generates an irony which Mann would have been the first to applaud; the operatic Aschenbach must sing words, yet it is only music which can faithfully represent his state of mind and serve as surrogate for his own fictitious art of literary expression. So what kind of words? While Myfanwy Piper and Britten[5] are very largely successful in crystallizing the complex processes of Aschenbach's mind into singable words without offending against Mann's own verbal music, it has to be admitted that the libretto does occasionally stray less than comfortably from Mann's characteristic idiom. One suspects that it may have been an understandable concern to put the narrative across as plainly as possible to an audience subject to powerful musical and visual impressions, that prompted the sometimes rather clumsy glossing of what Mann had been to great pains to ensure was no more than suggestion or allusion. To the Chorus's article of faith that the silent dead are about to 'enter into the house of the Lord' (Act I scene 1), Aschenbach is required to respond, 'Yes! From the black rectangular hole in the ground.' Equally unhappy are the words for the otherwise utterly compelling monologue, 'Mysterious gondola', which Aschenbach sings after the Old Gondolier has made off without waiting for his fare: 'Yes, he rowed me well./But he might have done for me,/rowed me across the Styx/and I should have faded like echoes in the lagoon/to nothingness.'

But for what style of musical setting were the words of the libretto destined? Britten had originally thought that Aschenbach's 'narrative' reflections should have been *spoken*. (See also Mitchell, pp. 4–5.) It was only after hearing Peter Pears sing the pitched but rhythmically free line in Schütz's Passions on a number of occasions close together, that he realized how apt this kind of narration could be for Aschenbach.[6] The Schütz-indebted soliloquies for Aschenbach give the singer enough room to improvise rhythmically, powerfully suggesting, as Peter Evans has pointed out,[7] that Aschenbach is not delivering well-prepared speech, but rather improvising thought (thinking aloud) and reflection from moment to moment, just as he actually does have to improvise the rhythmic delivery of the words. The melodic contour of the soliloquies, particularly as the opera progresses, makes frequent reference to the major/minor third of the principal musical cell which permeates the whole opera, and about which there will be more to say below (pp. 173–4). In authentically Mannian style, these references are, again in Peter Evans's admirable description, 'hidden in apparently free lines, creating . . . that impression of a constricting web which the rest of the music more elaborately delineates.'[8]

In the novella Aschenbach constantly alludes to great Classical writers, both for philosophical refreshment and illumination, and because he finds there the best expression of the battle between that Apollonian side of his nature which has governed his life and art, and the suppressed Dionysiac side which has now so disconcertingly erupted. Rather than risk over-burdening the soliloquies with this debate, Piper and Britten dramatize it by introducing roles for the

Voice of Apollo (counter-tenor) and, later, the Voice of Dionysus (bass-baritone). A further means which Britten uses to expand the external action in order to balance the drama of Aschenbach's calamitous inner life, is the beach games of Tadzio and his friends. These are shown, and arguably rather too extensively, as a complex mythological enactment which in the novella was only an association in Aschenbach's mind (the story of Hyacinthus is perhaps a less than likely choice of subject for a beach game by a group of young boys).[9] This is a balletic realization, with choral commentary, of an important mythopoeic aspect of Mann's conception. The presiding Voice of Apollo is perhaps a more credible, because uncompromisingly mythological, interpolation than the Piper/Britten requirement that the Hotel Guests should assume new masks (and perhaps that is precisly what they *should* do) in order to supply a well-schooled Classical commentary on the games.

Britten appears to leave it open whether this extended episode is to be staged 'for real', or as a fantasy of Aschenbach's – and it is perhaps not even necessary to choose between the two. The important thing is that these games, though conducted as an Apollonian celebration – 'Beauty is the only form of spirit that our eyes can see' – undermine Aschenbach's self-control to the point where he is plunged into Dionysiac passion and the waiting abyss. Later in the novella, Aschenbach's nightmare which 'left the whole cultural structure of a lifetime trampled on, ravaged, and destroyed' (DVP, p. 74) is undilutedly Dionysiac in its horror. But in the opera Piper and Britten sustain the dramatic tension by reinventing the episode as a contest for Aschenbach's soul (enacted over his sleeping body) conducted between on the one hand Apollo, and Dionysus and a chorus of his followers on the other: the 'dream' becomes a mime of Aschenbach's losing battle to reassert control over himself.

Dionysus is one of seven roles in the opera taken by a single bass-baritone. He introduces himself to Aschenbach as the Traveller standing on the steps of the mortuary chapel in Munich. With his very first phrase, 'Marvels unfold', summoning up a tropical landscape, threatening yet enticing in its untamed exuberance, he also unfolds the most important musical motive of the opera, the four notes D–C–E–D sharp, whose principal characteristic is the major third contracting to the minor (see P. Evans, Ex. 1a, *passim*). As we have seen, this 'fate' motive permeates Aschenbach's soliloquies, and is later especially associated with the plague. But although it is 'planted' by the Traveller and closely identified with him in his subsequent roles as the Elderly Fop, the Old Gondolier, the Hotel Manager, the Barber, the Players' Leader, not forgetting his impersonation of Dionysus, the motive is by no means his exclusive property. It would be an offence against its protean nature, its diabolical ambivalence, to label it definitively, or to associate it too closely with any one idea. For, in its various transformations, it comes to be associated with all those forces which conspire to bring about Aschenbach's downfall.

There can, of course, be no doubt about the concerted role which the Traveller-figure plays as Aschenbach's tempter. Here there is another significant adaptation of Mann's own scheme. For whereas in the novella (drawing on Mann's own experiences of a holiday in Venice) the man in the portico of the cemetery chapel, the obstinate gondolier, and all the other sinister figures are separate characters, each contributing his own variant of Kafkaesque unease to the story, in the opera Britten compounds them into but a single character – the Traveller – who, as it were, then diversifies by playing many roles. Obviously the advantage of this in a staged drama is that it sets up a pervasive conflict reminiscent of that, say, between Mephisto and Faust. It is only at the very end that the Traveller, now taking the part of the Hotel Manager disengaging himself from his guest, reveals himself openly as manipulator of events, and perhaps even their judge: '. . . who comes and goes is my affair . . . it is the time of departure . . . our work is nearly done. /No doubt the Signore / will be leaving us soon?/ We must all lose / what we think to enjoy the most.'[10] Such a transparent metaphor is more apt for Britten's stage than the allusive, tacitly understated pages of Mann's novella. In the opera it draws together and knots the strands previously unloosed, whereas in the novella this would have been too crude in its technique and moral sentiment. It is interesting that in her invention of this 'proprietor's farewell', Mrs Piper draws on Mann's characteristic ability to turn the banalities of social discourse to ironic and even sinister effect, though phrases like 'who comes and goes is my affair' and 'our work is nearly done' run the risk of straining at significance.

We have seen how, in the opera, the omnipresent Traveller is a means of dramatizing the tension between Aschenbach and the world about him. But the factor that contributes most powerfully to that tension is the totally unexpected effect on Aschenbach of the boy Tadzio. This is the principal theme of the story, and because Aschenbach and the boy do not exchange a single word but only glances – and at the most a smile, that fatal smile – this set Britten the serious problem of how such a relationship could be presented in an operatic context, where singing is generally the primary means of expression.[11] Britten's solution is quite masterly and is the pivot around which the success of the opera revolves. If we do not yet know whether the notion that Tadzio and his family should be dancers (a balletic mime within the opera) preceded the idea of giving them a gamelan-like music quite outside the musical language of the rest of the opera, or vice-versa, perhaps that does not greatly matter (see however Mitchell, pp. 4–8). What there can be no doubt about is that the mime and the music create a world of oriental, seductive beauty as unexpected and overwhelming in its immediate musical context as it is, in the novella, in Aschenbach's well-ordered mental world. Tadzio's A major-ish theme with its prominent major seventh, A–G sharp, scored for vibraphone and other percussion, is quite literally a shimmering, vibrant and vibrating sound aura, its apartness signalled not only by its exotic instrumentation but by its inbuilt harmonic stasis, such fan-like harmonies as there are being derived virtually exclusively from the notes of the melody.[12] It sets up a hermetic world in the opera, almost as though Tadzio and his family are a vision in a glass box at the heart of the drama. By and large Britten has composed intensely naturalistic operas (excepting *The Turn of the Screw* and *Owen Wingrave*, both of which are permeated with premonitions of the supernatural, and the ritualistic Church operas), but the representation of Tadzio and his family by sounds and gestures that are foreign to the immediate context is both an altogether fitting idea at the naturalistic level – the portrayal of people who, in their Polishness, *are* strange to Aschenbach, in a combination of music and gesture that is articulate only in its beauty, its alien exoticism – and a sounding–visual metaphor for something that is going on only in Aschenbach's mind, his idealization of the beautiful Tadzio.

But why *oriental* sound for Tadzio, rather than some strain evocative of his Polish origins? The naturalistic fact (in the novella) of his being Polish is of small importance compared with his being foreign, quite outside Aschenbach's experience. Obviously the Far East is a far cry from Poland, but this was a golden opportunity for Britten to draw on his longstanding fascination[13] with oriental music (*The Prince of the Pagodas, Curlew River*) to create a more potent musical metaphor of an unearthly, beckoning beauty than could have been achieved by a medley of Chopinesque mazurkas, for example.

In Mann's novella there is a possible cue for such a musical interpretation of Tadzio in the suggestion[14] that the Orient is the common source of the ecstatic, libidinous cult of Dionysus and of the Asiatic cholera which is the physical cause of Aschenbach's death. But in giving Tadzio's music an oriental character – and in the opera it is of course the prime carrier of the *idea* of Aschenbach's bewitchment – Britten adds his own emphasis by bringing into the foreground the notion that the story can be understood as that of a Western Platonic psyche undone by the Orient.

While Tadzio's music remains the unchanging centre around which the opera turns and with which it ends, it subtly influences and interacts with the other principal motivic elements – and most particularly those associated with Aschenbach and the Traveller. Britten's prodigious use of motive gives the work a unity, a homogeneity as potent as that in a strict serial composition where melodic and harmonic space are one and the same. And indeed, as we have seen, the characteristic harmonies of *Death in Venice* are derived from its melodic contours. The musical drama is enacted not through the opposition of key centres (as in the majority of Britten's operas) but through the spinning of a net of motives which entraps Aschenbach as he becomes aware of their ominous significance. With Mannian irony, the most deadly and pervasive four-note motive (a major third collapsing to a minor third), which symbolizes the plague and its several manifestations, seems when first introduced (accompanying the Traveller's words, 'Marvels unfold!') to be as blameless as the enticing glamour of a travel brochure. This motive functions both openly and insidiously, representing in its various guises the physiological, psychological and mythological dimensions of Aschenbach's downfall. These dimensions are already delineated with contrapuntal mastery by Thomas Mann: although his story necessarily unfolds in linear prose, the reader is always aware not just of a 'realistic' narrative, but of much wider resonances. Mann's use of literary leitmotifs as such – the repetition of a phrase to alert the reader to some previous occurrence explaining or illuminating the immediate context – is, for him, relatively, but deliberately, restrained. In reclaiming the device for music, Britten is able to deploy it far more subtly and suggestively than can be attempted in prose. With its help he achieves a unity in the musical fabric without sacrificing either variety or the contrast between the world of Aschenbach's music and the unchanging pentatonic A major of Tadzio's.

This pervasive use of motive is uncannily reminiscent of a piece of fictitious music which Mann described in his late novel *Doctor Faustus*, where it is not a scholar who makes a pact with the devil but a composer. Mann tells us that the entire musical fabric of Adrian Leverkühn's final work, the *Lamentation of Doctor Faustus*, is permeated by a five-note motive. This is itself derived from letters with musical equivalents found in 'Hetaera esmeralda', the name given by Leverkühn to the prostitute from whom he acquired the disease which served both as inspiration for his art and to bring about his eventual madness and death. (Visconti slyly has 'Esmeralda' painted on the bow of the steamer which, in his film, brings Aschenbach to Venice.) Although it is not known for certain whether Britten ever read *Doctor Faustus*, the parallel between the constructional principle of Leverkühn's fictitious composition, and Britten's actual practice in his *Death in Venice* opera, is truly remarkable.

By permeating Mann's *Death in Venice* with a musical web, Britten fully articulates that half-hidden 'musical dimension' implicit in the novella, while giving it a quite different style and flavour from that which Mann might have recognized or intended (had he been the composer that he sometimes wished he was). If, as we have seen, music in its Wagnerian sense of a voluptuous art, supremely sensual and subversive, is an underground presence in Mann's *Death in Venice*, it emerges cleansed to new life in Britten's transformation. The novella is a supreme literary work by a writer steeped in music; the opera is a musical masterpiece by a composer steeped in literature. For Mann, music is a metaphor; for Britten, the language of his art.

14 Aschenbach becomes Mahler: Thomas Mann as film

PHILIP REED

Problems inevitably emerge when transferring any great artwork couched in one medium for consumption in another format. The suitability of the source material for adaptation is a prime consideration. With regard to Mann's *Death in Venice*, this is as true for Britten and Myfanwy Piper's operatic presentation as it is for Luchiano Visconti's more liberal film version. As raw material for cinematic art, the type of philosophic fiction which *Death in Venice* embodies (whose chief occupation is the projection of ideas rather than action) is not what we might expect to find apt for the screen; yet film-makers have sought to project this kind of literature with great success. There is, of course, always a tendency to judge any new version (be it film or opera) by merely comparing it with the original. In some respects this is a false premise, since any declared adaptation will not necessarily also claim to be an accurate representation of the original. However, such can be our identification with, and affection for, the source work that we find ourselves completely unable to divorce our feelings (and our critical faculties) about the adaptation from the original itself. How easy it is to claim that a cinematic version of a classic work of literature – whether by Austen, Dickens, Hardy, Tolstoy, or by Thomas Mann – is but a pale shadow of its literary antecedent, a monochromatic impression in comparison with the blazing glory of the full colour of the original.

Visconti's own account of *Death in Venice* (1971, with a script by Nicola Badalucco and Visconti himself) is guilty of alterations to Mann's conception which qualify it as being very much more Visconti's version than Mann's own. It incorporates changes which at times appear to be nothing short of perverse to admirers of the novelist's genius. The purpose of this brief essay is not to criticize the film too unfavourably in the light of the novella's achievements – at least, not exclusively that – but to provide an opportunity to explore some of the reasons which led Visconti to alter Mann's framework.

26 From the film of *Death in Venice* by Luchiano Visconti ©1971 ALPHA CINEMATOGRAFICA S.R.L.

The most striking feature of Visconti's *Death in Venice*, and one which impels us to view his film in a completely different light from the novella (and, indeed, from the opera), concerns the identity of the chief protagonist, Gustav von Aschenbach, who is transformed from a distinguished man of letters into an equally distinguished composer. This change of profession is, in itself, perhaps not so heinous a crime; but what is more puzzling is that Visconti bestows upon Aschenbach (played by the actor, Dirk Bogarde) the persona of the composer Gustav Mahler. At first sight this translation from one creative discipline to another, from literature to music, seems at best odd and at worst without reason; however, Visconti was aware of a precedent to be discovered in Mann himself which partly justifies or, more accurately, explains this fundamental alteration of Aschenbach's identity.

In a letter dated 18 March 1921 from Mann to Wolfgang Born (1894–1949), a Munich painter and graphic artist, the novelist revealed something of the genesis of *Death in Venice*. Born had produced a sequence of nine coloured lithographs for *Death in Venice*, and Mann's letter congratulated the artist on his impressive achievement.[1] It was Born's last picture, entitled 'Death', which provoked the most interesting response in Mann:

The conception of my story, which occurred in the early summer of 1911, was influenced by news of the death of Gustav Mahler, whose acquaintance I had been privileged to make in Munich and whose intense personality left the strongest impression upon me. I was on the island of Brioni at the time of his passing and followed the story of his last hours in the Viennese press bulletins, which were cast in royal style. Later, these shocks fused with the impressions and ideas from which the novella sprang. So that when I conceived my hero who succumbs to lascivious dissolution, I not only gave him the great musician's Christian name, but also in describing his appearance conferred Mahler's mask upon him.[2]

What surprised Mann about the final lithograph was that Born had managed to make Aschenbach's features possess qualities which were distinctly Mahlerian. The influence of Mahler – the minimal influence of Mahler[3] – upon Mann's work had been quite unwittingly uncovered by Born.

Having transformed Aschenbach's persona into that of Mahler, Visconti amplified his particular conception of the Aschenbach–Mahler figure by incorporating in the film whole episodes derived from Mahler's life. For example, Visconti employs a chain of flashbacks to Aschenbach's quarrels with a character who does not appear in the book (named Alfried), but who is presumably intended to represent Arnold Schoenberg. Their discussions appear to be derived in part from Alma Mahler's *Memories and Letters* with its recollections of Mahler and Schoenberg and their disputatious relationship, in Visconti now transferred into vehement confrontations around the piano. One commentator has suggested that Visconti plundered Mann's novel, *Doctor Faustus* (whose protagonist, Leverkühn, *is* a composer) for material for Aschenbach's spoken 'explanations'. In the film the steamer on which Aschenbach arrives in Venice is called 'Esmeralda', as is the prostitute whom Visconti has Aschenbach take in a brothel; 'Esmeralda' is, of course, the name of the prostitute in *Doctor Faustus* who gives Leverkühn syphilis. The Mahlerian biographical correspondences continue: in the film Aschenbach grieves for the death of a daughter, not a wife as in Mann. This can be explained by the fact that Mahler's own daughter, Maria, had died in 1907, and the composer was stricken with grief. Finally, Visconti's clinching stroke was to use Mahler's own music as the film sound-track, the Third and Fifth Symphonies but especially the Adagietto from the latter. But is Mahler's score the music of an artist who found himself frozen in his feelings, or are we to suppose the Adagietto is the product of Aschenbach's liberated feelings in relation to Tadzio? David Denby, in a perceptive critique of the film entitled 'Movies: the sense of period',[4] is in no doubt about the 'conceptual chaos' resulting from the manipulation of Mahler's music as representative of the art of Mann's Aschenbach. In Visconti, Denby writes,

We get a character named Aschenbach who happens to have written Mahler's music, but then that music is described in terms that fit the work of Mann's literary artist – serene, perfect, Apollonian. Visconti and Nicola Badalucco, who together perpetrated the screenplay, seem to think that the audience is unaware of the character of much of Mahler's music. He was anything but serene; in fact, most of his work has a deep emotional turbulence.

The way Visconti uses Mahler on the soundtrack makes his personal attitude toward the composer clear enough. The beautiful *Adagietto* from the Fifth Symphony returns again and again in moments of crisis, the emotional climax of the movement surging forward as the camera moves in on Bogarde for the devastating close-up. (Poor Bogarde has to attempt to execute, against the music, one of the most miserable clichés of classy filmmaking: a Great Ironic Laugh as he collapses in a Venetian square.) In other words the *Adagietto* is used like the thick sludge of string tone composed in imitation of Mahler by the various Central European refugees who worked in Hollywood in the thirties and forties. The movie composers stole from him or watered him down to make money, but Visconti undoubtedly thinks that his corruption of the music is part of a great honor rendered to the composer.

Such is the naivety of Visconti's conception and his confusion of Mahler and Aschenbach that he is able to imagine that Mahler's music is the proper kind of aural stimulation to accompany the opulent visual images.

What kind of critical interpretation can be placed upon Visconti's film? One commentator has argued that Visconti's *Death in Venice* is an allegory of his own life and experiences. Visconti certainly identified with Thomas Mann's work and saw something of himself reflected in the Mahler–Aschenbach figure. The film version becomes, then, an explicit recollection of Visconti's own life, gloriously revived by Piero Tosti's costumes and décor. An analogy can be drawn between Visconti's own mother, Donna Carla Visconti, and Mann's Polish mother; the well-disciplined Polish children, and particularly Tadzio, are analogous to the severely brought-up Visconti brood.

The undercurrent of homosexual awakening in Visconti's life is mirrored in both Tadzio and Aschenbach (as Mahler), with the curious notion that Visconti is able to manipulate the Aschenbach–Tadzio relationship in such a way as to suggest the old Visconti watching his innocent, young self. In this interpretative stance the flashbacks can be seen to suggest elements of Visconti's own life, doubts and preoccupations rather than those of Mahler. In the film Aschenbach is often shown as a solitary figure, isolated in a crowd (a Brittenesque theme here!); for Visconti this image suggests much of the condition of his own life. Visconti expands Aschenbach's fear of old age – a symptom of his own fear of aging and dying. The longing for youth is enlarged upon, often by means of the film's imagery; for example, when Aschenbach is pursuing the Polish family through the streets of Venice, there is an emphatic image of an hour-glass presented by a background of balustrades which repeats the hour-glass shape.

Part of the problem – indeed, one of the many anxieties about the film – concerns quite simply Dirk Bogarde's unconvincing physical portrayal. In spite of Visconti's insistence on the Mahler figure, Bogarde has the air of an absent-minded provincial professor, slightly eccentric, rather than the great writer experiencing what Mann himself described as 'lascivious dissolution'. No time is allowed to insinuate Tadzio into Aschenbach's consciousness as delicately as does Mann, but then one might argue that that type of problem lies at the heart of filming this kind of novel. The image of the handsome Björn Andreson (who plays Tadzio) is thrown at us: in Mann, Tadzio's glances are recorded through the filter of Aschenbach's point-of-view; in Visconti, they now appear much too explicit, almost consciously seductive. Whereas in Mann an emphasis is placed upon the nature of love rather than on the love object as a primary goal (achieved via Platonic references in the text), in Visconti we are not wholly sure that this same degree of subtlety is present. This, I feel, partly explains their relationship's lack of credibility.

Even with all these deficiencies (and the allusion to Mahler is undoubtedly the most regrettable) the film is still remarkably expressive in its own right; the cinematic analogy cannot be a complete treachery to Mann since it does not presume to be the original, but whether it is a great film is open to question. Perhaps it is best to say that it succeeds in as much as it is complementary to Mann though hardly superseding him, for it struggles inside a literary work of great original vigour and resonance.

15 'I was Thomas Mann's Tadzio'[1]

In *Death in Venice* we read of the beautiful hero who made such a deep impression on the writer Aschenbach:

Aschenbach listened . . . to the boy's voice announcing his coming to his companions at the sandheap. The voice was clear, though a little weak, but they answered, shouting his name – or his nickname – again and again. Aschenbach was not without curiosity to learn it, but could make out nothing more exact than two musical syllables like Adgio – or, odder still – Adjiu, with a long drawn-out *u* at the end.

Today [1965] there lives in a one-family house in the Mokotow district in Warsaw a man whom Thomas Mann's well-known Polish translator, Andrzej Doegowski, has identified – by pictures and many family details – with that beautiful boy who was the indirect cause of Aschenbach's death from cholera in Venice.

'I am that boy! Yes, even then in Venice I was called Adzio, or sometimes Wladzio . . . But in the story I am named Tadzio . . . this is how the Master must have understood it. . . .' Of course it is not the similarity of name that Wladyslaw Moes, as he is now called ('origins and title are no longer of any importance'), produces as evidence. He remembers exactly when he first read the description of himself in *Death in Venice*. At a big dance in Warsaw in 1922 his partner Gabriella Czesnowska teased him – 'You are a hero, Adzio – have you read Thomas Mann's new story and discovered what a strange family you belong to?'

Wladyslaw Moes swallowed the bait – with the result that his memories of that visit to the Lido became sharper and more precise than they would ever have become simply from reading his family history. 'In the story I found everything described exactly, even my clothes, my behaviour – good or bad – and the rough jokes I played on the sands with my friend.' Moes cannot even today, however, remember Aschenbach's (or Thomas Mann's) appearance; but at sixty-seven he knows exactly how closely the famous author must have observed him.

'My friend Janek was also in Venice with his family at that time. He appears in the story as "Jaschiu", which is what we always called him. I enjoyed playing with him, though I did not like his rough way of playing – when we were fighting, he used dirty tricks and this brought our friendship to an end.' Aschenbach observed this accurately and Thomas Mann describes it thus:

Jaschiu was evidently overtaken by swift remorse; he followed his friend and tried to make his peace, but Tadzio motioned him back with a jerk of one shoulder and went down to the water's edge.

Doegowski, the Thomas Mann expert, had many conversations with 'Tadzio' Moes. He carefully verified Moes's accounts and compared them with the history of Moes's family in 1911–12. The two agreed pretty closely about the sudden departure of Tadzio and his family from Venice when cholera made its first appearance and about the striking clothes that Tadzio's mother bought for the beautiful boy that made such an impression on Aschenbach (Thomas Mann) on the beach.

Wladyslaw Moes remembers:

I was considered a very pretty child and women admired me, stopping in the street and kissing me . . . I was painted and drawn, but in my memory all that is a matter of indifference. I was in many ways a typical spoiled and precocious child, childishly indolent as is often the case. The description in *Death in Venice* is better than any description of mine . . . My unusual clothes must also have made a great impression on the writer, who describes them exactly and in detail – a striped linen suit with a sort of red bow and my favourite blue coat with gold buttons. The thing that I still find most interesting is the fact that the writer then saw me and described me as I really was – my characteristic movements, which have not changed, and a certain elegance of bearing . . .

Another thing that still amuses me and my family, and that I remember best of all, is the ceremonial order in which we always marched into the foyer of the hotel before meals – Mama, my three sisters (the youngest still in the charge of her governess) and last of all I, the boy. The light irony with which Thomas Mann describes this etiquette is delightful.

Later that summer, when we were at home again, we heard of the ghastly proportions of the epidemic which we had just managed to escape and of the many deaths that it caused . . .

In the mind of Andrzej Doegowski, who has had a long correspondence with Erika Mann (the writer's daughter) on the subject, there is no doubt that the Tadzio in the story is identical with the distinguished elderly gentleman from Warsaw called Moes.

[Translation: Martin Cooper]

16 *Critical reception*

Britten's Venice[1]

by Ned Rorem

For two centuries after the death of Henry Purcell in 1695, England produced no music of consequence. With Benjamin Britten's birth in 1913 the land awoke like Sleeping Beauty and picked up where she had left off. As though reincarnated, Purcell himself was Britten's main influence and love.

Britten in turn is the main influence, if not love, of English musicians today. Like a huge magnetic tuning fork his conservatism sets their tone: some resist, but by that resistance acknowledge the tone which they cannot shut out long enough to move toward other fields of attraction. In a sense, Britten even influenced his immediate predecessors (Vaughan Williams, Berkeley, Tippett, Holst, Walton, Bax, forever awash in the so-called modes of Hellenism and of Renaissance Albion) since he bettered them at their game and they knew it.

He is the utter eclectic. Not conventional so much as traditional, he does not fall back on the set grammar but pulls it up into his special syntax. It would be difficult to find in Britten's catalogue any measure not somehow attributable to another composer, yet each measure is somehow stamped with his technical trademarks just as each overall work is redolent of his human fixations.

His trademarks are metaphors. Like all artists, Britten does the undoable. In giving nonvocal music a recognizable meaning beyond its 'abstract' meaning he becomes, more literally than Debussy ever dreamt of being, an impressionist, a metaphorist rather than a similist. This he manages through orchestrational *tours de force* and through obsessional rhythmic patterns. (In his new opera, for example, his brushed drums *are* what you hear – not *like* what you hear

186

– from vaporetto motors; his dipping viola patterns *are* what you hear from dripping gondola paddles.) His vocal music too is metaphoric. He treats speech values more eccentrically, investing them with the personal pulse of tension and release, convincingly filling the empty areas of pure music with the impurities of literature.

His human fixations are chiefly aquaphilic and pedophilic. Not only is water more than mere décor in operas like *Peter Grimes*, *Billy Budd* and the first Church Parable, *Curlew River*, the sea, as a presence or image, can be found in a diversity of his nontheater works as well, in *Holiday Diary*, *Friday Afternoons*, *On this Island* and *Nocturne*. Young males are the *raison d'être* in such operas as *Peter Grimes*, *Billy Budd* and *The Turn of the Screw*; they cast a central glow over some chamber and choral works (*A Boy was Born*, *Saint Nicolas*, *Canticle II*, *Spring Symphony*) and, by Freudian extension, upon some strictly instrumental pieces too, like *The Young Person's Guide to the Orchestra*. Britten has never set a drama on urban ground, nor on a theme of romantic love between man and woman.

For an eclectic rather than an innovator to dominate a country's art is fruitless: his followers in aping mere manner lack the verve of outright thieves. England's youngish explorers, such as Birtwistle and Davies, seem not to possess the force of true discovery and so have remained in the shade of the old. Suddenly the shade starts to shimmer with new slants. Music's recent global style of willful opaqueness is clearing away. A modernistic brand of ugliness that everyone hated without admitting it is no longer being manufactured with the hope of being unpopular. The pendulum swings back to the right. Since Britain, thanks to Britten, always *was* right, British conservatism ironically is becoming the current avant-garde, and is represented by the 'representational' scores of Bennett and Maw, who are in no way revolutionary or even resistant. They sprang full-blown and affectionate from the head of their foster parent, Sleeping Beauty. That parent meanwhile continues producing children of its own.

Benjamin Britten's musical language, cold for some, for me has always seemed warm and contagious, open to every dialect of mind and soul. But I was miffed, at first, by Britten's latest work, *Death in Venice*.

In preparation for the dress rehearsal I dutifully pondered the vocal score and couldn't make much of it. It did stress the trademarks and fixations – sea, youth, 'forbidden' love – more candidly than ever, the metaphors turning psychoanalytically, if not musically, verbose as though the composer were forcing his dead collaborator's Germanisms onto his own native restraint. But the aftermath, at least on paper, looked sterile, padded, colorless, simplistic and, yes, lazy, with endless recitative on neumelike signs speckling an over-extended text. However, since this was a reduced blueprint (even Britten's full scores don't readily yield their secrets in print) by a musical dramatist who was nothing if not experienced, probably there was method in his drabness.

Sure enough, at the rehearsal the hall brimmed with noises of skill and beauty. What for the eye was a skeleton became for the ear, when fleshed out by an orchestra, a wealth of *trouvailles* which unexpectedly shined up the dusty narrative.

Since then, I've returned often to both live performance and the score, and realized I'd originally missed some basic points (a reader's speed is never precise). Each verbal phrase, regenerated through live performance, exemplifies and redefines Britten's claim as the world's supreme melodist. If that claim was not immediately obvious in *Death in Venice* it was because the tunes were honed to microcosms. Those recitatives weren't recitatives at all, but total melodies refined to lowest terms. The elaborate book, filled with logical contradictions, could thus be imparted without sounding silly. If this music never 'opens up' in the usual sense, it does so in reverse, like explosions in some galaxy seen through a microscope.

Melodists are those who flow rather than build, who let happen rather than make happen, who write tunes rather than figures – arched lines that feel singable rather than playable, lines that sound 'sung' whether planned for human voice or for mechanical instruments. Melody is the surf in which Puccini bathed, as did Ravel and even Hindemith, breathing passively, propelled by nature more than by calculation.

Fragmentists whittle more artificial, more *complex*, pieces, since fragments, like cells, innately lend themselves to rearrangement and self-renewal.

Thus Chopin, who never composed for singers, was a melodist; Beethoven was not. Mahler, primarily an orchestral composer, was a melodist; Debussy, so happy with voices, was not. Thus Webern too was a melodist, not because his pieces aren't compact like Beethoven's (they are), but because his material is not reworked and developed.

(Which, finally, is more economical, the melodist or the fragmentist? A motive is a perennial which reblossoms in endless shapes, a piece of glass in a kaleidoscope. A melody can be heard a single time, spacious and inevitable, before, like a Cereus, it dies.)

Benjamin Britten is the only living composer equally skilled at melody and fragment, whether writing opera, small songs, or 'pure' instrumental works of every shape. He merges these assets in combination.

Like Mozart, Britten has a knack for making mere scales more than mere. Consider the questioning dream before the phantas-magoria in Act II, wherein four E major modes set forth diatonically from low pitches, separate and float at different speeds to four unstable branches, alight, turn to solid silver and glitter fixedly, a frozen harmony derived from liquid counterpoints, a static place upon which a roaming soliloquy is now etched. Again the modes ascend, and still again, each time climbing higher on the same common tones, each time arresting to form frames for the nervous words.

This simultaneity – this doing of more than one version of the same thing at the same time (literally the same thing, not variations, like a canon at the unison unfocused from too-closely-staggered entrances) – is Britten's metaphor at its most eloquent. Listen again to the scene in San Marco where the identical litany is chanted at two tempos, evoking not only the cathedral's echoing walls but a different (though simultaneous) viewpoint, or soundpoint, in the minds of Aschenbach and Tadzio. With traditionalists, newness plays no part; novelty lies in perception more than in what is perceived. In *Death in Venice* Thomas Mann (also a traditionalist, carrying on rather than breaking through, so that, like Britten, he seemed to predate certain of his elders) did not tell what had never been seen, but what had always been seen and not noticed. In his opera, Britten, by telling what we've always heard without listening, revirginates our ears. Such perception is a thrilling and dangerous gift, a gift which both the novelist and the composer 'lend' to their respective visions of Aschenbach, and which kills him.

The transfer of Thomas Mann's self-contained and well-known story into another medium could have been, at the very least, superfluous. Britten almost turns the trick because he has *framed* the text. Retaining intact the famous words, he has focused private colors on them from all around, and transported the finished tableaux for us to see and hear upon a stage. What we experience is a kind of masterpiece, although I'm not sure why, beyond the fact that it was composed with a marvelous ear for taste and tension.

Nonetheless, two extraneous elements help to explain the special-
ness. First is the well-timed collaboration of a dead and a living
artist. Although Thomas Mann, whose hundredth birthday will
soon be celebrated [1975], was the first novelist to write with sensible
intelligence (as opposed to emotional intelligence – for there was
Proust, after all) about the musical creative process, none of his con-
temporaries ever set his fictions to music. Although ostensibly about
the pull between a creator's sacred duties and profane desires or, as
Mann put it, between Apollo and Dionysus, the subject is the waning
of productivity as symbolized by the 'mystery' of pederasty. Britten is
the only composer ever to depict that matter centrally in opera. The
matter needs his British understatement, not because homosexuality
is the bizarre vice it seemed in 1912, but because today it is so very
normal. We go along with myths like *Tristan* or *Turandot*, but
stigmas of the not-too-distant past remain ticklishly close to our
nominal magnanimity. Who any longer, when so openly all is said
and sung, could possibly utter, and get away with it, the words of an
old man suffering from a love that dare not speak its name?

Which brings up the second extraneous element: Peter Pears, the
English tenor and Britten's lifelong friend, in the role of Aschenbach. Pears, who has realized most of the composer's vocal works in
Europe, is now [in 1974], at sixty-four, making his Metropolitan
Opera debut. For one hundred and forty minutes he does not leave
our view or our attention. What some call his lack of opulence paradoxically lends his nonvoice a dimension of expressivity unknown to
more standard tenors. His sentences are intoned with enviable clarity
as though invented on the spot. For Pears is a thread of the score's
very fabric: he appears to belong to the composer's living concept,
and to the dead author's too, so serious and touching is his portrayal.
To imagine another in the role is to imagine a harpsichord piece
played on an organ.

Myfanwy Piper's adaptation is faithful to a fault. She includes in
the libretto nothing not in the novella, down to the last subnotion
and symbolic echo. With transposition from art to art, certain
weights, while keeping balance, switch emphasis. A strawberry
vendor, ominously recurrent in the story, becomes on stage an airy
refraineuse risking comparison to another in *Porgy and Bess*.

Riskier still is Tadzio's realization. To make flesh of the ineffable is
always a miscalculation. The success of parables like *Parsifal* or
Suddenly Last Summer, or of characterizations like Kafka's petty-
bourgeois K or Auden's great poet Mittenhoffer, lies in the invisible

ideal. Tadzio inhabits our fantasy no less than Aschenbach's. To find him now in person, a *dancer*, is to find a perfectionist intent on selling his craft. Observed as a ballet *sans* text (which the opera is for anyone ignorant of English), *Death in Venice* becomes the saga of a flirty boy who lusts for an old man but whose mother interferes so he drowns himself.

If the Silent Ideal must be depicted within a medium whose very purpose is noise, then mime, while a bit illegal, is probably the only solution; indeed, Britten has effectively based at least one previous opera around a mute but visible child. But actually to choreograph vast portions of the piece, as Frederick Ashton was hired to do, in the set-number style of Rameau is deadening for a modern mood piece; and when the Silent Ideal is rendered as a champion athlete the careful craft of Thomas Mann, without a word changed, is utterly violated. Mann's Tadzio is no winner, but the passive recipient of everyone's love earned not through excellence but through innocence and beauty.

[Revised 1986]

Reviews of the first performance (16 June 1973)

Desmond Shawe-Taylor in The Sunday Times, 24 June 1973

A useless piece of advice, I fear, but the best preparation for Benjamin Britten's *Death in Venice* – which had its first performance on June 16 at the Aldeburgh Festival – is *not* to have seen the too celebrated film. In this we should only be emulating the composer, who knew nothing of the film when he began to consider the operatic possibilities of Thomas Mann's famous novella a few years ago, was somewhat disturbed when he learned of its existence, and has since made a point of avoiding it. For all the visual attractions of Visconti's treatment, there is much in his superficial approach to the theme, in his misguided identification of Aschenbach with Mahler, and especially in the grossly overblown Mahlerian sound-track, that places the film at the furthest remove from Britten's distinguished score.

What works to the composer's disadvantage, however, may be useful to the critic, who can at least safely assume that by this time the story will be familiar to all. Eminent, elderly author (in point of fact, about 53) falls for stunning Polish boy of fourteen on the Lido, and makes an ass of himself? Ah no! Whatever incidental reservations may arise as we watch and listen, it is a measure of the artistic

success of Myfanwy Piper's libretto and Britten's score that both
have risen to the level of Mann's subtle and elaborate scheme: that is
to say, the ambiguous role of the creative artist caught between
Apollonian order and Dionysiac licence, the gradual disintegration
of a fine spirit, and the parallel idea of Venice itself as a symbol of
beauty rooted in corruption and decay. Here again, as in *The Turn of
the Screw*, Britten has reshaped a complex literary subject into a
genuine musical composition.

The planning is masterly. Britten has always been the type of artist
who instantly perceives the technical solution to a given problem;
and in this case he has again turned old formulas to pointful new
use. Recitative and aria, for example. What more natural, and what
in the event more successful, than to let Aschenbach, the practised
literary observer and self-communer, 'speak' his thoughts and diary
entries in all the supple freedom of piano-accompanied quasi-
melodic recitative, here given a further freedom by the device of
writing pitched notes without duration-symbol like those for the
Evangelist in Schütz's Passions – and then to allow orchestra, chorus
or other solo voices to enter as the writer's notebook is put away and
he himself (increasingly, and in the end disastrously) becomes
immersed and enmeshed in the action?

Then there is the old French tradition of *opéra-ballet*, revived in
order to present not only Tadzio, the Polish boy, but the whole group
of his family and associates, on another level. This device is very
telling: for instance, Aschenbach's failure to speak to Tadzio in the
natural way of friendliness, and subsequently to the boy's mother to
warn her of the spreading cholera, can be seen as due in part to his
sense of guilt, but also to the fact that they inhabit different worlds.
And in casting so many of the sinister lesser roles (Traveller, elderly
rouged 'Fop', Hotel Barber, Leader of a troupe of Strolling Players,
and so forth) for the same baritone, Britten not only picks up a hint
implicit in many of Mann's descriptions but seems to adapt to his
purpose the multiple disguises of the *commedia dell'arte*, and of the
highly operatic figures of the Mephistopheles legend and of E.T.A.
Hoffmann's tales.

All this ingenuity of handling, however, would be of no avail if the
material – the sheer musical stuff – were not in itself of absorbing
interest. Fortunately, it is. The score is rich, fresh, and, notwith-
standing its tight organization, varied and spontaneous-sounding.
There is here none of the dryness that, for me, spoilt the abundant
skill and resource of *Owen Wingrave*, nor even, despite sundry

advance hints to that effect, is there much of the spareness of the Church Parables. Even Aschenbach's initial sense of creative staleness is conveyed in a rising, then falling, twelve-note theme, constantly turning in on itself, which proves paradoxically fertile; while the minor episodes and figures are touched in with a rapid, glowing brush worthy of the city that inspired Guardi and Turner.

With Aschenbach, we approach Venice from the sea, and first hear the five-note phrase, 'Serenissima', that is to become the musical emblem of the city on the lips of a set of rowdy young trippers from the Adriatic coast. The following 'overture' seems to be murmuring the word over and over again against a lapping figuration, while a symphony of bells resounds through the golden haze. There is a moment of indolent, seductive magic as another boatload of singing boys and girls passes Aschenbach's gondola, heard but unseen; and there is a wonderful recurrent theme consisting of a rising octave and falling thirds that embodies the wide ocean horizons and all that they mean to the sensitive writer.

Tadzio's exotic beauty is suggested by a complete change of colour: a quasi-pentatonic figure or chord, with gamelan-like orchestration. The children's beach games are lightly accompanied by celesta, glockenspiel, xylophone and *col legno* strings; and Tadzio's peculiar allure is additionally conveyed by the constantly repeated rising or falling sixths of his chorally called name. The first act rises to a musical climax in which Aschenbach, obliged to return to the hotel after the misdirection of his luggage, gives himself up to serene contemplation of the beach play, fancifully transfigured into games in honour of Apollo.

At an early stage of acquaintance with the opera, this scene strikes me as its sole misconception. The amplified off-stage counter-tenor of James Bowman does not adequately suggest to my ear the calm divinity of the sun-god, while the chorally accompanied games are too long, too close in tone to the Norwich masque in *Gloriana*, and (partly no doubt for that reason) too English-seeming to make their full intended effect; all Sir Frederick Ashton's choreographic skill could not quite hold us through the five stages of the pentathlon. But the climax of the act – Aschenbach's failure to speak to Tadzio, and his ecstatic but appalled 'I love you' – regains the lost dramatic impact.

In the somewhat shorter second act the impulse never slackens. There are brilliant Italian vignettes: the repeated quavers of the Barber's professional patter interspersed with his ingratiating 3/4 phrases *à la* Tosti or Denza; the piazza scene with the café trio playing a 'Tadzio tune'; the comic song and laughing-chorus of the Strolling Players. Underneath it all, the plague theme (first uttered by the mysterious Traveller seen in the Munich cemetery) spreads on the low soft tuba like a miasma.

After a Dionysiac nightmare in which the Bacchantes' cries seem to parody both the gondoliers' hoarse 'Aou'!' warnings and the yearning beach-calls of 'Tadziù!' there comes the most moving episode of all: that in which Aschenbach, although by now grotesquely transformed into the semblance of the painted old dandy of the earlier boat scene, sings the words of Socrates' tender dismissal of Phaedrus (which Mann took straight from Plato) to a harp-accompanied cantilena of direct and calm simplicity. In the final scene, on the beach, the slowly retreating Tadzio is revealed as the symbol of Hermes, messenger of Death and conductor of souls to the Underworld, while the faint rising calls of his name are heard once more, for the last time, from the unseen chorus and from the dying man himself.

As can be imagined, the part of Aschenbach offers an immense challenge and opportunity to Peter Pears, who was in fine voice and sang with wonderful skill and variety of tone; he will not be easily replaced. Nor will John Shirley-Quirk, who in the numerous sardonic roles revealed a histrionic versatility that I had hardly suspected in him. Although it is said that we shall not see John Piper's sets at their best until the opera reaches a real theatre (it goes to Edinburgh in September, and then to Covent Garden, Venice and the Metropolitan), his designs already offer an evocative impression of the Venetian scene, within which Colin Graham has deployed the action most cunningly.

Faced with the difficult task of directing a troupe of dancing adolescents, and with an accomplished but somewhat too old and muscular Tadzio in Robert Huguenin, Ashton acquitted himself admirably; and in the much regretted absence of the composer (whom audiences and his admirers everywhere will wish a full and speedy recovery from his operation) Steuart Bedford led the English Chamber Orchestra in what was surely a clear and faithful account of the intricate score.

Peter Heyworth in The Observer, 24 June 1973

Operatic history is full of trivial works based on famous books and great scores that have been raised on trivial libretti. But Benjamin Britten's operatic version of Thomas Mann's *Death in Venice*, which had its first performance at the Aldeburgh Festival eight days ago, is an attempt to take the full measure in music of a work that is itself a masterpiece. It marks Britten's return to the opera house after an absence of thirteen years and it is probably the most testing undertaking he has embarked on since the *War Requiem* of 1962. Whether it achieves what it sets out to do is another matter.

Needless to say, Britten's *Death in Venice* is in no sense 'the opera of the film'. In fact Britten has, I am assured, not seen the film, and it would hardly have appealed to a man of his literary perspicacity if he had. For Visconti reduced Mann's wonderfully rich and many-layered story to a trivial tale of a famous writer, Gustav von Aschenbach, who feels his creative powers to be flagging and goes on holiday to Venice in search of refreshment and renewal. At his hotel he encounters a young Polish boy of surpassing beauty and falls so desperately in love with him that when cholera breaks out he refuses to leave and eventually dies, watching the boy at play with his friends on the beach.

Described as baldly as that, *Death in Venice* sounds like a queer novelette, and that is just what Visconti made of it. Though the original story is in large part autobiographical, Mann is in no way evasive about the sexual aspect of von Aschenbach's infatuation, but with great mastery weaves into it a number of themes of wider moment.

Aschenbach is far from the neurasthenic queen with a ready eye for a pretty face that was presented by Visconti. He is a married man, self-possessed, even a shade self-important, highly disciplined and totally dedicated to his art. Indeed, part of his temptation lies in his awareness that abandonment to the suppressed Dionysian element in his corseted character may be a means of rekindling his creativity. He recalls Plato's words that beauty 'is the one form of spirituality that we experience through the senses'. It is only shortly before his death that he also recollects Socrates' warning that beauty leads to passion and passion to the abyss.

Myfanwy Piper and, one must assume, Britten himself have succeeded in fashioning a libretto that is faithful to the story in all its aspects and yet succeeds in weaving its many strands into a series of seventeen brief scenes that for the most part move with the rapidity of a film scenario. There is only one notable exception. To give dramatic shape to the days which Aschenbach spends watching

Tadzio and his friends at play on the beach, Mrs Piper has resorted to the device of a series of athletic contests which brings the first act to an end. This seems to me an error, for it introduces an element of *divertissement* (emphasized by Frederick Ashton's choreography) that is quite foreign to the introspective nature of the work as a whole.

In his setting of this scene, Britten skilfully indicates the gulf between Aschenbach and the boy, who remains barely aware of the emotions he has awakened, by using an extensive percussion section to produce a brittle, Balinese quality that is at once exotic and impersonal and stands in sharp contrast to the remainder of the score. Yet, it remains the one scene where he has failed to sustain the sense of pace which is such a notable feature of the opera as a whole.

On the other hand, Mrs Piper may in one respect be said to have improved on the original. Acting on what are no more than hints in the story, she has treated the various characters who edge Aschenbach on his path to destruction as a series of embodiments of a single Hermes-like figure. These characters are all taken by one singer (John Shirley-Quirk) and this gives the opera an additional element of unity.

In the book Aschenbach is both narrator and protagonist, and Britten has found an effective means of distinguishing between these two roles. In his meditative moments Aschenbach is given a melodic recitative. Its pitch is notated, but its note values remain free, very much as they do in Schütz's Passions, so that the rhythmic quality of each phrase is left to the performer's discrimination – a device that Peter Pears handles with matchless artistry. Only as Aschenbach's ironic detachment deserts him and he grows more a prisoner of his emotions does the music become more lyrical and a sparse piano accompaniment give way to the orchestra. The other problem is, of course, the boy himself. In the story he never speaks, for his magic lies purely in his appearance, and Britten has cunningly negotiated this hurdle by casting the part with a dancer.

Indeed, his consummate skill as an opera composer has never been more apparent. In scene after scene he establishes atmosphere and dramatic points with uncanny rapidity and sureness of touch. At the opening of the opera, for instance, Aschenbach's restless unease is instantly evoked in a brief rising vocal phrase, punctuated by varied rhythmic figures whose instrumental colour constantly changes. The means are simple, the result is haunting. A brief overture, which comes, not at the opening of the opera, but at the point of Aschenbach's arrival in Venice, brilliantly evokes the city's splendour in a climax dominated by bells and brass, and a sinister lapping figure accompanies his passage across the lagoon to the Lido. Later in the opera, a brief phrase for bustling bassoons exactly hits off the busy activity of the Hotel Porters and the song of the Strolling Players who entertain the Hotel Guests has a grotesque and menacing quality. Nor are these isolated details, for the whole score is bound together by a subtle web of thematic relationships, from which stems a strong sense of underlying unity.

Yet it is significant that most of the examples I have cited do not directly concern Aschenbach himself. And this, I suspect, is not mere chance, for as the story moves into deeper waters the music fails to keep pace with its gathering intensity. There is, admittedly, one striking exception, a nightmare scene, in which Apollo and Dionysus contend for the soul of Aschenbach, and Dionysus in the form of Tadzio hovers like a hawk over the sleeping writer's bed. Here Britten suddenly unleashes a violence that his music has hardly achieved since *Billy Budd*.

Elsewhere, it is Apollo who rules, and the most memorable passages directly involving Aschenbach are reflective. A long descending vocal line, accompanied by a fascinating pattern of sound that is repeated on flute, clarinet, horn and harp, movingly evokes Aschenbach's awareness of the remorseless passage of time. The setting of Socrates' dialogue with Phaedrus on the ambivalent nature of beauty has a classical simplicity that recalls the Hölderlin songs. But with the single exception I have noted, Britten does not penetrate far into the dark side of the subject matter, and it has called forth no notable extension of his expressive powers. Unlike Mann, he seems to flinch before the abyss he evokes, and in the latter stages of the opera the music lacks intensity, wildness and mystery – in short just those Dionysian qualities the story is concerned with. Aschenbach dies, but Apollo's rule is only momentarily threatened, and then, significantly one may think, in his [Aschenbach's] sleep.

Peter Pears sustains the arduous central role with an absence of strain that is astonishing in a singer in his sixties. Each inflection of his voice is stamped by that blend of intelligence and sensibility that is the hallmark of a great artist. Dramatically, however, it seems to me that he allows Aschenbach to lose his self-possession too early in the day and thus has little in reserve for the real disintegration that only occurs in the second act. As the Hermes figure, John Shirley-Quirk sings magnificently and offers a wide variety of telling thumbnail sketches.

Colin Graham's production is ingeniously conceived and clearly executed. But in spite of John Piper's evocative yet cliché-free back-cloths (his torrid seascape is a brilliant and original conception), the result is rather too disembodied for a work so firmly anchored in fact. No doubt the limited resources of the Maltings imposed restrictions, and it will be interesting to see how the production works when the English Opera Group brings it to Covent Garden later in the year. Steuart Bedford conducts with authority. But as an interpreter of his own music Britten, who had not sufficiently recovered from a recent heart operation to attend either the rehearsals or the first night, has, of course, no equal. May he soon be restored to health and enabled to let us hear his latest opera under his own direction.

Edward Greenfield in The Guardian, *18 June 1973*

Benjamin Britten, consistently perverse in his choice of opera subjects, has once again proved the impossible. Thomas Mann's *Death in Venice* a compressed and intense story, an artist's inner monologue, lacking conversation, lacking plot, has against all the odds become a great opera. Britten has turned it into one of the richest and deepest of operatic character-studies.

In the world première at the Maltings, Snape, on Saturday, Peter Pears in the central role of the writer, Aschenbach, exploited every dimension of a part that has few parallels. He is rarely off the stage. Not even the Pears parts in earlier Britten operas have quite the scope of this, a *tour de force* which inspired Pears to some of his finest singing ever.

Plainly the first problem facing the composer and his librettist, Myfanwy Piper (collaborator with him on the two Henry James operas), was that the unspoken thoughts of Aschenbach as reported in Mann have had to be externalized into sung monologue. Britten has cleverly varied his form of doing this, distinguishing between comments on the passing scene (verse with light orchestral accompaniment) and darker, more philosophical reflections (prose sung within free rhythm with dry piano accompaniment).

The result over a very long span (nearly two and a half hours of music with only one interval) is an intensification of emotion which firmly establishes the composer's right to impose operatic form. He has heightened the original. The portrait of the central character is only one aspect of that heightening process, the literal level of psychological story-telling. In formalizing the original, Britten and his librettist have enhanced the symbolic elements, too. They have done this most forcefully through having a single singer take the incidental parts, the characters whom Aschenbach meets before and during his trip to Venice. All these have it in common that they lead him towards sensuality. They represent in various ways Dionysiac temptation – the Traveller in the Munich cemetery, the Elderly Fop, the mysterious Gondolier, the Hotel Manager, the Barber. With the central character encountering the same singer (John Shirley-Quirk in superb form) at every turn, you could regard *Death in Venice* as the longest and greatest of the Church Parables, a story of a pilgrim and his tempter.

There is symbolism, too, of course, in the vision of the beautiful boy, something which in lesser hands might have seemed selfindulgent or even coy. As it is, with finely judged production by Colin Graham and choreography by Frederick Ashton, the balletic playing of the children on the beach (no vocal parts at all for Tadzio and his family) rightly remains an incidental, a heightening of the aging Aschenbach's inner vision. Casting the part of Tadzio must have provided headaches, but it was right to have an older boy than the story would allow, Robert Huguenin, one whose poised movements are calculated enough to be sensual without overstepping a very delicate frontier. Deanne Bergsma as Tadzio's mother conveys fine patrician detachment, setting the whole family apart as an unapproachable object of obsession.

Predictably Britten's music intensifies the symbolism on every level. For example, the arrival of the plague (symbol ultimately of Dionysiac indulgence) is felt subconsciously, long before the idea is made explicit in the text, through Britten's sinister use of the tuba in crawling bass figures. That is typical of his simple ingenuity. Even a brief study of the score shows how subtle the web of musical motives is, but even an unprepared listener will note the broad contrast of chromatic contortions (temptation music of every kind) set against the relative purity, often pentatonic, of the music of true beauty, the music of Tadzio with magic overtones on the vibraphone, the music of Apollo with the offstage voice of the male alto, James Bowman, giving an other-worldly quality, or the music of the playing children on chattering xylophone.

The actual idiom owes something to the Church Parables, but this is a score which relates much further back to the vocal and instrumental beauty of such works of Britten as the Michelangelo Sonnets ('innocent' bitonality often recurring here), the *Serenade* and above all the *Nocturne*.

Death in Venice positively invites rehearing, presenting as it does a long sequence of moments to look forward to, whether of richness – the antiphony of brass and bells in St Mark's or the first scene on the beach with horns and strings richly expansive in Tadzio's call motive; whether of sinister power – the forceful dream sequence when the orgiastic vision of Tadzio among the black revellers horrifies Aschenbach at his own subconscious; whether of simple eloquence – the broken but stoic Aschenbach remembering a Socratic dialogue. After that the final death scene is brutally and powerfully foreshortened to intensify its power, the trap snapping shut. The contrast with the film version is at its strongest there.

On the open Maltings stage the fluidity of the story and its setting are beautifully conveyed. The restraint may be judged in that only after fifty minutes does John Piper's full Venetian canal-scape emerge for the first time, swivelled into view on enormous triangular columns in the manner of the Maltings *Midsummer Night's Dream*. Piper has also done charming backcloths, and the Edwardian costumes of Charles Knode are wonderfully atmospheric.

This is the first Britten opera which the composer himself has not helped to produce on its first presentation. On doctor's orders he could not even be present on Saturday, but Steuart Bedford as conductor was a splendid deputy, while the superb duo of Peter Pears and John Shirley-Quirk made one fear for any rival singers attempting to take over their roles.

Though I still reserve judgement on one or two of the ensemble numbers, there is a richness in simplicity throughout this score which more than anything in years takes us back to the first full flush of Britten's early success. Aschenbach when he reflects on his first sight of Tadzio says: 'There is in every artist's nature a wanton and treacherous proneness to side with beauty'. In *Death in Venice* Britten has certainly 'sided with beauty'.

Bayan Northcott in The New Statesman, 22 June 1973

Despite memories of its incomparable acoustics and the halcyon outlook down the Alde's rushy estuary, I must confess I approached the Maltings, Snape, last Saturday evening for the first performance of Benjamin Britten's latest opera with real misgivings – some of them frankly musical. As a young man, Britten's facility was notorious but in more recent years he himself has spoken of increasing difficulties in composing. How far this is the cause, how far the effect of a declared attempt further to simplify a technique that was never complex is impossible to say, but the etiolated and mechanical procedures of some of his more recent scores have made depressing listening for those who value the plangent lucidities of the earlier ones. Was he really going to eke out his longest work since *A Midsummer Night's Dream* of 1960 with textures that even the sympathetic Peter Evans in his preview in *Opera* magazine[2] described as looking 'dangerously thin on paper'? And while Peter Pears, now in his mid-sixties, has been singing perhaps better than ever over the last season, could he be expected to sustain the almost continuous part of Aschenbach for the best part of two and three-quarter hours? And what about the subject matter? In tackling as overt and ripely obsessive a treatment of a theme so long latent in his output, was Britten not risking self-parody?

In the event, my forebodings proved not unfounded; there *are* miscalculations, ineffectualities and some exquisite embarrassments. Nevertheless, by the end of the evening, I was convinced not only that Britten had picked just the right kind of narrative to make the best of his musical resources at the moment – and composed his least hide-bound score in ten years – but also that he has adumbrated a new operatic formula in the process.

Indeed it could well have been the formal possibilities as much as the content that suggested the choice of Mann's story. In at least three of Britten's earlier operas the action is surrounded by an element of separate commentary in the form of prologues and epilogues, but I can think of no operatic precedent for the almost complete reversal of traditional narrative priorities in *Death in Venice*. Faced with the problem of providing the protagonist of a book in which there is virtually no speech with a singable stream of consciousness, Myfanwy Piper has, I think wisely, avoided any suggestion of 'realistic' groping for thought. The bald formality with which her Aschenbach announces his preoccupations – prose for detail, verse for more sustained feeling – takes a little getting used to as a convention but proves not inappropriate for so initially stiff and detached a figure. At first the actual incidents of the story are seen merely as an intermittent background to the ceaseless reflective monologue. Gradually, however, a secondary continuity is established by the reappearance of a second singer – in this performance John Shirley-Quirk, superbly varied and increasingly sinister of aspect – in that sequence of figures who conduct Aschenbach on his fateful path: the Traveller, the Elderly Fop, the Old Gondolier, the

Hotel Manager, and so on. As involvement grows, the stage action moves into the foreground, gathering pace and variety of allusion: the repeated gondoliering between Venice and the Lido derives from Britten's Church operas in its stylized Japanese staging, the unreal beauty of the Polish family is underlined by casting them not as singers but dancers (with Deanne Bergsma exotically fragile as the Mother), while in the milling crowds and rapid scene changes surrounding Aschenbach's pursuit of Tadzio through Venice at the beginning of Act II, Colin Graham's direction against John Piper's sets realizes just that fluid, televisual directness that *Owen Wingrave* failed to achieve.

Thereafter, by way of a theatrically somewhat old-fashioned nightmare scene, the stage empties and events slow down again – perhaps a little too much? – for the elegiac close. Yet the only real disaster in this whole scheme is surely the extended children's beach ballet. Coming at the end of an Act I running an hour and a half and glorifying Robert Huguenin's rather glum Tadzio, the prep-school nostalgia of this lengthy Ancient Greek sports day strikes me as both dramatically gratuitous and disturbingly at variance in spirit with what is for the most part so faithful a transposition of Mann's original.

Britten, of course, has always worked in closest collaboration with his colleagues from the moment a new opera is conceived, and I have the strong impression that this wide range of dramatic techniques was deliberately invoked here as a framework for a corresponding retrospective, a summation even, of his own musical evolution. After years of scoring that has clung to the upper registers, there is a welcome reactivation of lower pitches, not least Britten's special feeling for tuba tone; Aschenbach's recitatives with piano hark back to the *Cantata Academica* and the children's gamelan-like music to *The Prince of the Pagodas*, while the Noh-like cries of the gondoliers and other voices-off recreate that sense of vast spaces behind the stage which was a feature of several of the earlier operas. When the Hotel Manager praises the sea view from Aschenbach's window, the orchestra fans out in a great *Peter Grimes*-like texture of piled-up thirds; and not least, the choral commentary to the dances and the stricken Aschenbach's little aria about Socrates and Phaedrus recall the euphony and grace of some of Britten's first successes.

What binds these varying idioms together is an intervallic scheme, largely based, as Peter Evans has demonstrated, upon the various ways of filling in a major third, which Britten has found himself able to deploy in a pervasive, free-flowing complexity that runs far deeper than the dry little patterns of so many of his recent works. I have often found in the past that the lasting harmonic felicities of his music are those that at first hearing sounded the most fugitive and ambiguous. Often surprisingly cloudy in chordal implications, despite its textural clarity, *Death in Venice* is full of such moments, and certain dense, chorale-like passages, such as the climax of the Venice Overture or the Hotel Manager's theme, represent a sound quite new in Britten's music. Moreover, the conjunct source-intervals generate a vocal line for Pears's Aschenbach, less athletic, perhaps, than of old, but as exemplary a vehicle for his current vocal artistry as those of Grimes and Peter Quint were for his early and middle years. For verbal clarity and sympathetic characterization it is difficult to imagine his performance in this role ever being surpassed.

Death is Venice was composed under the threat of severe illness and it shows signs, both in its subject matter and technique, of having been executed as the last and supreme effort of an artist's final period. In Britten's absence, Steuart Bedford has prepared and conducted a doubtlessly faithful performance. Yet now, as Britten convalesces, can he not take heart from the suggestion that his ordeal may not only have represented, rather, a purgation but also that it has resulted in a score that opens up new possibilities for a composer who is after all still under sixty?

[Afterthought, 1985: The above demonstrates the dangers of describing a complex new work on the basis of a single performance and without recourse to a score: the climax of the Venice Overture and the Hotel Manager's music, for instance, are not actually 'dense' so much as strikingly spaced. More seriously, the review now betrays an embarrassing condescension of tone. This may have been partly an unthinking reflection of the cooler critical attitudes towards Britten of the late 1960s, partly a (temporary) personal disaffection from a composer who had meant so much to me in my youth; I would certainly not today describe as 'etiolated' or 'mechanical' the *Building of the House* Overture, the Second Cello Suite, the best of the Pushkin and Soutar songs or the first act of *Owen Wingrave*. Indeed, the last now seems to me compositionally, musico-dramatically, rather richer than either act of *Death in Venice* – an heretical view in this context which I shall only attempt to support by mentioning the extent to which the leisurely continuities of the latter depend upon scalic material, conjunct motion and heterophonic

204   *Death in Venice*

superimposition, and how little (a few obvious passages apart) upon genuine counterpoint. Those who understand the work more deeply than I do will doubtless feel that this very lassitude of musical thought is part of its character and message. And maybe what has inhibited frequent productions to date is rather the practical problem of finding tenors of the range, artistry and insight to measure up to the main role – a problem the work seems destined to share with another operatic testament, Pfitzner's *Palestrina*. Yet this in turn could be a blessing; while *Peter Grimes*, *Albert Herring* and *A Midsummer Night's Dream* will always stand up to the ravages of the repertory system for which they were created, *Death in Venice*, by its comparative rarity, should retain its special meta-musical luminosity undimmed. B.N.]

Notes

1 An introduction in the shape of a memoir

1 See Donald Mitchell, 'Montagu Slater (1902-1956): who was he?', in *Peter Grimes*, compiled by Philip Brett, Cambridge University Press, Cambridge, 1983, pp. 41-3.

2 See also Donald Mitchell, '*Double Portrait*: Some personal recollections', in *Aldeburgh Anthology*, ed. Ronald Blythe, Aldeburgh and London, 1972, pp. 431-7. It was typical of Britten that even with a first performance (of the song cycle *Who are these children?*) on his hands he was still able to talk in such detail about his plans for the new opera. This was an example of the many levels he lived on simultaneously.

3 See Carol J. Oja, 'Colin McPhee: composer turned explorer', *Tempo*, 148, March 1984, pp. 2-7. Since publication of this article Ms Oja has completed her doctoral thesis: 'Colin McPhee, 1900-1964: A Composer In Two Worlds', City University of New York, 1985. See also Douglas Young, 'Colin McPhee's music: (I) From West to East', *Tempo*, 150, September 1984, pp. 11-17.

4 See David Matthews, 'Act II scene 1: an examination of the music', in *Peter Grimes*, compiled by Philip Brett, Cambridge University Press, 1983, pp. 122-4, and Christopher Palmer, 'The colour of the music', in *The Turn of the Screw*, ed. Patricia Howard, Cambridge University Press, Cambridge, 1985, pp. 104-11. See also Donald Mitchell, 'What do we know about Britten now?', in *The Britten Companion*, ed. Christopher Palmer, Faber, London; Cambridge University Press, New York), 1984, pp. 39-45.

5 Mr Cooke is currently engaged on a doctoral thesis (Cambridge University) which has as its topic the oriental influences on the music of Benjamin Britten.

6 I quote from this letter by kind permission of Mrs Piper and the Trustees of the Britten Estate.

7 The gramophone recording of the opera adheres to the unrevised version of this passage.

8 See Christopher Isherwood, *Christopher and His Kind: 1929-1939*, Farrar, Straus and Giroux, New York, 1976, pp. 267-8.

9 See the vocal score of the opera, published by Faber Music, London, 1975, p. 15, and Appendix, p. 265. The only other optional cut authorized by the composer is marked on p. 125, the so-called 'Hyacinth' dance

for Tadzio and Jaschiu. It is important to note, however, that this cut, unlike that of the first recitative for Aschenbach, was *not* made on the recording, though the dance was dropped from the original production (including the Met) after the first year of performances (1973–4). It has been adopted generally in performances of the opera since the first production. But in a production at the Grand Théatre de Genève in March/ April 1983, directed by François Rochaix and conducted by Roderick Brydon, the 'Hyacinth' dance was revived; and it reminded many of us how essential this mythological enactment of the Tadzio/Jaschiu rivalry is to understanding, at its profoundest symbolic level, the Tadzio/Jaschiu struggle in which the opera culminates at the end of Act II. After all, it is precisely this Apollonian 'game' which Aschenbach has witnessed *from his deck chair* during the early stages of the beach scene, and with his classicizing eyes and mind 'reads' as the fate of Hyacinth (Tadzio), dispatched by 'Zephyr's mighty breath'. The rivalry is re-enacted at the end of the opera, with Aschenbach *again in his deck chair* (a vital visual symmetry this, which itself embodies a reminder of and reference to the larger mythological symmetry) as an involved witness. But this time he is not perceiving the struggle in an objective, classicizing, Apollonian spirit, but as a painful, because passionate, participant. What a brilliant irony it is that at the end of this struggle, it is not Hyacinth/Tadzio who is struck down, but Aschenbach, the hapless lover, perhaps as much a victim of the gods as of his own infatuation. Much of this marvellously ironic symmetry is lost if the 'Hyacinth' dance is not done. Surely all serious productions of the opera should disregard the composer's optional cut, made, I believe, out of a needless fear that the beach scene was too long, and give this crucial episode its proper emphasis. Steuart Bedford recalls Britten having doubts about the music of the dance, but these were evidently not serious enough for him to discard the dance in the recording.

A quite commonly encountered criticism of the opera was that 'The Idyll' was 'too long' – hence no doubt Britten's mistaken offering of the 'Hyacinth' dance as an optional cut. It is interesting that he did not – could not – do the obvious thing and knock out one of the actual games, which itself speaks for the integrity of their architecture. These non-specific arguments about length are hard to combat. I would make this point, however, in defence of the extended proportions of 'The Idyll': that the hair-raising impact of what follows 'The Idyll' – Aschenbach's 'The boy, Tadzio, shall inspire me' (which Peter Pears once memorably and truly described as a *duet* for the singer and dancer); the smile; and the grinding dissonance of Aschenbach's confession, 'I love you' – is entirely dependent on those events being preceded by a substantial stretch of idyllic music (the only music of its kind in the opera) which almost lulls Aschenbach (and the audience) into a false sense of calm and detachment. It is the one moment in *Death in Venice* when, so to say, time is arrested, and along with it, Aschenbach's otherwise inescapable fate. To achieve that 'The Idyll' needs the time and space Britten allotted it.

10 That Britten continued to be anxious about the shape and pacing of

Act I after the recording had been made was evident late one evening in the summer of 1974 when he was spending a few days in Sussex. Quite unexpectedly, he asked to hear Act I of the opera on the gramophone before he went to bed (the only time, I think, that I found myself listening with him to a gramophone recording of one of his own works for a purpose of this kind). He was clearly still bothered by the first recitative (or by its absence, rather, from the recording); and if I remember aright, it was after this listening session that he made up his mind that the recitative ought to be reinstated. This was the summer preceding the production of the opera at the Metropolitan, New York. The interim vocal scores had already been modified and thus conform with the cut made in the recording. This was now countermanded and a supplement issued, restoring the recitative (see Strode, p. 43), which, after all, formed part of the Met performance. (But see also p. 16 above.) The 'Hyacinth' dance, however, was omitted in New York and thereafter.

11 Tadzio's theme is omnipresent throughout Act II. But it is only at fig. 325 that we hear it in its original form, and for the last time. I have not overlooked it emerging at fig. 284 as the climax of 'The dream', but there it is massively distorted by the accompanying (and dissonant) harmony. (See also Palmer, pp. 150–2.)

12 See Donald Mitchell, *Britten and Auden in the Thirties: The Year 1936*, Faber, London, 1981, p. 25.

13 Ibid., pp. 160–3.

14 The quotation is made with the permission of the Trustees of the Britten Estate and Mrs Elizabeth Welford.

15 Britten once remarked to me, somewhat out of the blue: '*Death in Venice* is everything that Peter and I have stood for.' I have often wondered since whether in saying that he was not just referring to the opera's frank avowal of his own Tadzio-oriented homosexuality but also to the obligatory consequential constraints, the absence of which – of the 'carefully chosen' and shouldered 'discipline' – was ultimately Aschenbach's undoing. Britten *stood* as much for that, the discipline, as for the unequivocal acknowledgement of a principal and sometimes overriding – but not exclusive – source of inspiration.

16 See Donald Mitchell, 'Catching on to the technique in Pagoda-land', in *The Britten Companion*, ed. Christopher Palmer, Faber, London, 1984, pp. 192–210, and 'An Afterword on Britten's "Pagodas": the Balinese sources', *Tempo*, 152, March 1985, pp. 7–11. See also Somsak Ketukaenchan, 'The Oriental Influence on Benjamin Britten' (part of MA submission, University of York, March 1984). I regret to find on looking back to the *Musical Times* of nearly thirty years ago, to the February issue, 1957, p. 91, in which I reviewed the first performance of the *Pagodas* at Covent Garden, that it was precisely the gamelan element in this score that I singled out for adverse comment. The culture shock that the gamelan music in the *Pagodas* presented was altogether too much for me, which may explain, though not excuse, my inept response to it – an indication, however, of how novel the experience was that Britten's gamelan offered and how sharp was its impact.

17 The replica of the ship's siren reminds me of the care Britten took in *Who*

are these children?, in the eleventh song, 'The Children', to remind himself of the authentic wailing pitch of the air raid sirens heard during the
Second World War. This was then transferred to the keyboard and is a
central sonorous image throughout the song. The composer's attention
to detail of this sort was infinite. To return to the ship's siren again: has
anyone noticed how, in the first recitative after Aschenbach has reached
the hotel, Britten reintroduces the siren at its original pitch (cf. Palmer,
Ex. 1, p. 132) in the piano, just before Aschenbach asks himself, 'A
pleasant journey did he say?' (fig. 64, my italics):

That little recapitulation of the siren's blast – the sonority qualifying the
adjective to come – wonderfully conveys the disorienting impression
made on Aschenbach by the boat trip.

2 A *Death in Venice* chronicle

1 Sources: In preparing this chronology I have, with the full agreement of
the Executors and Trustees of the Britten Estate and the Trustees of the
Britten–Pears Library, consulted the following materials in the Britten
archives at The Red House, Aldeburgh:

Libretto drafts of *Death in Venice*, and related correspondence between
Myfanwy Piper and Benjamin Britten.

Britten's composition sketch (including discarded pages) and the original
manuscript full score of the opera, also the Red House master dyeline of
the manuscript full score containing all corrections, 1973–6.

Numerous early state dyelined copies of the original vocal score (1972–3)
and later interim vocal scores (1974–5) in particular those used by Peter
Pears, Benjamin Britten and myself.

Archive files of official papers, correspondence, newspaper cuttings,
programmes etc., kindly made available by Faber Music Ltd. Similar files

belonging to the Britten Estate (including engagement diaries and lists, and my own office files from 1970–6) and files from the English Opera Group archive now housed in the Britten–Pears Library.

John Evans's doctoral thesis *Benjamin Britten: 'Death in Venice': Perspectives on an Opera* (University of Wales, 1984), a copy of which is deposited in the Britten–Pears Library.

In addition I have greatly benefited from the recollections of many friends and colleagues who were also involved in one way or another with the origins and first production of *Death in Venice*. In particular I would like to thank Steuart Bedford, Isador Caplan, Colin Graham, Colin Matthews, Donald Mitchell, the late Sir Peter Pears, Myfanwy Piper, and Stephen Ralls (orchestral pianist in the first production) for their help and advice.

2 A letter from Mrs Piper of 11 September 1970 (now in the Britten Estate archives) makes this point clear, although she herself had previously recalled that November 1970 was the crucial moment. See *The Operas of Benjamin Britten*, ed. D. Herbert, Hamish Hamilton, London, 1979.

3 Colin Graham has told of his own scenario for *Death in Venice*, which (having heard Britten mention the story more than once) he had prepared soon after the filming of *Owen Wingrave*, and then handed to the composer. At the time he was completely unaware that the work was already under discussion with Myfanwy Piper. See *The Operas of Benjamin Britten*, ed. D. Herbert.

4 The duet at fig. 239 between the Young Players is set to another Italian tune – 'Giovanottino mi garbate tanto' by M. Ferradini. The use of this tune was authorized by its publishers, with entirely satisfactory business arrangements.

5 See also Steuart Bedford's illuminating and entertaining 'The Struggle with the Word', in *Peter Pears: A Tribute on His 75th Birthday*, ed. M. Thorpe, Faber Music, London, 1985, pp. 5–7.

3 The libretto

The quotations from *Death in Venice* and *Tonio Kröger* are taken from translations by H.T. Lowe-Porter, Penguin Modern Classics, London, 1955. The quotations from Thomas Mann's letters are from *The Letters of Thomas Mann*, Vol. I, selected and translated by Richard and Clara Winston, Secker and Warburg, London, 1971. This chapter first appeared as part of 'Writing for Benjamin Britten', in *The Operas of Benjamin Britten*, ed. D. Herbert, Hamish Hamilton, London, 1979, pp. 8–21.

1 To Wolfgang Born on 18 March 1921, pp. 109 and 110.
2 To Kurt Martens on 28 March 1906, pp. 50 and 51.
3 To Erika and Klaus Mann in 1932, p. 187.
4 Quoted by permission of the Trustees of the Britten Estate.
5 T.J. Reed, Introduction to *Der Tod in Venedig*, Clarendon German Series, Oxford University Press, Oxford, 1971.

4 The Venice sketchbook

1 Three movements from this projected suite were revised and performed in 1936 as *Three Divertimenti* (published posthumously by Faber Music, London, in 1983). [Ed.]

2 This work was completed but abandoned while the finale was under revision. Two of the sonatina's movements were published posthumously by Faber Music, London, in 1986. [Ed.]

3 'Sketch' is, of course, an ambiguous term, since it can also be applied to the main compositional process which, in Britten's case, with very few exceptions, took the form of a two or three stave through-composed 'composition sketch'. For *Death in Venice* (as with all Britten's operas) the layout of the composition sketch is very close to the published vocal score. (A folder in the Britten–Pears Library labelled 'Sketches' contains pages rejected from the composition sketch for the opera, and not advance sketches.)

Mention should be made here of two sketchbooks used by Britten from 1974 onwards. These contain very detailed workings for Opp. 90–95: but the change in working methods was due to Britten's declining health rather than the experience of the Venice sketchbook.

The music examples throughout this chapter are exact transcriptions of Britten's original sketches with all their idiosyncracies and 'mistakes' retained.

4 In Murray Schafer, *British Composers in Interview*, Faber, London, 1963, p. 123. See also 'Mapreading', Benjamin Britten in conversation with Donald Mitchell, in *The Britten Companion*, ed. Christopher Palmer, Faber, London; Cambridge University Press, New York, 1984, pp. 90–1.

5 These are the first Players' song 'O mio carino', and the first version of the Leader's song, 'La mia nonna'. The latter could not be used because of copyright problems, and Britten had to rewrite the whole song using another tune. (See Strode, p. 38.)

6 I have a memory, unfortunately imprecise, of Britten saying that this theme came to him while sitting in the back of a car – it was certainly a reaction to a specific view, although as John Evans points out (in his article on the sketchbook in *Soundings*, University of Cardiff, No. 12, Winter 1984–5, pp. 7–24) the theme has much wider implications. (See also Mitchell, pp. 2–3.)

7 Changed at an interim stage to 'Come but here to seek to revive me', but the (far superior) original version was reinstated.

8 'yearning' in the sketchbook.

9 The rhythms of this passage derive from the rising scales at fig. 34 (not in the sketchbook), but there the scales are diatonic.

10 Page 30 contains the new tune for the Players' scene. See n. 5 above.

5 The first production

1 This chapter originally appeared as part of 'Staging first productions 3' in *The Operas of Benjamin Britten*, ed. D. Herbert, Hamish Hamilton, London, 1979, pp. 55–7.

2 Colin Graham refers to the passage between figs. 94 and 96. [Ed.]

6 Synopsis: the story, the music not excluded

1 This chapter originally appeared as part of the notes accompanying the Decca gramophone recording of *Death in Venice* (SET 501-2), released in 1974. [Ed.]
2 The circumstances relating to the inception of the 'view' theme are outlined in C. Matthews, n. 6, p. 210, and Mitchell, p. 3. [Ed.]
3 For the particular history attached to the creation of this theme, see J. Evans, pp. 110–11 and Plate 19, p. 110, C. Matthews, pp. 59–60, and Mitchell, pp. 3–4. [Ed.]
4 See also Strode, p. 36: Britten had some difficulty in deciding where to introduce the end of Act I. [Ed.]

7 Tonal ambiguity in *Death in Venice*: a symphonic view

1 Alban Berg, *Letters to his Wife*, ed., trans., and annotated by Bernard Grun, Faber, London, 1971, p. 147.
2 See Myfanwy Piper, 'Some thoughts on the libretto of "The Turn of the Screw"' in *Tribute to Benjamin Britten on his Fiftieth Birthday*, ed. Anthony Gishford, Faber, London, 1963, p. 79.
3 See Denis Arnold on the theoretical basis of Monteverdi's works in 'Monteverdi', *The New Grove Dictionary of Music and Musicians*, Vol. 12, ed. Stanley Sadie, Macmillan, London, 1980, pp. 514–34. 'He [Monteverdi] . . . turned to Plato's general artistic ideas, the most important of which seemed to him to be one discussed by Zarlino that Ficino has rendered from the Greek as 'melodia ex tribus constare, oratione, harmonia, rhythmus'. [Literally, 'the text, the combination of notes and rhythms are the three elements which constitute melody'. Denis Arnold notes this statement in connection with Monteverdi's view that music should be second in importance to the words.]
4 Such a device – very simply and clearly used here by Britten – is distinctly Bergian. Both *Wozzeck* and the *Lyric Suite* (which Britten admired throughout his creative life) contain fascinating examples – both local and large-scale – of this reflective, overlapping means of continuity. Britten's earlier 'Wozzeckian' opera, *Peter Grimes*, contains many interesting examples of 'linkage technique'. Perhaps the most memorable (both long-range and local) is the D major seventh chord, first heard when Peter takes the oath in the witness box in scene 1 and then returning at the end of the opera as an image linked to the doleful fog horn and the cries of Peter's pursuers in the 'Mad Scene'. (The very use here, by the way, of a single chord for a whole scene is a no less Bergian device.) However, one should not discount the possible influence of 'linkage technique' (also Berg-derived?) in Shostakovich's Fourteenth Symphony which Britten conducted at Aldeburgh in 1970, only a year before work on *Death in Venice* began. In this case Shostakovich links certain numbers (see especially the sequence 'Loreley' – 'The Suicide' – 'On Watch' – 'At the Santé-Jail') by means of common single pitches, the end of one twelve-note melody or formulation forming the beginning of the next.
5 As partner to Peter Pears in Schubert's *Winterreise* and lifelong Mahlerian (cf. Mahler's Sixth) Britten was well acquainted with this expres-

sive symbol. It is striking that Schubert's A major vein in *Winterreise* always carries the connotation of illusory happiness. Perhaps this, coupled with its classical, Mozartian connotations for Britten, was not without significance in his choice of A major for Tadzio? See also Donald Mitchell's comment on A major as the 'Apollonian' key of Britten's *Young Apollo*, for piano and orchestra (1939), and its role in *Death in Venice* (sleeve note for EMI recording, ASD 4177).

6 Although in this respect – as Donald Mitchell has pointed out – the orchestral song cycle, *Nocturne*, of 1958 is a notable precursor. The *Nocturne*, moreover, provides some musical images and gestures which strikingly anticipate *Death in Venice*. Compare, for example, the exotic vegetation/bassoon imagery of 'The Kraken' and the timpani cadences of the Wordsworth setting with their conflation in 'Marvels unfold' (fig. 14), and the A major characterization of the 'Beauteous boy' (strings and harp) with the Tadzio motive on its first appearance (fig. 73).

7 Generally speaking, Britten's blend of tonal, 'free atonal' and twelve-note elements in this opera are unmistakably Bergian, though Bartók's handling of bi-tonality, mixed mode and mediant relationships are also a well-digested influence in Britten's style.

8 Britten's sheer delight in the amassing of 'genre' elements in this opera is precisely what gives such scope to his musical irony – as it did to Mahler, for example. Consider their multiplicity in random order: military fanfares (shades of *Owen Wingrave* and *War Requiem*, and, of course, Mahler); popular band; vamping accompaniments; recitative; aria; 'overture'; street cries; 'barcarolle'; choral dance; twelve-note melody; bell music; gondoliers' cries; passacaglia; ternary form (even 'sonata form' itself!); chorale; Mahlerian Adagio; Delphic Hymn; heterophony; operatic 'big tune', and so on. (See also Mitchell, pp. 23–5.)

9 However, Hans Keller has forcefully argued that, no matter what the composer thought he had achieved, or was trying to achieve, the first movement of the quartet unfolds in fact an extremely subtle and innovative sonata scheme. For his alternative point of view see Hans Keller, 'Britten's Last Masterpiece', *Spectator*, London, 2 June 1979, pp. 27–8; this was also discussed in his BBC Radio 3 talk about the work broadcast on 11 June 1978. See also D. Matthews, pp. 159–60. [Ed.]

10 Cf. Mahler's deceptive tonal symbolism in the finale of his First Symphony – especially the premature return of D major which opens up the huge retrospective retransition at fig. 34.

8 Twelve-note structures and tonal polarity

1 Arnold Whittall, *The Music of Britten and Tippett: Studies in Themes and Techniques*, Cambridge University Press, Cambridge, 1982, p. 261.

2 F sharp is the tonal point of departure for scene 2. F sharp is also highlighted at the top of each phrase in the instrumental texture where the canonic alignment of two contrapuntal strands brings together E (the region of departure) and F sharp (the goal towards which Aschenbach's vocal line is directed).

3 One might press into descriptive service here Adorno's 'unscharfe

Unisono' [unfocused or indistinct unison], 'in which identical parts are rhythmically a little out of step with one another', the term he introduced into his discussion of the peculiar counterpoint of Mahler's *Das Lied von der Erde*, of 'Der Abschied' in particular. See T. W. Adorno, *Mahler: Eine musikalische Physiognomik*, Suhrkamp, Frankfurt, 1960, p. 194. [Ed.]

4 Peter Evans, *The Music of Benjamin Britten*, Dent, London, 1979, p. 527.

5 Cf. in Mann's novella Aschenbach's frequently expressed sense of Tadzio as *sculpture*, created by the 'pure, strong will which had laboured in darkness and succeeded in bringing his godlike work of art to the light of day. ... Was not the same force at work in himself when he strove in cold fury to liberate from the marble mass of language the slender forms of his art which he saw with the eye of his mind and would body forth to men as the mirror and image of spiritual beauty?' (*Death in Venice*, trans. H. T. Lowe-Porter, Penguin Modern Classics, p. 50.) Mann's image is strikingly matched here by the actual musical process. [Ed.]

6 Peter Evans, op. cit., p. 526.

7 In the context of what Dr Evans writes here about Exx. 14–16, Mervyn Cooke's observation (p. 126) that when Ex. 15 is recapitulated by Aschenbach in Act II (fig. 300), it is *Tadzio*'s theme, conflated, which now forms the accompaniment, is particularly telling. By this means Britten marvellously fulfils the prediction made at fig. 40 + 4 and at the same time identifies Tadzio as the 'pretty little darling' who is the cause of Aschenbach's downfall. Aschenbach's own lacerating identification? Or a turn of the screw devised by the composer for the ears of the audience, the spectators of Aschenbach's painful metamorphosis? However one cares to read this passage, the ironies built into it are so many layered as to be beyond the reach of words. [Ed.]

8 Peter Evans, op. cit., p. 527.

9 Myfanwy Piper, 'Writing for Benjamin Britten', in *The Operas of Benjamin Britten*, ed. David Herbert, Hamish Hamilton, London, 1979, p. 16.

9 Britten and the gamelan: Balinese influences in *Death in Venice*

1 See Prince Ludwig of Hesse's *Ausflug Ost*, Darmstadt, privately printed, 1956, pp. 50–1: 'Here is another fairly large orchestra with boys of up to fourteen years old as musicians. The instruments sound somewhat tinny, the players are splendid' [16 January 1956]. The ensuing quotation from Britten's letter to Roger Duncan is made by kind permission of the Trustees of the Britten Estate and Mr Duncan, © 1987 The Britten Estate.

2 Cf. *Gloriana* and *A Midsummer Night's Dream*, both choreographed by Cranko.

3 Beryl de Zoete and Walter Spies, *Dance and Drama in Bali*, Oxford, 1938, p. 16.

4 An ensemble including at least four wooden xylophones (*gambang*) employed exclusively in cremation rites. Several sketches labelled 'cremation' were made by Britten in Bali on his visit to the island.

5 The group accompanying the 'Joged' dance and comprising wooden xylophones known as *rindik*. Britten took part in a typical 'Joged' on 14 January 1956.
6 Britten would have heard this effect with particular clarity on his long-playing record of a 'Legong' by the Pliatan gamelan (Argo RG1).
7 A flute-like instrument constructed from bamboo tubing with open fingerholes.
8 A set of ten gong-chimes mounted horizontally which had traditionally functioned as the melodic leader before the advent of the *kebiar* style.
9 Cf. *Pagodas*, Act II, fig. 75. Identical scoring is employed to represent *kendangs* in Colin McPhee's *Tabuh-tabuhan* (1936).
10 The *gong lanang* (male gong, high pitch) and *gong wadon* (female gong, low pitch).
11 Conversely, the presentation of the 'Serenissima' motive by the gamelan at fig. 228 is an equally pertinent illustration of Aschenbach's growing obsession: Venice for him now means only one thing – Tadzio.
12 Britten recalled that this mode came to him entirely unconsciously, an impressive vindication of his empathy with Balinese music. See Mitchell, p. 3, C. Matthews, p. 60 and J. Evans, pp. 110–11.
13 The serenity of Tadzio's mode is, of course, restored in the opera's orchestral epilogue. (See Palmer, Plate 23, p. 142.)

10 Britten's Venice orchestra

1 Britten made two commercial recordings of Elgar: *The Dream of Gerontius* (Decca, SET 525–6), with Pears as Gerontius, and the *Introduction and Allegro* for strings (Decca, SXL 6405).
2 Cf. Donald Mitchell in the third volume of his Mahler study, *Gustav Mahler: Songs and Symphonies of Life and Death*, Faber, London, 1985, p. 96: 'It is not on the counting of heads that an assessment of what is – or what is not – chamber music should be made. The determining factor is the quality of the invention and the imagination, which in turn determines the degree of intensity of attention exacted from the listener. If it is a very high degree, then it seems to me that chamber music is what we are probably listening to, whether it is a Beethoven quartet or part of Wagner's *Tristan*.'
3 For more on Elgar, Britten and the orchestra, see my chapter on Britten's orchestral works in *The Britten Companion*, ed. Christopher Palmer, Faber, London; Cambridge University Press, New York, 1984, pp. 393–410. My contribution ('The colour of the music') to *Benjamin Britten: The Turn of the Screw*, ed. Patricia Howard, Cambridge University Press, Cambridge, 1985, pp. 101–25, comments on certain aspects of Britten's 'chamber-music' orchestration not discussed here.
4 See Donald Mitchell's account of this movement in his work on Mahler cited in n. 2 above.
5 Britten wrote to Henry Boys in 1937: '. . . ['Der Abschied'] passes over me like a tidal wave – and that matters not a jot either, because it goes on for ever, even if it is never performed again – that final chord is printed on the atmosphere.'

Perhaps if I could understand some of the Indian [sic] philosophies I might approach it a little. At the moment I can do no more than bask in its Heavenly light – and it is worth having lived to do that.' For the complete letter see Mitchell's *Mahler*, Vol. 3, pp. 339–40.

6 See Mitchell, nn. 3, 4 and 16, pp. 205–6. See also his '*Death in Venice*: The dark side of perfection', in *The Britten Companion*, pp. 238–49.

7 The double-bass reinforces – adds weight to – the bassoons and does not register as a stringed instrument in its own right (it is often usefully employed in this capacity, e.g. in a military band context, where it adds, invaluably, breadth to the bass).

8 See Donald Mitchell, *Britten and Auden in the Thirties: The Year 1936*, Faber, London, 1981, p. 37.

9 I remember very clearly Britten telling me how hard he had had to work on this passage, getting the *dis*-synchronization of the scales exactly as he wanted it. [Ed.]

10 See also *The Britten Companion*, p. 258.

11 Mitchell's *Mahler*, Vol. 3, p. 347.

12 See also my chapter on *Death in Venice* in *The Britten Companion*, pp. 250–67, where I stake a tentative claim for Britten as a quasi-Wagnerian composer in relation to *Death in Venice* and *Tristan*. The empathy between Britten and Mann *had* to have some Wagnerian element as intermediary, however unconscious it may have been on Britten's part.

13 See J. Evans, *Soundings*, University of Cardiff, No. 13, Spring, 1987.

14 The irony bites deep here. Aschenbach is dismissed in E (one bar before fig. 319), i.e. in the tonality which is his own, which has defined his character, and was the agent of his undoing at the end of Act I: 'I love you'. (But see also J. Evans, p. 107 and Plate 18, p. 108.) [Ed.]

11 *Death in Venice* and the Third String Quartet

1 And by the time he came to work on the Third Quartet Britten's unsuccessful convalescence after his heart operation must have been another source of the self-identification to which David Matthews refers. Hence for example the 'autobiographical' quote in the quartet (Ex. 1h) of Aschenbach/Britten's Ex. 1g. [Ed.]

2 Act II was originally intended to follow on without a break; musically, it is still regrettable that it does not. See the reproduction of the composition sketch at this point in Rosamund Strode's chapter, Plate 5, p. 37.

3 For a fuller account of this process see my article 'The String Quartets', in *The Britten Companion*, ed. Christopher Palmer, Faber, London; Cambridge University Press, New York, 1984, pp. 389–92.

4 Peter Evans, *The Music of Benjamin Britten*, Dent, London, 1979, pp. 340–1.

12 Mann and his novella: *Death in Venice*

1 This chapter appeared in *The 26th Aldeburgh Festival Programme Book,* 1973, pp. 5–6.

13 The novella transformed: Thomas Mann as opera

1 The quotations from Golo Mann's letter are made by kind permission of Professor Mann and the Trustees of the Britten Estate. There is no copy of *Doctor Faustus* among Britten's books and Peter Pears thought it unlikely that he had read it. [Ed.]
2 A selection is included in *Thomas Mann pro and contra Wagner*, the novelist's collected writings on the composer, trans. Allan Blunden, Faber, London, 1985.
3 *Buddenbrooks*, trans. H. T. Lowe-Porter, Secker, London, 1930 edn., pp. 348–9.
4 *Death in Venice*, trans. H. T. Lowe-Porter, Penguin Modern Classics, Harmondsworth, 1955, p. 24, subsequently cited in this chapter as DVP. This was the translation through which Britten and his librettist Myfanwy Piper approached the novella, and it is for this reason that this version is quoted here. Britten's principal working copy, now in the Britten–Pears Library at Aldeburgh (along with five other editions of the novella in German and English), was the New Adelphi Library edition of 1929. It is not known when he acquired this or when he first read the novella (see also Strode, p. 26). A greatly improved version of the Lowe-Porter translation has been made by Kenneth Burke (Random House, New York, 1970, rev. edit.). For copyright reasons it is unfortunately not published in the United Kingdom.
5 Myfanwy Piper (see pp. 45–54) makes clear that Britten himself often played a crucial role in shaping both the structure and detailed content of the libretto.
6 See John Evans, 'On the recitatives of *Death in Venice*', in *Peter Pears: A Tribute on his 75th Birthday*, ed. Marion Thorpe, Faber Music, London, 1985, p. 31.
7 *The Music of Benjamin Britten*, Dent, London, 1979, p. 528.
8 *Ibid.*, p. 528.
9 See Mitchell, n. 9, pp. 205–6, where it is suggested that the 'Apollo and Hyacinth' dance has a more important function to perform than that of a beach game. [Ed.]
10 This latter phrase sounds an echo of a central condition in the pact that Goethe's Faust makes with Mephisto. As long as Faust's thirst for experience and knowledge kept him on the move there was hope for him, but should he once experience contentment and be so struck by some beautiful moment that he would wish it to last for ever, then from precisely that moment he would be damned.
11 A rare precedent is the central role played by Fenella, the seduced Neapolitan maid, in Auber's *La Muette de Portici* (1828), who communicates only through dumb-show and dance. Britten himself had already confronted a not dissimilar challenge in *Peter Grimes*, where the apprentice's silence is eloquent enough of Grimes's relationship with him.

12 Mervyn Cooke (see also pp. 121–4), in an unpublished M.Phil. dissertation ('Britten and Bali: a study in stylistic synthesis', University of
Cambridge, 1985) makes a highly important contribution to our understanding of the influence of oriental music on Britten and shows that
'Tadzio's theme is constructed from a variant of the *saih pitu* mode which
corresponds to two sketches Britten made in Bali in 1956'. I am indebted
to Mr Cooke for his kind permission to quote from his dissertation.

13 Dating back as far as his first encounter with Balinese music in New York
during 1939–42. See Mitchell, nn. 3, 4 and 16, pp. 205 and 207.

14 See T. J. Reed (pp. 164–5) and also the introduction to his edition of
Der Tod in Venedig, Clarendon German Series, Oxford University Press,
Oxford, 1971.

14 Aschenbach becomes Mahler: Thomas Mann as film

1 Mann's appreciative attitude in this letter sharply conflicts with his
earlier, private (and probably) initial reaction to Born's lithographs.
In his diary entry for 26 May 1920 Mann recorded:
Born, whom I mistakenly caused to be turned away at the door, brought
his colour illustrations for *Death in Venice*. I find them stiff and unat-
tractive.
(See Thomas Mann: *Diaries 1918–1939*, selected by Hermann Kesten,
trans. Richard and Clara Winston, André Deutsch, London, 1983, p. 98.)

2 *The Letters of Thomas Mann 1889–1942*, Vol. I, selected and trans.
Richard and Clara Winston, Secker and Warburg, London, 1970, p. 110.

3 That minimal influence was transformed, alas, into a major fantasy. It
was not sufficient, it seems, that Mann had had the physical appearance
of Mahler in mind when imagining Aschenbach. There was some further
and hitherto hidden 'truth' to be revealed; and revealed it was by Hollis
Alpert, in 'Visconti in Venice', in the *Saturday Review*, New York,
8 August 1970, pp. 16–18, whose source ('invaluable and infallible') was
Dirk Bogarde:
There is an extraordinary amount of certainty among those involved in
the production that Mahler was a prototype for the Mann story. . . . 'It's
a story Visconti once heard,' Bogarde said. 'I'm not sure whether it was
from Mann himself, or from a member of the Mann family. At any rate,
Mann is supposed to have divulged to *someone* that in 1911 he was
coming back from Venice on a train and with him in the same compart-
ment was this fifty-one-year-old weeping man with dyed hair, terrible
makeup, eyelashes falling off, absolutely hideous, and obviously in great
distress. Mann spoke to him – so the story goes – and learned he was
Mahler, who said, "I've just come from Venice, and I've fallen in love with
a boy of thirteen." They went on to discuss it, and Mahler is supposed to
have said that it wasn't the boy per se, but the beauty he represented. The
boy became the symbol for all that he'd lost – beauty, purity, innocence.
Visconti, therefore, is basing the film very lightly on an early twentieth-
century composer who could conceivably be Mahler, and, perhaps more
pertinent, this gives him the opportunity to use Mahler's music throughout on the soundtrack. At the very end, I'm on the beach, watching the

boy, who is about to leave plague-stricken Venice, and I'm composing, I suppose, an unfinished Mahler symphony.'
Even Mr Alpert himself came to the conclusion as he wrote that there was little to substantiate the Visconti assumption (i.e. that Aschenbach *was* Mahler). But the damage had been done and for an appreciable period this grotesque invention, which cannot even be described as a falsification, so remote was it from any kind of reality, gained wide currency, causing much embarrassment to the Mann family and to Mahler's surviving daughter, Anna. Monica Stirling, in her biography of Visconti, *A Screen of Time* (New York, 1979), does not resurrect the story, but adds (p. 210) a remarkable gloss of her own on the film's relationship to Mahler: '. . . millions of spectators would . . . hear Mahler's music for the first time while watching Venetian landscapes, and would, as a result, contribute to the popularity of Mahler's music, which began spreading soon after *Death in Venice* was released [*sic*].' So much for the Mahler revival of the 1950s and ensuing decades. As for Tadzio, it was not Mahler who encountered him in Venice, but Thomas Mann, during the early summer of 1911. The real-life Tadzio made himself known in 1965 (see 'I was Thomas Mann's Tadzio', pp. 184–5), though as a result of the publicity surrounding the film his identity was more widely reported (see *Frankfurter Rundschau*, 21 October 1975; and *Die Welt*, 276, 26 November 1977, Welt-Report, p. 7). Nothing false, then, about Mann's Tadzio. He was there, on the beach, in 1911. [Ed.]

4 *Atlantic Monthly*, September 1971, pp. 109, 113.

15 'I was Thomas Mann's Tadzio'

1 This article first appeared in *Twen*, Munich, Vol. 7, No. 8, August 1965, p. 10.

16 Critical reception

1 'Britten's Venice' first appeared in *The New Republic* (Washington, DC), 172/6, 8 February 1975, pp. 31–2. This was a review of the original English Opera Group production given at the Metropolitan Opera House, New York, on 18 October 1974.

2 Peter Evans, *Opera*, 24, 1973, p. 490 *et seq.*

Bibliography

Adorno, T. W., *Mahler: Eine musikalische Physiognomik*, Suhrkamp, Frankfurt, 1960

Alpert, Hollis, 'Visconti in Venice', *Saturday Review*, New York, 8 August 1970, 16–18

Bedford, Steuart, 'The Struggle with the Word', in *Peter Pears: A Tribute on his 75th Birthday*, ed. Marion Thorpe, Faber Music, London, 1985, 5–7

Berg, Alban, *Letters to his Wife*, ed., trans., and annotated by Bernard Grun, Faber, London, 1971

Britten, Benjamin, *Death in Venice*, An Opera in Two Acts, Op. 88, libretto by Myfanwy Piper, based on the short story by Thomas Mann, vocal score, Faber Music, London, 1975

   Death in Venice, Op. 88, full score, Faber Music, London, 1979

   'Mapreading', Benjamin Britten in conversation with Donald Mitchell, in *The Britten Companion*, ed. Christopher Palmer, Faber, London; Cambridge University Press, New York, 1984, 90–1

Cooke, Mervyn, 'Britten and Bali: a study in stylistic synthesis', M.Phil. thesis, University of Cambridge, 1985

Evans, John, 'Benjamin Britten: 'Death in Venice': Perspectives on an Opera', PhD, University of Wales, 1984

   'Britten's Venice Workshop: Part I: The Sketchbook', *Soundings*, University of Cardiff, No. 12, Winter 1984–5, 7–24

   'On the recitatives of *Death in Venice*', in *Peter Pears: A Tribute on his 75th Birthday*, ed. Marion Thorpe, Faber Music, London, 1985, 31–3

   'Britten's Venice Workshop: Part II: The Revisions', *Soundings*, University of Cardiff, No. 13, Spring 1987.

Evans, Peter, *The Music of Benjamin Britten*, Dent, London, 1979

Graham, Colin, 'Staging first productions 3', *The Operas of Benjamin Britten*, ed. David Herbert, Hamish Hamilton, London, 1979, 44–58

Isherwood, Christopher, *Christopher and His Kind: 1929–1939*, Farrar, Straus and Giroux, New York, 1976

Keller, Hans, 'Britten's Last Masterpiece', *Spectator*, 2 June 1979, 27–8

Ketukaenchan, Somsak, 'The Oriental Influence on Benjamin Britten', part of MA submission, University of York, March, 1984

Ludwig, Prince, of Hesse and the Rhine, *Ausflug Ost*, Darmstadt, privately printed, 1956

Mann, Thomas, *Buddenbrooks*, trans. H. T. Lowe-Porter, Secker, London, 1930 edn.

Death in Venice and *Tonio Kröger*, trans. H. T. Lowe-Porter, Penguin Modern Classics, Harmondsworth, 1955

Death in Venice, transl. Kenneth Burke, Modern Library College Edition, Random House, New York, 1970, rev. edn.

Diaries 1918-1939, selected by Hermann Kesten, trans. Richard and Clara Winston, André Deutsch, London 1983

The Letters of Thomas Mann 1889-1942, Vol. I, selected and trans. Richard and Clara Winston, Secker and Warburg, London, 1970

Thomas Mann pro and contra Wagner, trans. Allan Blunden, Faber, London, 1985

Matthews, David, 'Act II scene 1: an examination of the music', in *Peter Grimes*, compiled by Philip Brett, Cambridge University Press, Cambridge, 1983, 122-9

'The String Quartets', in *The Britten Companion*, ed. Christopher Palmer, Faber, London; Cambridge University Press, New York, 1984, 383-92

Mitchell, Donald, '*Double Portrait*: Some personal recollections', in *Aldeburgh Anthology*, ed. Ronald Blythe, Aldeburgh and London, 1972, 431-7

Britten and Auden in the Thirties: The Year 1936, Faber, London, 1981

'Montagu Slater (1902-1956): who was he?', in *Peter Grimes*, compiled by Philip Brett, Cambridge University Press, Cambridge, 1983, 41-3

'Catching on to the technique in Pagoda-land', in *The Britten Companion*, ed. Christopher Palmer, Faber, London; Cambridge University Press, New York, 1984, 7-11

'*Death in Venice*: The dark side of perfection', Ibid., 338-49

'What do we know about Britten now?', Ibid., 39-45

'An Afterword on Britten's "Pagodas": the Balinese sources', *Tempo*, 152, March 1985, 7-11

Gustav Mahler: Songs and Symphonies of Life and Death, Faber, London, 1985

Mitchell, Donald and Evans, John, *Benjamin Britten: Pictures from a Life, 1913-1976*, Faber, London, 1978

Oja, Carol J., 'Colin McPhee: composer turned explorer', *Tempo*, 148, March 1984, 2-7

'Colin McPhee, 1900-1964: A Composer In Two Worlds', PhD, City University of New York, 1985.

Palmer, Christopher, 'The Orchestral Works: Britten as Instrumentalist', in *The Britten Companion*, ed. Christopher Palmer, Faber, London; Cambridge University Press, New York, 1984, 393-410

'The colour of the music', in *Benjamin Britten: The Turn of the Screw*, ed. Patricia Howard, Cambridge University Press, Cambridge, 1985, 101-25

Piper, John, 'Designing for Britten', in *The Operas of Benjamin Britten*, ed. David Herbert, Hamish Hamilton, London, 1979, 5-7

Piper, Myfanwy, 'Some thoughts on the libretto of "The Turn of the Screw"', in *Tribute to Benjamin Britten on his Fiftieth Birthday*, ed. Anthony Gishford, Faber, London, 1963, 78-83

'Writing for Benjamin Britten', in *The Operas of Benjamin Britten*, ed. David Herbert, Hamish Hamilton, London, 1979, 8–21

Reed, T. J., 'Death in Venice', in *The 26th Aldeburgh Festival Programme Book*, 1973, 5–6

Introduction to *Der Tod in Venedig*, Clarendon German Series, Oxford University Press, Oxford, 1971

Rorem, Ned, 'Britten's Venice', in *The New Republic* (Washington, DC), 172/6, 8 February 1975, 31–2

Schafer, Murray, *British Composers in Interview*, Faber, London, 1963

Stirling, Monica, *A Screen of Time, A study of Luchino Visconti*, Harcourt Brace Jovanovich, New York, 1979

Whittall, Arnold, *The Music of Britten and Tippett: Studies in Themes and Techniques*, Cambridge University Press, Cambridge, 1982

Young, Douglas, 'Colin McPhee's music: (I) From West to East', *Tempo*, 150, September 1984, 11–17; '(II): Tabu-Tabahan', *Tempo*, 159, December 1986, 16–19

Discography

1974   (under the supervision of the composer)
Pears *Gustav von Aschenbach*; Shirley-Quirk *The Traveller*; *The Elderly Fop*; *The Old Gondolier*; *The Hotel Manager*; *The Hotel Barber*; *The Leader of the Players*; *Voice of Dionysus*; Bowman *Voice of Apollo*; Bowen *Hotel Porter*/ Members of the English Opera Group, English Chamber Orchestra/ S. Bedford

Decca SET581/83
London OSA13109

Suite (compiled Steuart Bedford)
1984   English Chamber Orchestra/ S. Bedford

Chandos ABRD1126 ④
ABTD1126
CD: CHAN8363

Index

Figures in *italic* type refer to illustrations or music examples. Unless otherwise indicated, works are by Benjamin Britten.

223